Towards
a theory for
UDC

Towards a theory for UDC

essays aimed at structural understanding and operational improvement

J M PERREAULT

Director of the library
University of Alabama in Huntsville

ARCHON BOOKS & CLIVE BINGLEY

FIRST PUBLISHED 1969 BY CLIVE BINGLEY LTD LONDON
THIS EDITION SIMULTANEOUSLY PUBLISHED IN THE USA
BY ARCHON BOOKS THE SHOE STRING PRESS INC
955 SHERMAN AVENUE HAMDEN CONNECTICUT 06514
PRINTED IN GREAT BRITAIN BY R E GORDON & CO LTD
COPYRIGHT © J M PERREAULT 1969
ALL RIGHTS RESERVED
208 00874 8

CONTENTS

Acknowledgments

My acknowledgements are due to the following sources for permission to revise and reprint the essays named : to *American documentation* for 'Documentary relevance and structural hierarchy' and 'A new device for achieving hospitality in array'; to *College & research libraries* for 'Comparative classification for administrators: a short sermon'; to the Classification Research Committee of the Fédération Internationale de Documentation for 'Categories and relators: a new schema', 'On the colon in UDC and on the Boolean operators', and 'Towards explication of the rules of formation in UDC'; to the Graduate School of Library Science of the University of Illinois for *Reclassification: some warnings and a proposal*; to *Libri: international library review* for 'Automatized retranslatability of UDC codes'; to the Marine Technology Society for 'Citation order – presuppositions, structure, and function'; to the School of Library and Information Services of the University of Maryland for 'The Universal Decimal Classification as candidate for reclassification either on the shelf or in the catalog'; to Mr Einar Öhman for the letter quoted in *Reclassification: some warnings and a proposal*; to Pergamon Press for 'Documentary relevance and structural hierarchy' and 'On the articulation of surrogates: an attempt at an epistemological foundation'.

JMP

Preface

by Geoffrey Lloyd

To be asked by the author to introduce this volume of essays was at once a surprise an honour and a challenge: a surprise because, although we have corresponded recently on UDC problems, we have met only once — and that rather fleetingly, at the FID seminar on UDC and Mechanisation in Copenhagen in September 1968; an honour, because in classification theory I am the apprentice, he the master; and a challenge, because I want here to try and make a positive contribution, however small, towards our common goal, rather than vociferate ineffectually from the touch-line. The goal, in short, is so to improve the Universal Decimal Classification that it will be recognised everywhere — including the United States and English-speaking world at large — not only as the best available general system for the library shelf and catalogue, but also as the standard unifying or 'switch' language for linking otherwise incompatibly indexed or classified documents and references in mechanised information systems. Many will find this conception altogether too grandiose, even utopian, but it is one that I believe I share with Jean Perreault, with an ever-increasing number of his countrymen, and indeed with a vast company of UDC apostles throughout the world. Let the sceptics take note of the recent work by Rigby and Russell, Atherton and Freeman (of AIP/UDC Project fame), Caless and other workers who have demonstrated the feasibility of UDC as a machine-indexing language. Let them mark well, too, these essays of Perreault — showing clearly that cool heads are at work to improve the UDC. It is on such efforts as these that the FID Central Classification Committee (FID/CCC) bases its confidence in the future of the classification.

Jean Perreault himself needs no boosting: he has already made his name in our field. With or without promotion, this book will be read by thousands, because he writes on a subject of topical interest in a manner that is lively and sincere — if sometimes overlaid with philosophical phraseology and classificationist jargon, and because he has often some fresh view to put across or some new battle to fight. Still, the main aim of an introduction should be to introduce — not reminisce or divagate: to introduce at least the author and, if possible, support his argument. Unfortunately, although we have easily fallen into a familiar forename relationship in our correspondence, of Jean Perreault, the man, I can draw no intimate portrait, so it must remain for readers who know him no better than I, to picture a rather gaunt, but genial, mixture of Sherlock Holmes and Don Quixote. Not that he is 'quixotic', for his idealism is not unrealistic or ludicrous, but blended with an unusual pragmatism — enabling him to probe deep and carry his logical arguments to fruitful conclusions. Perhaps it is the French ancestry implied by his name that has endowed him with such admirable precision and semantic tenacity: maybe it is even more his obvious enthusiasm for so many aspects of civilisation and culture that I can share: whatever it is, the image I have is particularly appealing to my romantic — perhaps too romantic — Anglo-Celtic temper. But this is taking us into the realm of surmise, and I must turn to the content and intent of Perreault's essays.

The title *'Towards a theory for UDC'* is apt, in that it implies that UDC still lacks a sufficient, consistent body of theory; and indeed this has been recognised by FID/CCC, who have just set up a second subcommittee CCC-F (Fundamentals) to complement CCC-M (Mechanisation). But the book is not pure theory, of course: it has its practical aspects and often reveals a polemic — even crusading — spirit, which I find enjoyable, though others may not. In the opening essays, we are given rather philosophical discourses on general retrieval/

classification theory and encounter (in IV) the principle of tripartition and triads, so consistently used in the Relator schema (VIII and IX). Those who at first find these indigestible should persevere, for they contain much that is fundamental and valuable for the understanding of later parts of the book. In the next few essays, we are plunged deep into UDC waters — rules of formation, the colon and Boolean operators (an appendix to the Copenhagen seminar), transparency and self-definition — in which we learn the importance of context (KWIC, thesauri, etc), of facet analysis and synthesis (with special reference to Ranganathan's pioneering work), and of Perreault's own ideas on classificatory relationships.

Then come to the two contributions VIII and IX — 'Categories and relators: a new schema' and 'Emendations to the relator schema' which, more than any others, have made the name Perreault familiar even amongst the most orthodox UDC users. Espoused by FID/CCC after limited testing and a rather wide enquiry, the emended relator-schema has been issued in the form of an FID proposal (P-note 958): if accepted for the proposed 5-year trial period, • it is hoped that further experiences of the use of the schema will lead to the official adoption of some such enrichment of the relational indicator (: colon) in the UDC. There are, however, those, it must be added, who fear that the schema (which is designed also for use in systems other than UDC) goes too far in its detail, and may lead to confusion if applied in parts of the main schedules where other relational devices already exist.

Several further essays deal with faceting and notational devices — including the suggested use of 'comma' divisions in place of Ranganathan's 'octave device to achieve maximum hospitality in array, and a new colon-dot (:.) device to replace the apostrophe, and here we can only admire the skilful manner in which Perreault combines ingenuity with his customary logic, even if we cannot always accept the results.

The three last essays XV to XVII, by way of contrast, are of a more practical and polemical nature: they are directed mainly towards those who must decide what system to adopt for initial classification or reclassification of a document collection — favouring strongly a general rather than an ad hoc (special) scheme and pleading specially with those having to reclassify from the Dewey DC to adopt the UDC (as next of kin) rather than the Library of Congress (LC) or some other classification. 'What is needed', says Perreault in the last paragraph of XVII, 'is a classification capable of discriminating between documents dealing with unusual and narrow topics. . . such a classification will almost certainly also be capable of dealing with documents on ordinary and/or broad topics . . . the system that is best able to handle the unforeseen is that most appropriate as our reclassificatory choice, and in this UDC is ahead of DC, LC and LCSH.'

I may conclude by reaffirming the conviction of FID/CCC that the UDC, already adopted by tens of thousands of institutional users the world over, is — even in its present state — a viable candidate not only for traditional library shelving and (subject) cataloguing, but also for the unifying or switching function so essential to any mechanized information retrieval system or network — whether at international, national or enterprise level, whether general or specialised in scope. With men of the calibre of Jean Perreault working to improve it, the UDC could well become *the* standard unifying classification in every country of the world.

Apocalyptic, utopian and unrealistic this may seem to many, just as did the 'Cite mondiale' of the UDC pioneers Otlet and LaFontaine; but we — some 70 years later, swept by the blast of an even greater information explosion than they — have both the hardware and the software to help us control and harness the effects for the benefit of society and human progress. If Jean Perreault still be dubbed a modern Don Quixote, let me straightway ride with him as Sancho Panza!

Geoffrey Lloyd

Head, FID Classification Department
and Secretary to FID/CCC

Introduction

What this volume contains is n o t a treatise. Perhaps (unlike Ranganathan's or Bliss's treatises, which cast so much helpful light on the systems of classification which they have each nearly single-handedly worked out) there can be no such thing as a treatise on UDC. Perhaps not, but to me it seems to be something that should be tried, but I have not tried it here — at least partly because UDC has arisen in a way so much less unified than is the case with the genesis of CC or BC.

This is something that UDC shares with LC: that they have arisen out of the efforts of a multiplicity of classificationists and subject specialists and their very disunity gives rise both to strengths and to weaknesses. Strengths, in that subject specialists could expend their energies on the particular problems of a class that they were passionately interested in; weaknesses, in that a rather looser grip is evidenced in the way in which they are to be used.

To teach BC or CC — or for that matter, DC — is an easier matter than to teach LC. UDC is less difficult than LC to teach, because it does have a great deal less disunity; but it is difficult to use, because *policies* can have a stronger impact on it as a *system* than is the case with BC, CC or DC.

This is so, at least so some extent, because for it to be t r u l y a system there needs to be a *theory* through which the learner/ teacher/user can see it, a view that gives a grasp of a manifold of particulars in a structured whole, a means to render the details of the 'system' unitarily transparent. Some of the essays below represent at least splinters of such a transparency, splinters in which can be seen reflected a general theory about classification and search strategy in general. And since that general theory is far more easily visible to the author than to the reader of any such particular essay, it seemed well to precede the whole with a few more general essays in which that theory had been developed.

These having been read, a frame of reference is formed that, it is hoped, will eliminate the necessity to rewrite the specifically UDC-oriented essays in such a way as to help that frame to become visible. (That they have not been rewritten as if to form a treatise will be seen in the more than occasion redundancy.)

The essays — all of them which have been published before — have been strenuously revised, though not to the extent of making me back out of ideas I now might not quite so enthusiastically champion. For instance, the two essays 'Categories and relators' and 'Emendations to the relator-schema' might well have been assimilated, so that points of view enunciated in the earlier would simply drop out of sight in favour of the appropriate emendation; but part of my intention is to make it possible to refer to this volume as a compilation of previously published papers in a perfected form, at the same time making reference to the original periodical sources unnecessary

It may well be noted that a significant hiatus obtains in this volume: the lack of discussion of the substantive situation of UDC in terms of up-to-dateness, terminological clarity and accuracy, appropriateness of collocation, *etc.* This is not to indicate that no questions need be raised over these matters; I can only beg the reader's indulgence, hoping to absolve myself by saying again: what this volume contains is n o t a treatise.

J M PERREAULT

GENERAL THEORETICAL BACKGROUND

A basic consideration on the theoretical analysis of any system of search strategy is the structure of the relations between its elementary parts. In the essay 'Documentary relevance and structural hierarchy' I have stated my preference for a certain sort of notation, but more importantly, have argued for a parity between the method of content analysis and of formulation of classificatory structures. Documentary hierarchy arises from two sources: our *Wesensschau* of ideas, and our observation of the attributes of the documentary population. Neither must be allowed to dominate the other.

The structure of a hierarchy is far from the only essential structure in classification – at least in d o c u m e n t a r y classification –; to it must be added the formal structure of the expressions that arise from its application to the documentary population. Since retrieval is our final cause, since retrieval is effected by consultation of a file, since consultation of a file depends on predictable order therein, and since such order (if the file is made up of conceptual complexes rather than of mere conceptual elements) depends on the order internal to the filed conceptual complexes; since I accept these premisses, a precise determination of such internal order is a fundamental part of a theory of classification. Again, since classification a s applied is a means of revelation of the content analysed as relevantly present, and since meaning depends largely on the order of conceptual elements, the same conclusion arises. Thus the cruciality of the essay on 'Citation order' in a general theory of search strategy.

The application of search-strategic systems involves the expectation that a file will be searched by persons unaware of the precise level of generality of documents surrogated therein. An objection is raised in 'Reflections on the relation between *general* and *special* in verbal search strategies' to certain unhelpful restrictions placed on the clear view available to the searcher in a verbally-based file; a preference for a classed file can be seen to motivate this argument.

Finally, looking at a search-strategic system as an artificial language (as I do), there arises the need for an understanding of the fundamentally linguistic problems involved in the formulation of surrogational reductions of a document's analysed contents. What is it that motivates the use not of conceptual elements m the construction of a file of surrogates, but of conceptual c o m p l e x e s? This is the problem of the essay 'On the articulation of surrogates' The theory therein put forward stands opposed to the linguistically agnostic arguments of Eric de Grolier; I am aware that in large measure what I propose is not really proved but only asserted; far fuller philosophical investigation would be necessary to arrive at such a full proof.

I

Documentary relevance and structural hierarchy

There is no writer today more closely identified with research into the idea of *relevance* as operative within the field of documentation than Donald J Hillman. It is not certain that he sees any real hope for arrival at any sort of technique capable of producing document surrogates relevant to real queries — thus excepting those that satisfy queries derived from 'source documents'. Yet in his paper 'The notion of relevance (1)'[1] he cites, presumably because it is relevant to his own discussion, a paper by B C Vickery, 'The structure of retrieval systems'[2]. No classifier, surely, probably not even an indexer, would have thought of using any such conceptual indicator as 'relevance' for Vickery's paper. If (and it is really conditional) we agree with the proponents of citation indices, it must be that Vickery's paper is relevant to Hillman's topic. But why? Even more, h o w can a technique be devised capable of mechanically tracking down Vickery's paper as a result of the query 'What is available on relevance?'?

Hillman puts the idea of relevance into question, but it seems to me that even so no one would be unable to say quite a bit about the idea, or at least to decide 'whether document Z is relevant to query A'. The term itself has become fashionably popular since Cleverdon's test results were phrased in such a way as to emphasize precision and recall above all other possible criteria of the evaluation of retrieval tests[3]. Yet it cannot be

1 D J Hillman, 'The notion of relevance(I)' (*American documentation.* xv (1964), 26-34); *cf* in general J E L Farradance, 'Classification and mechanical selection' (*Proceedings,* International Study Conference on Classification for Information Retrieval, Dorking, 1957 (London, ASLIB, 1957), 65-69, 106-107).

2 *Proceedings,* International Conference on Scientific Information, Washington, 1968 (Washington, National Academy of Sciences, 1959), ii, 1275-1289.

3 For a much broader list of such criteria, see *Summary,* Study Conference on Evaluation of Document Searching Systems and Procedures, Washington, 1964 (Washington, National Science Foundation, 1965), 6-10.

evaded that some things which someone thought (when he indexed a particular document) were relevant to certain topics were (from the querists's point of view) not so [4] ; it is the disparity which lowers the precision ratio. Such disparity is also called (in conformity with another fashion, that of 'information theory') *noise*. Also, some things the querist would (presumably, if he were able to get at them) call relevant, but which the indexer did not, are missed, lowering the recall ratio [5] . This disparity could also be called (in conformity with the same fashion) *silence*.

But another factor enters, which most reference librarians have encountered many times: purely conceptual relevance (match, fit between query and document orientation) is not enough for a patron in the real world, even if it may be good enough in a test situation. Even if all+only (conceptually) relevant documents are retrieved, they may not each be of use to the querist; formal and/or nominal considerations [6] may make even what is conceptually relevant inappropriate to a particular query.

One characteristic of relevance, then, as anyone could have seen, is that a judgment on it is a *value* judgment.

In both cases of disparity noted, leading either to *noise* or to *silence* — or in cases of formal or nominal inappropriateness — there is a sort of block involved; a block which the temporal nature of storage and retrieval brings with it, since it is describeable as 'long-duration information handling' or as a 'delayed message center'. A situation could of course be imagined where the creator of surrogates was in possession of all the queries that were to be allowed, before analysis of the corpus; it would now be unnecessary to create surrogates, but instead

---

4 Or which were retrieved because of faulty syndetic trails.

5 The fact that, in the 'real world' of patrons and reference librarians, the condition is that the querist can n o t get at all the relevant documents unless the system reveals them to him, and that therefore the only legitimate technique for evaluation of performance is reading, by the querist, through the whole corpus to determine which (additional) relevant documents ought to have been supplied, and which supplied documents ought to have been omitted, effectively vitiates all critiques of the source-document-based 'artificial' questions used by Cleverdon.

6 See J M Perreault, 'The catalog and the problems of bibliography' (*Libri*, xv/4 (1965), 291-301), § D (4).

7 See the work cited in fn 3 for a statement which,while certainly putting relevance among values, tends to make it so subjective as to be quite ineffable: "Relevance cannot function as a criterion since there is no standard against which relevance judgments can be measured."

only to check each document for relevance to each query. But even in this situation the querist, having delegated the relevance-judgments, could be disappointed by the results i f h e t o o h a d a c c e s s t o t h e c o r p u s.

The future query, though, in the normal situation, cannot be anticipated in its own concreteness (as the past/present one can be), so the surrogate-creator attempts to indicate instead the orientation(s) o f t h e d o c u m e n t. 'Concreteness' in this context is taken in the technical philosophical sense, signifying that an entity is actual when it has received ('is concretized out of') all its formal and material perfections — or, that an essence or nature is made up of several intersecting or overlaid formalities. From this point of view, the c o n creteness of a document which could be d i s cretely coded as A, B, C, D, could be exemplified (in particular by the punctuation) thus: $A:([B + C](D))$, or the like. The concreteness of the query is postulated as unlikely ever to match such a notation, but instead to be $B(E) + F$, or $A_1 : C(\delta)$, or the like. There are quasi-intersections between individual (discrete) formalities in each of these configurations, such (perhaps) as to make the document relevant to the queries [8].

The desideratum in mechanised retrieval is this, that the 'perhaps' be validly removeable; that, in other words, formal conformity be equivalent to material relevance (and hopefully, by the aid of formal and nominal elements in the document surrogate, appropriateness as well); and, in still other words, that the only operation required of the mechanism be a clerical one. But, the real problem is not 'that' or 'whether', but 'h o w'.

If, in our example A_1 signifies a species of the genus A, what are the conditions under which the document $A: ([B + C](D))$ would be relevant to the query A_1 (ignoring the rest of the original query example for the moment)? It is simply this, stated as a binding convention:

The concepts $A_1, A_2 \ldots \ldots A_n$ are so named because of the normality of their treatment together ($=A$). Where thus treated together, A is the indicator. Where treated in only partial

---

8 The difference between this situation (storage for future retrieval) and the hypothetical one outlined where there is no storage, is, besides the lack of futurity-based modes of effort, a wholly different attitude of analysis, depending on the possession or lack of the queries that are to be satisfied; what the proponents of natural-language whole-text 'retrieval' are really striving for is removed of the 're-' by putting the computer in the place of the non-surrogate-creating analyst. Again, the lack of (at least some future) queries is what leads to the creation of surrogates, and is what forces analysis according to all that the analyst c a n have at hand: the document itself.

togetherness, A is no longer totally appropriate, and must be
omitted in favour of those of its species actually present.
For instance, if in the upper genus 'dogs' there is a division by size
at least one middle genus will result as 'miniature dogs' —
besides other such middle genera. If the middle genus
'miniature dogs' is itself divided into Pekinese, Chihuahua, *etc,*
it can itself be validly applied only when all the named species
are present in the document. The second part of the binding
convention is thus:

No genus may be pre-scribed as including a set of species
without literary warrant for the normality of such
generalisation; no species may be pre-scribed as included
in a genus except for converse reasons. Nor may any
genus be in-scribed unless the document so in-scribed
treats the various species pre-scribed to that genus; nor,
mutatis mutandis, any species.

Hence, if the example above reads such that A is 'miniature
dogs' and A_1 is Pekinese, our convention indeed insures that
$A: ([B + C](D))$ is relevant to A_1. But, probably, other formalities
— as in the example $A_1 : C(\delta)$ — will be present in each query.
Postulating that the document-surrogate can be translated as
'influence of cold (B) and insufficient nutrition (C) as characteristic of high altitudes (D) upon miniature dogs (A)'; and
postulating the query to be translatable as 'influence of
insufficient nutrition (C) as characteristic of abnormal
environments (δ — the upper genus of D) upon Pekinese (A_1)',
it can be seen that a purely clerical operation of the mechanism
will produce the document in response to the query, and that
its relevance is guaranteed by the convention.

Unfortunately, this solution extends no further than to what can
be called 'explicit relevance'. Such a case as was the starting
point of this paper may not be included in it. But we do catch
a glimpse of another characteristic of relevance, that a judgment
on it is a *hierarchic* value judgment.

However, another look at what underlies the convention may
furnish additional clues for a fuller solution. It has been proposed
that classification is not necessarily hierarchical [9]. I cannot agree
that it is a legitimate use of the word 'classification' to apply it
to a mode of document-surrogation which does not have the

9 For instance by O F Taulbee in 'New mathematics for a new problem'
Electronic information handling (Allen Kent and O E Taulbee *ed* , London,

characteristic 'hierarchical'. This presents the problem of an explicit distinction between (hierarchical) classification and those modes I would characterise as 'indexing' — in any case, a clearer distinction has been needed for some time [10].

Indexing itself can be of at least two types, depending on whether it is controlled or uncontrolled in its vocabulary; this distinction could be put also as 'whether its vocabulary is external or internal to the document(s)'. If controlled, it *a*-scribes concepts to a document, if uncontrolled, it *de*-scribes the document by the words in it. Thus, the use of controlled subject headings [11], just as much as the setting up of a concordance, is indexing; they are both (−)scription of e l e m e n t s o f t h e d o c u m e n t s.

Classification, on the other hand, is not concerned with the detection of concepts or words within documents, at least not as a final purpose. It is concerned instead with *pre*-scription positions within a systematic conceptual organisation, and with *in*-scription of the documents to such positions and of such position indications to documents and surrogates. Thus classification too is (−)scription, not of the elements of documents, but o f d o c u m e n t s a s w h o l e s a n d o f t h e c o r p u s a s a w h o l e. This may connote the marshalling function of traditional library cataloging classification, or, on the other hand, the c o n c r e t e p r e - s c r i p t i o n (recall that concreteness is defined by the intersection of formalities) of articles in the *Revue internationale de la documentation, Referativnyi zhurnal, Nachrichten für Dokumentation, etc,* to complex UDC numbers.

The systematic-conceptual-organisation aspect of classification is also characteristic, to some extent, of controlled thesaural subject headings, where, if fully graphed out [12], the syndetic aspects would result in a systematic conceptual organisation, however inadequate or difficult to follow through. It is not classification, though, in that it avoids going beyond the discrete level of indication of topical orientation — except

10 *Cf* for instance J Mills, 'Classification as an indexing device' (International Study Conference on Classification Research, *Classification research* (Copenhagen, Munksgaard, 1965, (428-444).

11 In the sense that they are controlled, then, what Mooers call *d e s criptors* must be re-named '*a*scriptors', since if controlled they are n o t taken *from* ('de-') the document, but are ascribed *to* 'a-') it.

12 This is done in J M Perreault, 'The conceptual level in bibliography' (*Libri*, xv/4 (1965) 302-310).

insofar as the idea of roles and links has been adopted by indexers.

Diagrammatically, the new terminology would fit together thus:

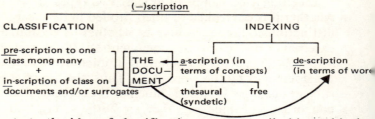

(As a note to the idea of classification as necessarily hierarchical, I will not deny that, even within a hierarchical classification, classes do not stand in a hierarchical relation to e v e r y other cl; Thus, in such a *schema* as this:

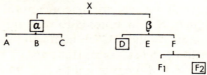

the blocked in classes are not a m o n g t h e m s e l v e s hierarchically arranged. But, just insofar as these notations are conceptually filled and are used in a verbal system (if then, ϖ = fishes, D = felines, F_2 = Pekinese), there are i m p l i c i t (systematic [13] relations between them which constitute hierarchicality a s s o o n a s t h e r e m a i n i n g t e r m s a r e u s e d (if x = anim β = mammals, F = canines, *etc*).)

Going back to the beginning, it can be said that relevance is a sort of double negative. I might very well be able to find a Biblical passage relevant to this paper, just as Hillman found a passage in Vickery; that is, without the thematic orientation of the cited bibliographic entity being such as to indicate the relevance. The Bible is further off, granted, but that is not really why I did not go to it in search . . . I have not done so, not because it is not (possibly) relevant, nor because it is not particularly appropriate, but most of all because there is a fairly

13 *Cf* M Scheele, *Punched-card methods in research and documentation, with special reference to biology* (New York, Interscience, 1962 , 114-127: 'Significance and problems of the theory of order'.

plentiful supply of more clearly relevant material nearer by —
mostly because of the work of Hillman himself. Hillman, on the
other hand, desirous of locating a relevant source by a
documentalist (rather than more citations from Carnap,
Goodman, or other philosophers — note the need for a p p r o-
p r i a t e relevant documents), looked for a double negative: a
document on documentation that was not not relevant to relevance.

Again, though, how can such a process become purely
clerical, in order to be fit for the delicate constitution of the
computer? What good (in line with my own predilections) can
hierarchy be for such a need?

Utilising a hierarchicality that is *structural notationally* as
well as conceptually, the mechanism can easily find the relevant
documents for the Pekinese query (the subscript 'l' is analogous
to a decimal structurality) — of course assuming the binding
force of the convention. This can be reinforced all the more if
the document-surrogate, in place of a merely conjunctive colon
(='mutual influence of some sort'), uses a more precise relational
term (*eg* 'is destroyed by'), and if the query is in such terms as
(instead of its colon) 'is injured by' in a system where not only
substantives but relatives are notated structural-hierarchically [14]
such a query could likewise be satisfied by the document-
surrogate mentioned, because of a subordinate relation between
the query's relational term and that of the surrogate; besides
helping prevent this document's becoming *noise* for a query
where the relation is strongly variant from that mentioned, but
the substantives remain the same.

The necessary factual condition that would now lead to the
discovery of the Vickery document because of the insertion of a
query phrased however Hillman did phrase it, is this: there is a
particular system of document-surrogates organized
conceptually into substantive classes and sub-classes; capable of
being mechanico-clerically manipulated because of the structurality of its notation; and capable of each part within it
becoming modulated by any other part, in accordance with a
relational *schema* similarly structural, hierarchical, and
general-categoric; — such that the terms of the query are
related to the terms of the document-surrogate by pre-established

14 *Cf* J M Perreault, 'Categories and relators: a new schema' (*Revue
internationale de la documentation,* xxxii (1965), 136-144, reprinted below).

paths. Such a condition might, in this case, be met by classification 'X' but not by 'Y' [15], yet tomorrow there might be another query for which 'Y' would produce far superior results. It is impossible therefore to say that any particular substantive organisation (for, since the other characteristics should be made to obtain in a n y classification intended for use with the computer, t h i s is what distinguishes one such system from another) is always best (LC? UDC? CC? *etc*); from this many have validly but wrongly [16] concluded that classification − indeed, the creation of any kind of surrogate − is inadequate as the basis for mechanised retrieval, and that some means of automatic extrapolation from the full text of the author's own verbalization of his thoughts is necessary[17]. But it can be fairly conclusively shown by the testimony of those favorable to such a technique [18] that even such automatic means of creation of document-surrogates is far more successful in regard to classifying than in regard to indexing. And we must take our pick − there are no other available modes of conceptual bibliography. So our previous criteria still stand. We see that even a computer-pre-scribed classification will not necessarily always do for our querists what they would like (though, here as otherwise, *silence* is golden in comparison to *noise*: if the querist doesn't know the answer already − for instance by having read the whole corpus prior to his query − not telling him anything will not reveal the defects of the system as much as will telling him something he c a n see is irrelevant). The question then is: can there be one 'perfect' computer-produced pre-scription? Or, is it just like the 'manual' classifications, a matter of some kind of taste or predilection which guides the creation of such a systematic conceptual organisation? Does factor analysis result in invariably reliable structures − or does associative mapping? Note at once the essential point: if one technique of automatic pre-scription is indeed invariant (so that queries can be constructed in accordance with it), there is surely

15 A substantive factor that would prevent retrieval of the relevant document for the Pekinese question would be, for instance, the non-inclusion of high altitudes (*D*) in abnormal environments.
16 As E H Gilson puts it, 'in so far as logic is concerned, one may be faultlessly wrong as well as faultlessly right', *Being and some philosophers* (Toronto, Pontifical Institute of Mediaeval Studies, 1949), 100.
17 See footnote 8, above.
18 *Cf* M E Stevens, *Automatic indexing: a state-f-the-art report* (Washington, USGPO, 1965) (= National Bureau of Standards Monograph 91).

no need for another technique unless the second results in advantages n o t found in the first — even if while omitting some of the first's advantages.

The task ahead then is to classify classifications, both 'manual' and automatic, a: in accordance with their degree of satisfaction of our criteria, b: in accordance with the substantive structural primordia upon which they are based, and c: (which may be but another way of putting b) in accordance with their attitude towards and provision for relevances.

II

Citation order —
Presuppositions, structure, and function

1.0: Citation order is a set of rules for the ordering of the terms in an artificial-linguistic expression applied to the creation of searchable surrogates in an information storage and retrieval system. One of its earliest expressions is that of Kaiser: concrete + process. More recently, Ranganathan has analysed the terms of all complex artificial-linguistic expressions into membership in one of his five fundamental categories (personality, matter, energy, space, and time), and has argued for a concomitant rule that the terms should combine in that order; Vickery has expanded this set of five fundamental categories to a set of ten: thing, kind, part, property, material, process, operation, agent, space, time, with a similar concomitant rule of order.

Do such rules have a solid foundation, either in theory or in fact? Does their application result in advantage or disadvantage? I wish to outline several fundamental assumptions underlying the idea of such rules, and then to draw conclusions about the effects of their application. This application, I feel, is not restricted just to systematic (or notational) information languages, but should equally appropriately be analysable in regard to verbal information languages.

I. 1 (a): The first fundamental assumption behind citation order is really even further back than that; it is a fundamental assumption behind every information language that has any degree of what is sloppily called 'pre-coordination', or better, articulation or the presence of complexes. The opposing position is that of Taube in his more radical proposals for the use of 'uniterms'. In such proposals no complex was envisioned any more close-knit than the constellation of terms predicated of a particular document. Each term that could be reasonably extracted from or ascribed to a document was something that document was about. We find undigested echoes of such ideas in such a statement as this by Philip Corrigan, that ' a book of

maps descriptive of economic conditions in Europe has three
distinct subjects: MAPS
                       EUROPE
                       ECONOMIC CONDITIONS' [1]
The fact is, of course, that while the document is about economic
conditions and Europe, it is in no sense a b o u t maps, as is implied
by calling maps one of its subjects. But a better way of saying
what it is about is that it is about the economic conditions o f
Europe, and that the kind of information it conveys is of the
sort one expects from maps. Thus we avoid the misleading idea
that it is about Europe in general or about economic conditions
in general, but is only about these two ideas as they modify and
restrict each other.

Another witness to the same point is the tendency, in thesauri
(historically strongly dependent on Taube's theory and on the
practice of the firm he led, Documentation Inc), for potential
error to be avoided by the construction of already-bound
complex 'terms'[2].

What we are led to by all this is that meaning is not a property
of each term taken in isolation, but that meaning arises in the
relatedness of terms; in a word, in *complexes* of terms.

I. 1 (b): The second fundamental assumption is rather closer
to home: if meaning arises in complexes of terms, and if our
means of communication of meaning is temporal, *viz* one-
dimensional, then the order of the terms that make up the
complex must be the determinant of their relatedness. This has
already been implied in that along with the development of a
two-five, or ten-category membership-analysis of the terms of
every complex, there is a concomitant decision as to the order
in which such terms may be combined. The hoariest of the
several hoary jokes about this is the difference between 'blind
Venetians' and 'venetian blinds'. Examples could be amassed
unconscionably; I will rest content with one favoured by
Ranganathan: 'history of classification' and 'classification of
history' – which, by the way, is a far fairer test, resting on no
internal (semantic) ambiguities as with the first example, but
being an ambiguity of external relation only, and being

1   P R D Corrigan, *An introduction to Sears list of subject headings*
    (London, Bingley, 1967), 32.

2   See for instance several mentions and exemplifications in K G B Bakewell,
    Classification for information retrieval (London, Bingley, 1968), 48-50,
    67-69, 78, 91, and in the introduction to the *Thesaurus of ERIC
    descriptors* (Washington, USOE, 1967), XIII-XIV.

brought about by a change of order alone.

Thus, if the document conveys a meaning that would be falsified by a variant order in the terms of the information language used to construct the complex expression referring to it, that variant cannot be allowed. Yet this most crucial of all points in regard to citation order is often masked beneath a discussion of citation order as a factor in the convenience of use of one information language as against another.

I. 1 (c) For instance LC and DC are often compared in their organisation of the literature-collection in favor (resp) of the scholar and the general reader. It is assumed for the sake of the argument that the scholar is interested in finding all the works of a particular author together, and all the secondary works devoted to him; and, further, that in proximity to the works by and about one author should be those of other authors of the same period. Thus the citation order for literature in LC is Language: Period: Author: Form of work. On the other hand, it is assumed that the general reader is more concerned to find together all those works in a language which are in the same form, since he desires not to study but to read. Thus the citation order for literature in DC is Language: Form: Author. These variants do not suffice to introduce any change of meaning; since ambiguity is avoided, convenience can be sought. Whether the convenience attained is universally accepted as such, however, is a very open question: surely some general readers a r e interested not in a form of literature but in a period, and DC gives them no help in locating it; similarly, the scholar may well need convenient access to all representatives of a form, and LC gives no help in providing it. (It is surely largely from this non-universality that the attempt of Taube has sprung, an attempt which favors no one but in the process allows the destruction of meaning.)

I. 2 (a): From these fundamental assumptions (complex meaning, orderedness with complexes, and variability for the sake of convenience) there flows an important operational feature. The variability allowed under the third assumption, as well as the subordination called for under the second, gives rise to distributed relatives. These terms are not easy to detect in the browsing of a file or shelf, since they determine the position of entries or of documents only as modifications of previous, more prepotent [3]

3   See S R Ranganathan, *Headings and canons; comparative study of five catalogue codes* (London, Blunt, 1955), 59-63.

term(s) in the complex. Yet these terms may occur as direct modifications of the class itself; and the important point to note is that when they do, they will invariably be considered to be more general than those terms which could intervene between them and the class. From this arises the important operational feature of the inverse relation between citation order and filing order. This has been adequately discussed by Jack Mills in his *Modern outline of library classification* [4], but he centers almost the whole of his attention on the citation order, treating the filing order as a reverse of it. The fact is that from the desired filing order (generated from the nearly most fundamental of all fundamental classificatory assumptions: *general before special*) there can arise i t s inverse, the citation order, just as well as the other way 'round.

The inversion itself, by the way, is not difficult to grasp; what i s difficult to grasp is the fact that the general-before-special principle does not contradict the citation-o r d e r principle of decreasing concreteness. This last can be seen exemplified in all three (Kaiser, Ranganathan, Vickery) mentioned categoric-analyses and especially in their concomitant citation orders: 'concrete' is more concrete than 'process', 'personality' is more concrete than 'matter', which in turn is more concrete than 'energy', *etc*; 'thing' is more concrete than 'kind', which in turn is more concrete than 'part', *etc*. Therefore the least concrete category will necessarily fall last in the citation order, but, because it is the most general at the same time, it will be first in the filing order when it occurs without any of the intervening terms.

I. 2 (b): Another interesting observation can be made about this inversion relation. It is that each category in the order can be determined as being more concrete than another by virtue of its divisibility by that other; in fact this could be called a corollary of the second fundamental assumption, since its negative is not true. Thus it can be stated as a negative condition: if the terms in category *P* can n o t divide those of category *Q*, then *Q* must precede in the citation order[5]; it would not be true, though, to

4 (London, Chapman and Hall, 1960), 11-20.
5 If, that is, neither is a dependent to some third category.

say that because the terms in category P c a n divide those of category Q, that Q must follow it in the citation order. Therefore the structure of a class with three categories of division is:

> X (class): A (least concrete category))
> X : B (next more concrete category)
> X : B : A
> X : C (most concrete category)
> X : C : A
> X : C : B
> X : C : B : A

I. 3: But this is an unnecessarily opaque way of visualising the matter (though we will see in a moment that its opacity is characteristic of verbal information languages when they attempt such complexes); let us instead envision a matrix coded as above, and we see at once that B is divisable by A, and that since C is divisable by B, it repeats the pattern of B-division; adding a yet more concrete category D shows it as divisible in the same manner as all the less concrete categories that preceded it:

X				
X				A
X			B	
X			B	A
X		C		
X		C		A
X		C	B	
X		C	B	A

X	D			
X	D			A
X	D		B	
X	D		B	A
X	D	C		
X	D	C		A
X	D	C	B	
X	D	C	B	A

Note that the double horizontal lines occur whenever a new (previously uncited) category comes into play. The structure subordinate to D is the same as the structure prior to the introduction of D; the structure to C is the same as the structure prior to its introduction; the structure subordinate to B is the same as the structure prior to its introduction; the structure subordinate to A is absent, which mirrors the lack of any sub-division prior to its introduction.

It is thus fairly easily seen that the filing principle 'general before special' is in no conflict with the citation order principle 'concrete (special) before abstract (general)'. Note too that the usual layout of the schedule is (and for good reason) the same as that of the filing principle; from this arises the dictum 'synthesize from bottom to top of schedule'. Imagine a schedule of the form.

class X
category A (most general in filing, most abstract in citation)
    term 1
    term 2
category B (most special in filing, most concrete in citation)
    term 1
    term 2

from which could be constructed such codes as $XA1$, $XA2$, $XB1$, $XB1A1$, $XB1A2$, $XB2$, $XB2A1$, and $XB2A2$. Both general-before-special filing and concrete-before-abstract citation work out fine with the dictum 'synthesize from bottom to top of schedule'. But to schedule the first cited, so that the dictum would become 'synthesize from top to bottom of schedule' would be disastrous. Imagine a schedule of the form:

class X
category A (most general in filing, most concrete in citation)
    term 1
    term 2
category B (most special in filing, most abstract in citation)
    term 1
    term 2

What has happened is that the original coupling (general filing + abstract citing, special filing + concrete citing), which could be symbolised '$A + 1, B + 2$', has been broken up into a pattern symbolisable as '$A + 2, B + 1$'. It may seem at first that this is of no great importance until it is noted that this now introduces a conflict: the general-before-special filing is not embodied in general-before-special concepts, but just the reverse: what files first is what cites first, and is accordingly the l e a s t general

(Of course it would equally be possible to rearrange the original coupling so as to retain the general-before-special filing in a meaningful sense, while upsetting the citation order formula so as to put the most concrete category last; but this would produce an unwarranted distribution of precisely those terms most likely to be desired to be easily searched out.)

I. 4: Thus far we have seen the three fundamental assumptions of citation order and have examined, with the aid of a matrix-model, the idea of filing order as the inversion of citation order. It should now be pointed out that citation order is occasionally unable to indicate the precise meaning of a complex of terms, and that this lack can be supplied, apparently, only by the use of an explicit symbol of relation. This topic, however, is outside the scope of the present paper; for discussions of many aspects of it and references to other discussions, see the *Proceedings* of the International Symposium on Relational Factors in Classification [6]. A few examples of this lack will arise in examples below.

II.0: Citation order is something within information retrieval systems; it is a rule; it depends on membership of the terms so ordered in categories such as 'process', 'agent', 'time'; it is the basis for the construction of all faceted and/or analytico-synthetic classifications; its implicit presence can be detected even in classification systems not constructed upon it.

There has been a considerable rise in interest in classification systems, both in terms of analysis of them and of their application, in the United States in the last few years. However, at least in the special library and information center field(s), there has been a historical attachment to the theory and practice of Taube, or to descendants thereof. This theory involves the use not of notational equivalents of concepts, but of verbal equivalents — in a word, words.

II. 1: Subject headings have long figured as the standard verbal search-strategisations; but subject headings are just as much attacked by Taube's theories as are notational classifications. This is not difficult to understand, since subject headings are also characterised by the incidence of distributed relatives, and thus can be criticized by Taube as favoritistic.

Can subject headings be analysed as implicitly containing citation order? Take such a heading as TIDES. This (in LCSH) has the indirect geographic subdivision allowed to it, as well as two special subdivision, — TABLES and

6   *Ed* J M Perreault (Oxford, Pergamon, 1967) (=*Information storage and retrieval,* iii/4 (1967)).

—UTILIZATION (which last is actually a *see* reference to TIDAL POWER). Surely then, for a document on tidal tables for the Atlantic Ocean there might be three possible configurations of entry:

a: 1.   TIDES–TABLES
       2.   TIDES–ATLANTIC OCEAN

b: 1.   TIDES–ATLANTIC OCEAN–TABLES

c: 1.   TIDES–TABLES–ATLANTIC OCEAN

One might argue for *a*, in that as against *b* or *c* it does not risk distribution of either subordinate term. But the fact of LC practice is that *c* is the solution used; what rule brings about this practice rather than that represented by *b*? I would analyse it as an unconscious adherence to an implicit rule of citation order which can be explicated thus: A topic may have indirect geographic subdivisions, and where these are allowed they are attached to the general topic; there may also be enumerated topical subdivisions, and where these are allowed they are considered to be more specifically divisions of the topic than are the geographic subdivisions; therefore the order of combination, when all three are called for by a particular document, is TOPIC– TOPICAL SUBDIVISION – GEOGRAPHIC SUBDIVISION.

Into this apparently neat configuration can be introduced a great deal of further difficulty, in those cases where the subdividing terms are not in a single alphabetical array but instead are grouped into more or less consciously recognised facets. The heading CHEMISTRY and its dashed-on and comma'd-on subdivisions is at least partially a case in point [7]: the sub-divisions introduced by the dash are more general, and are attached to the general heading CHEMISTRY; there is no geographic subdivision; the subdivisions introduced by the comma are more special, denoting kinds of chemistry (*eg,* resp, CHEMISTRY – EXPERIMENTS and CHEMISTRY, ORGANIC). Under CHEMISTRY, ORGANIC there is also enumerated the subdivision –EXPERIMENTS; but this sub-

7   An even more fully confused one is that for the heading ART: see my discussion of it in 'Approaches to library filing by computer (*Proceedings* of the 1966 Clinic on Library Applications of Data Processing (Champaign, Illinois Union Bookstore, 1966), 47-90), esp 59-63; the paper is also available in *The indexer,* v (1967), 169-187, esp 177- 180..

division is not found under CHEMISTRY, ANALYTIC or CHEMISTRY, LEGAL or several other such kinds of chemistry. It therefore is n o t freely combinable with such kind-headings. But it is clear that the system would be more likely, eventually at least, to tolerate a heading such as CHEMISTRY, ANALYTIC — EXPERIMENTS than CHEMISTRY — EXPERIMENTS — ANALYTIC, and this for two reasons. The first is the more basic: the meaning is not the same, since in each case the adjective 'analytic' modifies the term that precedes it. The second is also important, especially in a practical sense: a user who finds CHEMISTRY, ORGANIC — EXPERIMENTS has a perfect and logical right to expect to be able to shift his focus from *organic* chemistry to *analytic* chemistry without finding a new configuration of the terms making up the complex. These, even if not explicitly recognised, are the same as the second and third fundamental assumptions of citation order given above; and of course the mere existence of headings made up of multiple terms is enough to indicate agreement with the first basic assumption.

It is to be noted that here too, as in notational classification, the dictum 'synthesise from bottom to top of schedule' is operative; in fact, a third, even more special, layer of modifications of CHEMISTRY is to be seen in such headings as CHEMISTRY AS A PROFESSION — a layer which is at the very 'bottom of the schedule', filing after CHEMISTRY, THEORETICAL.

II. 2: But the least obvious application of citation order is precisely that at which the whole of the preceding discussion is aimed, as mere propaedeutic: citation-order rules for the construction of complex headings from the terms given in a thesaurus.

All that is practical for me to do at this stage is to point out what needs to be done to allow for such an application, and to try to show how the disadvantages usually attributed to non-unitermic (complex) headings can be avoided.

II. 2 (a): (1) The categories that can enter into the formation of complexes within the particular field must be assessed, particularly in terms of those modifications in meaning that depend on changes in order. It is then possible, but not necessary, to partition the vocabulary into these categories; if such partitioning is left undone, the various terms can be used as members of the various categories as needed. Such a term as 'bibliography', for instance, can denote either a *problem* (as in such a title as 'the need for exhaustive bibliography of Asiatic biological research') or a *form* (as in such a title as 'introductory bibliography on angiosperms').

Symbols to indicate the categorical membership of each term in the complex must be established.

(2) The vocabulary itself must be structured thesaurally, *ie,* hierarchically, and an index prepared to the position of each used term and to the terms synonymous to these used terms. This, is in regard to primitive (uni-)terms only, leaving aside the possibility that a primitive term is the equivalent of a phrase. Phrases in the thesaurus are to be allowed only when absolutely unitary in meaning.

(3) Rules must be devised for the treatment of relations between complex headings, analogous to the *see also* and *seen also from* references in subject headings.

II. 2 (b): The result of this structuring of the index language would be that a heading term in a complex heading would be seen to be followable by (say) a form-term, by a place-term, or by both; by a topical-subdividing-term, by a topical-subdividing term and a form-term, by a topical-subdividing-term and a place-term, or by all three. In a word, the matrix analysis previously applied to notational classification is seen to lend its transparent structure equally well to verbal information languages. Thus the general-before-special layout can be seen to apply to the terms subordinate to any leading term.

Permutation on each term constituting each complex solves the problem of distributed relatives; the fact that each such term will be shown to be a member of a particular category within the citation order thus assists in interpretation of its meaning And the fact that it will be permuted, *ie* shown as part of a greater whole, will add to each such term the same advantageous context that is added to each term of a title in a KWIC index.

Hierarchical thesauri (though not thematically appropriate to this paper) can prevent the need for 'generic posting'. But hierarchical clues, together with citation order applied to an unpartitioned vocabulary, can give the nearest approximation to the advantages of classification in a verbal system. And the non-partitioning of the vocabulary allows for the thorough analytico-synthetic nature of the application of such a system, as well as helping to keep the vocabulary itself compact and unredundant.

III

Reflections on the relation between *general* and *special* in verbal search strategies

The well known rule for *see also* references in subject heading system is

> Refer from a general heading to a related but more
> special heading; or from a heading to a related heading
> of about the same level of specificity; but n o t from a
> heading to a related but more general heading.

The *see also* references in the Library of Congress subject headings and in Sears' list of subject headings point out that·
this principle is actually practised, though it is not to be denied that there are occasional lapses.

These lapses are not, I believe, unfortunate. For instance, there are the appropriate general-to-special references in LC subject headings, from CLASSICAL LITERATURE to GREEK LITERATURE and to LATIN LITERATURE; but there are also special-to-general references from both GREEK LITERATURE and LATIN LITERATURE to CLASSICAL L LITERATURE. In light of the fact that it can surely be assumed that there can be no discussion of Classical literature that takes no cognisance of both Greek and Latin literatures, this practice is wholly justified; it provides that the searcher (say) for GREEK LITERATURE--COLLECTIONS not be prevented from finding the volumes entered under CLASSICAL LITERATURE--COLLECTIONS, which last could hardly avoid being collections of Greek literature, at least in part.

Another well known rule, this one in the realm of the punched card or computer documentalist (or − though the term surely also refers to what is done when subject headings are searched−: in the realm of information retrieval), is

> Accept documents coded A,B,C, or A,B,D, or
> A,B,E, when the search specification is A,B;
> do n o t accept, in such a search, documents
> coded A,C, or B,C or A,D *etc.*

The rationale behind this rule is similar to the rule favoring general-to-special *see also* references: Each special idea is composed of a general idea plus a specifying concept (man= animal+rational). In searching for A,B a special is being sought which is composed of two generals: A and B; and to leave either out is to allow for automatic retrieval of documents at a more general level. Again, the document entered under A,B,C must be a further specification of A,B; allowance for its retrieval is analogous to retrieving a collection of Greek drama or Greek poetry when the original need was for a collection of Greek literature as a whole.

The popularity of BT, RT and MT (*see also*) reference in so-called thesauri shows a full allowance of the un-traditional special-to-general *see also* reference, though such a structure may not have been conceived as explicitly anti-traditional. BT (broader term) references, though, flourish alongside the searching rule which prevents automatic generalisation: an example of not thinking a problem through to its final implications, an example all too characteristic even of 'modern' library and documentation work.

In respect of subject headings there would be no great difficulty in providing the patron and the reference librarian with information that is at present available only to the cataloguer: the *see also from* (*xx*) references could become the basis for such a mode of information, subject to the same rules about non-allowance of blind references that govern *see also* references. Care would need to be taken to prevent references which were in fact n o t special-to-general *xx*'s, and the adoption of the BT, NT convention might be desirable RT, on the other hand, is a very sloppy matter in many thesauri, and should be accepted in libraries only if it has been thoroughly purified).

In respect of searching in post-coordinate systems, it should be realised that added and unrequested specificity (A,B,C, in response to A,B) is no less dangerous than is subtractive generality. The argument in favour of the rule about references is that a wolf is at least a canine, though a mammal a s s u c h is not a canine; but the argument cuts both ways: the proposition 'a wolf is an animal' is n o t convertible into 'an animal is a wolf'. But the real crux in the case is that not every additional term is a specification; when the search is for 'a bibliography (A) on delta wing (B) aircraft (C)', B is a specification of C,

but A is n o t. Thus the search for A,B,C cannot allow automatic
elimination of A, lest a form of document be retrieved that is
not desired; but the specifying term B (or, if C is taken, as it might
be, to specify B, the specifying term C), if considered to be
automatically eliminable when the search for A,B,C fails to
retrieve any or enough documents, would retrieve documents
entered either under A, B, or A, C. And if the convention that
I have enunciated in 'Documentary relevance and structural
Hierarchy' [1] is followed out, there will be a guarantee that
the general document is relevant to searches for the special
idea as well. The convention reads

The concepts $A_1, A_2, \ldots A_n$ are so named because of the
normality of their treatment together ($=A$). Where thus
treated together, A is the indicator. Where treated in
only partial togetherness, A is no longer totally appropriate, and must be omitted in favour of those of its
species actually present.

No genus [A] may be pre-scribed as including a set of
species [$A_1, A_2, \ldots A_n$] without literary warrant for
the normality of such generalisation; no species may be
pre-scribed as included in a genus except for converse
reasons. Nor may any genus be in-scribed unless the
document so in-scribed treats the various species pre-
scribed to that genus; nor, *mutatis mutandis*, any species.

The convention, of course, is nothing new at all, but merely
makes explicit what all conscientious subject-catalogers and
classifiers know and do.

Since the logic that stands as support for the two rules (the
one against special-to-general *see also* references, the other
allowing for automatic retrieval of greater specificities but not of
greater generalities) is shaky to say the least; and since these
prohibitions are likely to lead to non-retrieval of items guaran-
teeable to be relevant – if the convention about generals and
specials is obeyed–; it must be seriously suggested
either *a*: that subject cataloguers re-examine the problem to see
whether xx references should not be made known to their
patrons, and that documentalists re-examine the tactics of
allowance and non-allowance in their search procedures; or
b: that explicitly classified systems of search strategisation be
considered as means for avoiding the arisal of such problems.

1   *Information storage and retrieval,* iii/1 (1966), 13-18 and *American
    documentation,* xvii (1965), 136-139, reprinted above.

IV

On the articulation of surrogates:
an attempt at an epistemological foundation

There are several levels at which I could discuss the underlying philosophical bases of syntactic relationship, which could be rather summarily enumerated (in order of progressive foundationality) as Psychology of Learning, Epistemology, and finally Ontology.

Rash as it may be, I would propose that the problem of the psychology of learning has been well enough understood already not to be dealt too much at length with: we know enough from genetic psychology [1] to be at least fairly sure of the role of classification in inductive and deductive thinking alike. And I would further propose not to attempt to penetrate even unto the ontological primordia of the problem of relationship, partly because it would necessitate an examination of far more than just syntactic relationship, but even more because such a penetration would have to presuppose a preliminary examination of the epistemological level of foundation. It is thus this epistemological level that it is my hope to examine and lay open.

Epistemology is, even if not thematic in relational systems, proposed or operational, at least strongly present in an implicit way. We can see this in the satisfaction, obtained by the use of relational factors both in classification and in abstracting, of the desire for *information* over and above *indication* [2] It is only in the transformation, by the use of syntactic elements of mere strings or constellations of semantic elements, that indication comes to be information.

To become aware that this is the perennial attitude of the theorist of knowledge, we need only advert to the history of the doctrine 'Truth is found in the judgment'; judgment, in its most

1 See J Piaget, 'Genetic psychology and epistemology' (*Diogenes*, no. 1 (1953) 49-63).
2 See the essay below 'Transparency and self-definition' §2-12.

elemental sense, is the mental act of positing a *relationship* between two (or more) concepts or beings.

It has been to reach this level that i n f o r m a t i v e abstracts have been urged as superior to i n d i c a t i v e, it is the same with the other complementary pairs of classes of concepts or of terms, as suggested by some of those here now: Syntagmata and Paradigmata, Morphemes and Semantemes, Correlators and Correlanda. In all these efforts has been the implicit or explicit recognition of the perennial theme 'truth is the judgment' — not, then, merely in the idea.

A tentative theory of truth

We are all used to the traditional opposition — one assumed to be quite self-evident—between the Objective and the Subjective. It is in fact the great claim of scientific methodology that it is entirely objective, that it does not allow for the intrusion of anything but the evidence of the object being investigated. Over against this claim we can then visualise Kierkegaard's position: 'Truth is Subjectivity'[3].

Now Kierkegaard was not opting for mere whimsicality in philosophy and theology; he was no anarchist bent on reducing science to a shambles of relativistic opinion — at least not 'science' in the broad sense of the virtue of true knowledge. He was, first of all, reacting (or perhaps over-reacting) to that most 'objective' of philosophers, Hegel. It was Hegel's claim, indeed, to have constructed a philosophical system w i t h o u t p r e s u p p o s i t i o n[4]; without in other words, anything that smacked of the intrusion of the implicit opinion of the philosopher; thus, an absolutely objective system, reflecting only the operation of the only really t o t a l system, reality a s a w h o l e, inclusive even of the subjectivity of the philosopher as he reflects upon this whole.

Impossible, perhaps; at least Kierkegaard thought so. His dictum, accordingly, indicates a passionate acceptance of the philosopher's own situation, of the stance of man as creature

3 See *A Kierkegaard anthology*, ed R Bretall (Princeton Univ Press, 1946 [repr. 1951]),210-231 (from *Concluding unscientific postscript to the 'Philosophical fragments'*).
4 See my thesis (unpubl) *The position of nature in the Hegelian system* (Marquette Univ, 1957).

(hence, surrounded by presupposition [5]); and, finally, indicates his acceptance of the principle that only in conscious choice and judgment (which cannot, after all, be else then subjective) can truth and value come forth.

Objectivity and subjectivity may, seen from this historical vantage, seem to stand over against one another; but this vantage may be (I propose 'is') too narrow; subjectivity can include objectivity, just as the reverse was proposed by Hegel. The mind must be receptive, it must be capable of receiving the other as other, for knowledge to be possible. But without subjectivity this 'knowledge' could never be characterised as 'truth', since truth implies (in the perennial dictum) the judgment, the self-moving act of the subject as subjective; or (in the existentialistic usage of Martin Heidegger): truth implies *sammeln* (to gather, to collect) [6].

This discourse on subjectivity is not indulged in for its own sake, but to prepare the ground for another distinction. We hear constantly that classification of documents is not adequate to the 'classification of knowledge'; or, alternatively, that such a sundering is a false and sterile one. I would like to present the *locus classicus* for the first position in the words of Aristotle [7]:

If genera are different and coordinate, their differentiae are themselves different in kind. Take as an instance the genus 'animal' and the genus 'knowledge'. 'With feet', 'two-footed', 'winged', 'aquatic', are differentiae of 'animal'; the species of knowledge are not distinguished by the same differentiae. One species of knowledge does not differ from another in being 'two-footed'.

—Nor does one species of documents from another.

From this we can make one of two conclusions: either those who advocate 'knowledge-classification' do not really know what such a classification would result in, or they mean something else entirely when they use the expression. Since the second

5   See the discussion of *ens creatum* in M Heidegger, *Sein und Zeit*, §6 (*tr*
    J Macquarrie & E Robinson: *Being and time* (New York, Harper, 1962), 46.
    Quotations from *SuZ* in this paper will be given, however, in my own
    version.

6   See W J Richardson, *Heidegger: through phenomenology to thought*
    (The Hague, M Nijhoff, 1963), II, iii. esp. 282 and the cited passages in
    Heidegger's *Einführung in die Metaphysik* (Tübingen, M Niemeyer, 1953).

7   Aristoteles, *Categories, tr* Edghill (*The works of Aristotle,* tr into English
    under the editorship of W D Ross, i (Oxford Univ. Press, 1928 [repr. 1963]). ʲ])
    1ᵇ16-19).

conclusion is not only the kinder but the more likely to be true, let us see whether there can be a justification for it.

One of the most fruitful modern attempts to bridge the apparent gap between objectivity and subjectivity is that erected by its originator into the new sub-fundamental discipline of phenomenology [8] – the work of Edmund Husserl. In his words [9] when we use the phenomenological method 'we direct the glance of apprehension and theoretical inquiry to *pure consciousness in its own absolute Being'*. Thus, dissolved in this pure consciousness, we cease 'subjecting what we experience, transcendent nature, to theoretical inquiries', but what we retain after this 'phenomenological reduction' is 'the whole of Absolute Being, which, properly understood, conceals in itself all transcendences, "consituting" them within itself' [10]. In the words of Heidegger, in his fine summary of what

8   See as a useful summary, I M Bocheński, *The methods of contemporary thought,* tr P Caws (Dordrecht, Neth, D Reidel, 1965), cap II. (His general discussion of epistemology in cap I is also lucid and refreshing.)

9   E Husserl, *Ideen zu einer reinen phänomenologie und phänomenologischen philosophie,*I. Buch, 'Allgemeine Einführung in die reine Phänomenologie'. §50 (tr W R B Gibson: *Ideas; general introduction to pure phenomenology* (London, G Allen & Unwin 1931 [repr 1952], 154-155). The original text is *ed* by W Biemel as Bd III of *Husserliana* (Haag, M Nijhoff, 1950).

10 We can see the fulfilment of Kierkegaard's dictum in as systematic a way as Hegel ever understood. K was sure that there could be no such thing as an existentialistic s y s t e m of philosophy, though there could be individual existentialistic insights; and Husserl's relation to the existentialists (Heidegger and Sartre, at least) has been challenged as tenuous, in view of their small concern for what he valued himself, *ie* a scientific philosophising. But we can see here how his method opens the way for the systematization of K 's original insights, though the ultimate systematization of subjectivity in his *Cartesianische meditationen* (Haag, M Nijhoff, 1959), *ed* by S Strasser as Bd i of *Husserliana* and tr, by D Cairns as *Cartesian meditations* (The Hague, Nijhoff, 1960), is hardly such as to attract latter-day Kierkegaardians to Husserl. Long after completion of this essay I came across the following in G Ballard's *analysis of his phenomenology* (Evanston, Northwestern Univ. Press, 1967), xviii: [Husserl] reduced the reality of the object to the 'seen.' Then that which is present with evidence is reduced to noematic unities of sense (the cogitata); the cogitata are integrated into the cogitationes or noeses, and the latter in turn are integrated into the monadic ego. Thus, though the world remains important as the transcendental guide in phenomenology, phenomenology as a whole becomes in the *Cartesian meditations* an egology, the explication of the self and of its self-constitution, of the Other, of the objective world, and of communities of persons. Thus, the idealism is completed by this reduction or leading back of all reality to its origin in performances of the ego. The weight of objectivity now comes to be shifted from the individuals,full perception of an intended object to an intersubjectively constituted sense which can give general validity to the presumption of objectivity.

phenomenology is [11]

The title 'phenomenology' expresses a maxim which can be formulated as 'to the things themselves!' — as against all free-floating constructs, accidental discoveries, against the acceptance of only apparently indicated concepts, against the illusory questions which are often perpetuated through a whole generations as 'problems'.

What mediation can this idea of phenomenology achieve in the apparent antithesis set forward by Aristotle? It consists in this, that if we obey the phenomenologists' injunction to go to the things themselves we eliminate the subjective/objective disjunction. It is not to deny the dual nature of knowledge, but to replace an external disjunction with a duality characterised by Husserl as 'noetic/noematic', thus [12]:

Intentional experience, one is wont to say, has 'objective reference'; but one also says, it is *'consciousness of something'*, consciousness, for instance, of an apple-tree in blossom here in this garden. We shall not find it necessary at first, in regard to such examples, to keep the two wordings apart. . . . to every noetic, in particular to every thetic-noetic phase, there corresponds a phase in the noema . . . the wording concerning the relation (more specifically the 'direction') of consciousness to its objective points towards a most inward phase of the noema.

Without pretending that we can penetrate the subtleties of this passage, or that in the space available here it can be placed in its context in the whole phenomenological system, this can be explicated — undoubtedly over-briefly — somewhat like this: Knowledge, or better pure consciousness, in itself contains, on (as it were) its two matching surfaces, the noematic reflection of the other, the 'object', and the noetic intention of the knowing (conscious) 'subject'; and that any attempt to separate them in a r e a l sense (as 'objective' over against 'subjective') can be nothing but a crippling aberration.

11 *SuZ* (Tübingen, M Niemeyer, 1953), § 7, 'Die phänomenologische methode der untersuchung', 27-28.
12 *Ideen . . .,* I. Buch, §129 (*tr*, 362-363); Gibson's use of 'phrase' and 'phase' to translate 'Redeweise' and 'Moment' is somewhat confusing, so I have substituted 'wording' for 'phrase'.

Thus, if we succeed in classifying the noetic intentions (knowledge as subjective), we simultaneously classify the noematic reflections of the other (knowledge as objective). Or, in a rather crude formulation, the classification of knowledge can become not merely the separation of facets such as 'methods of proof', 'modes of perception', and the like, but just what Aristotle refused to accept: it can become the classification of the noemata corresponding to the noeses of pure consciousness.

But, to recur to the perennial dictum, 'truth is found in the judgment'. Now, however much the phenomenological theories of Husserl may clear the way for a reconciliation of the classification of knowledge with the classification of documents, by pointing instead at the need for the classification of the various regions of noemata/noeses — this still only extends to the classification of 'isolates' (this last is not to be taken in Ranganathan's sense, but simply to avoid such terms as 'concepts', 'ideas', 'objects', and the like). If we accept the full implications of the dictum, we do not attain even in the profoundest acts of pure consciousness of noematic/noetic 'isolates' to truth [13] but only to the elements that can go to make it up. To listen once again to Aristotle [14]:

> No one of these terms [isolates from any category], in and by itself, involves an affirmation; it is by the combination of such terms that positive or negative statements arise. For every assertion must, as is admitted, be either true or false, whereas expressions which are in no way composite, such as 'man', 'runs', 'wins', cannot be either true or false.

Truth is the judgment, and that which makes judgment possible, given noemata, is, in traditional philosophy, the copula. 'John' is not a truth nor is 'dead'; but 'John is dead' is true, if such is the state of affairs. (We see of course that that which makes truth possible is what the same moment makes error possible; so, 'John' is neither true nor false, nor is 'dead', but 'John is dead' can be either, leading to the naive conclusion that the

13 R Sokolowski, *The formation of Husserl's concept of constitution* (The Hague, M Nijhoff, 1964) , 172, argues that '"Concepts" arise only in judgments. Before the categorical [= syntactical] act of judging takes place, there are only the fluid anticipations of meaning or sense, but such anticipations are not the same as fixed senses'.

Aristotle's conception, the origin of the perennial dictum in its common formulation, may accordingly be judged to be an over-rationalisation of the living reality of the process of conceptualisation/judgment.

14 *Op cit*, 2^a4-10.

41

copula is the sole instrument of the truthful judgment [15].

The copula 'is' is the most rudimentary of all syntactic relationships: it is mere juncture, intersection, conjunction in the Boolean sense. It could be attempted, as in the project of implementing all retrieval processes with Boolean logic, to reduce all relationships to 'is' and 'is not' [16]. But a more thorough linguistic analysis of propositions in natural language shows that the 'Boolean logic' of the documentalist is unutterably poor when compared with the real richness of syntax; indeed, if it were not so we might have succeeded better or more easily in achieving both mechanical translation and automatic retrieval processing of raw text.

'Syntax', etymologically considered, means the coupledness of the structured [17]. Its most rudimentary form may be the copula, but Heidegger — well known for not being willing to accept current understandings of 'is', in his search for the real meaning of 'Being' — shows us clearly that even the copulative 'is' is not a purely univocal concept [18] (besides which, of course, we must remember that 'is' need not always be a copula):

> We say: 'God is.' 'The Earth is.' 'The lecture is in the auditorium.' 'This man is from Swabia.' 'The cup is of silver.' 'The peasant is in the fields.' 'The book is mine.' 'Red is the port side.' 'There is famine in Russia.' 'The enemy is in retreat.' 'The plant louse is in the vineyard.' 'The dog is in the garden.' 'Over all the peaks / is rest.'

---

15 See Bocheński, *op cit*, 6-7, for a discussion of the fundamentality of the much abused two-valued traditional logic.

16 The more common elements of Boolean logic (despite the distance of their current formulation from their original state—*cf* W & M Kneale, *The development of logic* (Oxford, Clarendon Press, 1962, 404-420)—are 'and', 'or', and 'not', but these are capable of a further reduction, as proposed in the text, since 'and' can be taken to mean, in terms of the documents being coded, that class x and y are intersected in it— thus that x is y, extensionally at least, in this document—; 'not' and 'is not' are obviously enough assimilable; 'or' is the only member of the triad that gives trouble in the attempted reduction, but it too succumbs, since it can be seen as the pertinence to the document, discovered in a search for '$x \cap y \cap z$', of either the pair x, z or y, z. Thus 'or' means both 'is' and 'is not'; this, of course, is the basic meaning of alternation. (See also my essay 'Reflections ....').

17 From the Greek συντασσειν, from the latter part of which comes also the ταξις of 'taxonomy'.

18 M Heidegger, *Einführung. . . (tr* Manheim: *An introduction to metaphysics* (New Haven, Yale Univ Press (1959), 89-90). The quotation is modified in a few particulars.

In each case the 'is' is meant differently . . .
'God is'; i.e. he is actually present. 'The Earth is',
i.e. we experience and believe it to be permanently
there; . . . 'Over all the peaks /is rest'; that is to
say??? Does the 'is' in these lines mean, is situated,
is present, takes place, abides? None of these will fit.
And yet it is the same simple 'is'. Or does the verse
mean: Over all the peaks rest prevails, as quiet
    prevails in a classroom? No, that won't do either. Or perhaps:
    Over all the peaks lies rest — or holds sway? That seems better,
    but it also misses the mark.. . . .
    Regardless of how we interpret these examples, they
    show one thing clearly: in the 'is' Being discloses itself
    to us in a diversity of ways.. . . .
And we can go on from here to see that there are manifold
linguistic structures not congruent with even this apparently
simple declarative sort of proposition. But if syntax means
the coupledness of the structured, then the underlying aspect
which joins linguistic analysis to epistemological is *articulation*.
It is not simply that there are junctures in such an enunciation
as 'If John is dead, then Mary should be sad', but that these
articulating junctures do indeed articulate, just as do the sectors
in an arm or the cadences in a piece of music: Articulation is
what makes *discourse* [19] possible, and it is precisely in discourse
(as against the isolated proposition, which can be reduced,
perhaps, to the copulative 'is'—relation alone) that we come
upon the truth (or error) of documents.

To be a contribution to true knowledge (*scientia*), a
document must say something both new and true. Its
newness may not be an absolute newness — indeed many
claim that such is quite out of the question [20] — and its truth
may depend on conditions which are not themselves well
enough substantiated. But for all these modulations to

19 'Discourse' is what is traditionally posed as the capital characteristic of human
    discovery of truth, as well as of human communication — d i s c u r s i v e, as against
i n t u i t i v e and c r e a t i v e on the one hand, and as against merely
p e r c e p t i v e and i r r i t a b l e on the other. Etymologically, it stands very close
to articulation and syntax, since its springs from the need, in working toward the
truth, to gather a variety of insights (perceptions, intuitions, *etc*) togather in some
sort of order; and hence it implies the linear, durational, non-unilateral path of
thought. Aristotle's syllogistic and its successors do no more than predict these
paths.

20 The conclusion towards which a document tends may well not be new, but if
    no new evidence for that conclusion has been adduced, it might better have
    remained unwritten, and surely unpublished.

obtain within the document, it is necessary for it to consist of more than simple declarative propositions. Nietzsche can say 'God is dead', but the truth or falsity, newness or banality, of the content of this proposition depends upon a great many other discursive enunciations forming a whole into which the bald statement fits, and which support it more or less adequately — and which, more importantly, lead toward it from several directions. It is this multi-directionality which can be pointed out as the most essential characteristic of discourse. And just as it is not in pure consciousnesses that truth resides, except by virtue of the copulas (and other syntactic relations) which couple them into judgments, so do judgments unite into discourse and, in so doing, bring about truth of a higher order than 'declarative,truth: a r t i c u l a t e d   t r u t h [20a]

The articulation of surrogates

Just as the articulation of discourse is the revelatory aspect of the document as such, so do we all recognize the need for articulation in the surrogates of documents. It is from this recognition that all the systems of relational factors have arisen; what I hope to present next are some of the surrogational consequences of the foregoing epistemological (or better: aletheiological) discussion.

The articulation of discourse is given; what creates the possibility of an equivalent of it when we set out to create surrogates of this discourse? It was syntax which did so in the discourse itself; can there be such a thing as surrogational syntax? If the discourse can be reduced to its essential (or at

[20a]The question *In what does* b i b l i o g r a p h i c a l *truth consist* ? can be answered partly by saying that a surrogate for *Alice in Wonderland* is as bibliographically true as is a surrogate of a handbook of chemistry if the surrogates are equally well-formed and refer adequately to their respective documentary objects. To follow out the Husserlian references, see the discussion of the three strata of logic described in his *Formale und transzendentale Logik* (Halle, M Niemeyer, 1929) in S Bachelard, *A study of Husserl's 'Formal and transcendental logic,* tr L Embree (Evanston, Northwestern University Press, 1968), 4-24. These three strata deal (resp) with '[p] *ure morphology of judgments*' (namely the significations of the whole and of the parts of even a *confused* judgment), '[t] *logic of non-contradiction or logic : of consequence*' (namely of *distinct* judgments), and '[t] *he logic of truth*' (namely of *clear* judgments). Only this last demands evidential *fulfilment* in its proper Husserlian sense, and only in this stratum does a distinction between *Alice* and more 'factual' documents arise; bibliographical truth is accordingly a matter of no more than the first two strata-excluding, that is, all problematic of content-analysis.

least centrally thematic) pure conceptualities, then a similar reduction should be possible with the syntax. An articulation proportionate to the conceptually substantive elements of the surrogate is what is aimed at by the various systems that are represented at the present symposium.

In all transformations of conceptual complexes (as in explication, paraphrase, and the like), the one thing that must be avoided is oversimplification. It cannot be denied that the surrogate is a simplification of the document's discourse: it is what (we hope) will make it possible to retrieve the document when it is relevant — and not retrieve it when it is not — without having to read the whole document itself.(As Mills well puts it, 'The purpose of indexing is to tell us what we can afford to ignore ' 21.) By surrogational oversimplification I mean first that indicational storage of surrogates which stops short at what, in discourse itself, would be pure conceptualities; and second that addition to the pure conceptualities of such quasi-syntax as serves not to articulate the surrogate into discourse, but merely to qualify the pure conceptualities.

An example will aid in clarifying this. In the articulate propositional discursus 'If John is dead, then Mary should be sad', the whole can be characterised as conditional, and the antecedent and consequent conditions then can be characterised as the possibility of John's deadness and the moral certitude of the depressative effect of this antecedent upon Mary. But even this paraphrase remains articulated; whereas a paraphrase that merely qualified the substantive elements 'John', 'dead', 'Mary', and 'sad' could be later rearticulated into 'If Mary is sad, then John should be dead', or the like — which can mean two entirely different things, due to the ambiguity of 'should': *a*: ought to be, *b*: can be assumed to be. The articulation that can afford protection against the first-mentioned mis-articulation is such as is characterised as 'links' or 'interfixes': The second-mentioned is due to semantic ambiguity, and accordingly is outside my present conspectus.

In the larger picture of surrogational articulation as such, what links would prevent is the apparent reduction of the whole discourse to a single proposition; of the whole arm, as it were, to a single sector of it. In the surrogate, then, we need something analogous to the comma between 'dead' and 'then'. But we need

21 J Mills, 'Information retrieval: a revolt against conventional systems?' (ASLIB *Proceedings*, xvi/2 (1964), 48-63), 49.

more than that, we need an order which can prevent mis-articulations which could take place in more complex discurses. However, it has been proposed that since the addition of what I called quasi-syntax ('roles') to the substantive elements of the surrogate is both highly expensive and of little effect in retrieval, and since links are not expensive but a r e effective, these latter might well be retained even if the former be dispensed with 22. So, granted the need for links, let us set them aside and consider roles more closely, hoping to see why they can be called ineffective.

The role is that which attaches to each substantive element the delimitation of its function within the proposition. Without links, however, it is easy enough to see how little roles could accomplish since if there is more than one substantive with the same role attached to it, then it is no longer clear how this one substantive fits into the discourse, even though the function it performs there is clear and univocal enough. The link, though, if it sets these two identically 'role-d' substantives into separate sub-propositions, can serve to eliminate at least this one sort of ambiguity: it can, as pointed out, take the place of punctuation.

Note that roles must also be accompanied by links for a genuinely syntactic purpose to be fulfilled; roles, alone, lack something that we find even in the rudimentary copula: they do not unite, they simply modify. The link, also, is not by itself syntactic; it is no more than a phrase-marker, a means to a kind of mechanical articulation; but without the role it is rigid and inflexible. Why is this?

Let us return to the nature of syntax as such. It was proposed as 'the coupledness of the structured'. The substantives that enter into surrogates are themselves structured: 'John' is a name, and that which it names is a man, and to be a man is to be a certain element in a larger structure. So what syntax adds, by itself, is the *coupledness*. It is relationship — as is seen more easily in the rudimentary copulative syntax of simple declarative conjunction. But conjunction can be far from simple, it contains implicitly within itself a great many modularities. The essential point, however, is that conjunction, implying as it does a duality (or plurality) of conjoined substantives, is, as against the essence of the role, d y a d i c. The role is m o n a d i c, it

22 See F W Lancaster, 'Some observations on the performance of EJC role indicators in a mechanized retrieval system' (*Special libraries*, 1v/10 (1964) 696-701).

simply modifies, it does not couple. And this coupledness, join-
edness, is that which articulates; and articulation is what enables
discourse. 'Operators', 'Syntagmata', 'Morphemes', 'Correlators'
—all these are d y a d i c, they create an articulatedly discursive
string. 'Roles', on the other hand, being merely monadic,
further our understanding without setting forth an order. Thus
we can have roles added to substantives to give '$A1$', '$B2$',
'$C1$', and '$D3$'; and we can add links to give '[$A1, B2$] ($C1,
D3$)', but in either case we do not attain the flexibility or
articulateness of '$A \alpha B - C \beta D$ [23].

When we have dyadic relations, with the help of supra-
syntactic elements analogous to links, we can achieve to the
most complex of intentional structures. We can create surrogates
in the same way that discourse creates truth by the articulation
of (semantic) conceptual elements into flexible but unambiguous
wholes.

Surrogational articulation in retrieval

Postulating that all subject-analytic, notational, and storage-
organisational theories and practices are for one purpose only,
namely effective retrieval of information, I would like to project
the results of the foregoing articulation of the surrogate, which
itself followed the epistemological considerations with which I
began. And I shall assume that the ultimate desideratum is the
possibility of a system of the most thoroughgoing clericality or,
as I would prefer to call it, r i t u a l i t y, such as is the *unum
necessarium* with the computer as the 'clerk' performing the
retrieval operation. It is my belief (and, I am sure, not mine alone)
that the analysis of needs that can lead to the design of a
computer-based system of retrieval is beneficial in the light it can
shed upon all ritual retrieval operations, even those utilising the
services of human clerks. The retrieval operation, in such a setting,
is entirely dependent upon the quality of the strategy which has
been provided for it in the storage operation and even before, in
the design of the conceptual organisation which will be utilised

23 In the first case 'A, B, C, D' are 'John, dead, Mary, sad', and the numbers
indicate the appropriate roles; in the second the square brackets indicate the
antecedently conditional link, the parentheses the consequent; in the third the
roles and links are replaced by a series of symbols such that 'α' is the copulative
relation, 'β' the relation of moral certitude, ' $-$ ' the supra-relation antecedent/
consequent.

for both storage and retrieval [24]. There are two major aspects that must be considered in this strategic planning — and I must point out that I do not use the term 'strategy' to indicate what to me is more properly called 'tactics', namely the 'logical equation' or the like, set up by the querist or his delegate — and these two aspects are the same as have been mentioned earlier as 'complementary pairs' such as Operators and Analets, Syntagmata and Paradigmata, Relators and Substantives, and so forth. A great variety of organisational strategies for the semantic members (Analets, Paradigmata, Substantives) of each pair have been suggested: everything from the actual words of title, abstract, or text, to facet analysis. It is not my purpose to attempt an overall semantic analysis of this sort, as crucial as it surely is, but to concentrate on the operational similarity between them. What renders a system strategic is what we could dub its *adaptability*. Let me present an imaginary example. In a store of an indefinitely numerous set of surrogates, each with a single unique symbol (whether simple or complex) and with no sharing of orientations other than one shared by all, all that can be said to be successful in retrieval of query x is surrogate x_1. A simple match is all that is expected, and it is all that can be tolerated; failure to retrieve it is easy to detect, for obvious reasons. But in a store where there are even more partial similarities of orientation than there are separate surrogates — and in which the surrogational symbols are, accordingly, necessarily complex, not simple — there is crucial need for a strategy more potent than that which can seek for (and find) a one-for-one match. The necessary strategy must be able to seek out that which is *relevant*, that which can c o m e t o o u r a i d [25]. And this must be done on the basis of a ritualism which can substitute for the meaning contained in the words of the surrogates or in the notations to which they have been reduced. But the computer cannot recognise anything but

24 For background on these assertions, see my papers 'On bibliography and automation; or, how to reinvent the catalogue' (*Libri*, xv/4 (1965), 287-339) and 'Documentary relevance and structural hierarchy' (*Information storage and retrieval*, iii/1 (1966), 13-18),reprinted above.

25 Hence the crucial need for a precise mode of prediction of the relevance-distnace concepts: see Y Bar-Hillel, parts IV and V of *Language and information: selected essays on their theory and application* (Reading, Mass, Addison-Wesley, 1964), esp 'Theoretical aspects of the mechanisation of literature searching' (330-364), §§12-14(346-353). The most persistent more recent investigator of this problem is D J Hillman, whose reports (m any performed under NSF-G-24070) are too numerous to list here.

one-for-one matching; hence the need for a style of coding which can accomplish one-for-one matching (and 'greater than' or 'less than' comparisons) and at the same time enable manipulations which open up the possibilities of inclusions of relevances. But I do not intend to specify any more closely the characteristics of the semantic or notational structuration most appropriate, though I have expressed myself on this matter elsewhere [26].What we need to look for now is the *syntactical* aspects of this strategisation, namely: what is added to the ritual manipulability of surrogational codes by their articulation into discursive wholes, as against atomised clusters of meaning-bearing elements?

The most obvious gain is in the prevention of classic 'false drops'. But we must admit at the outset that it does not require a system as complex as, say, SYNTOL, to achieve this gain. The essential point, it is my belief, is that simple solutions such as linkages to prevent false drops are appropriate only when the semantic elements stand to one another in relatively rigid relations from the beginning. If, for instance, we have an element A which, in the context of the area of study being organised, is usually a causative or originative factor, another B which is usually an instrumental or catalytic factor, and a third C which is usually a goal or product factor, a simple link 'A,B,C' should be sufficient guarantee that the proper articulation of at least this sector of the surrogate can be assumed. But if we were to take an example of higher complexity, we find a : that simple links do not provide the guarantee we need, and b : that without more subtle linkage than just mentioned, s u c h a c o m p l e x c a n n o t b e s t a t e d t o s t a r t w i t h. Let the substantive elements of the surrogate be articulable in an 'abstract' such as: The document is partly by one author, who writes in German and publishes in 1902 that cultures are manifested in their attitudes with regard to war; and this is exmplified in Assyria attacking, and the response to it of, Israel; a supplementary section, by two joint authors, in French, and published in 1904, is in two parts: one giving archaeological evidence that substantiates Assyria's superiority with regard to military strength in relation to the whole fertile crescent; the other giving a secondary bibliography on the conceptual group 'Assyria attacking, and the response to

26 See the essay above, 'Documentary relevance . . . '.

it of, Israel'; the whole document being oversize and not
requiring security clearance for its use. Roles by themselves,
implicit or explicit, are unable to bring articulation into such a
mass — nor are links, by themselves. Indeed, with current
systems, such a surrogate would probably be reduced radically,
for instance to *DS73.8* (Asia/Mesopotamia / Sargon) or
DS70.96.17 (Asia/Mesopotamia/Relations/Israel) or *U21*
(War/Psychology) — as in LC classification; or to *1. Assyria—
Military History. 2. Palestine—Military History— to 70 A.D.
3. War and Society* — as in LC subject-headings: or to *LHAQ*
(Ancient History/ Jews/Conquest by Sargon) or *LJI* (Assyria/
Sargon) or *RMA* (War/Psychology) — as in Bliss; *or to
935.2: 933+ 355.01* (Relation of Assyria and Palestine +
War/Psychology) — as in UDC.

But the true operational goal in retrieval is clearer when we
attempt to process queries ritually against this surrogate,
queries such as themselves include relational factors not
reducible to simple linkages, such as 'something on the Middle
Eastern attitude toward war' (rel): 'something in German or
Italian on the pre-history of Israel's relations with her
neighbours of today' (rel); 'something on the cultural
relations of the Mesopotamian countries' (irrel); 'something
with bibliography dealing with Mesopotamian archaeology'
(irrel); 'something with bibliography dealing with ancient
wars' (rel); 'something published between 1875 and 1925 on
war s) in Asia' (rel).

The theoretical points implicit in this are *a:* the need to
cope ritually with the problems arising from the flexible — I
might say elusive — nature of discourse, by providing for
manipulations of similar flexibility in the course of the
retrieval operation; *b:* the need for further investigation of the
nature and function of relevance — from, I would suggest, the
point of view of the description of pure consciousness, and thus
by means of the phenomenological method; and *c:* the
advance beyond the 'merely' objective-oriented epistemology —
without undue concentration upon an exclusively subjective-
oriented epistemology either — to a noetic/noematic one
wherein the classification of realities and of knowledge is
adequately mapped one upon the other. And these three
desiderata — ritualisations of the flexible, systematic pre-vision
of relevance, and classification of pure consciousness — all

depend (to greater or lesser extent) upon the thoroughgoing analysis of syntactic relationships, without which there can be no flexibility, no relevance in the fully informational sense, nor any advance beyond ideal (noetic/noematic) perception to judgment.

In several of the relational systems mentioned below, there is to be seen a broad tripartition. These, however, do not map one upon another in a satisfactory way. The only one which is explicitly epistemological, or at least learning-psychological, is Farradane's operator-system, wherein the intersection of a dual tripartition of modes of knowledge gives rise to the nine Operators, each of which names a relationship between the beings known 27 ; in the case of SYNTOL there is a tripartition in the sense that both 'words' (Paradigmata) and 'relations' (Syntagmata) are derived in dichotomous three-level Porphyrian trees 28; in de Grolier's recent report *On the theoretical basis of information retrieval systems* (after pointing out the unsatisfactory almost-congruence between various such systems) the author surveys the rough tripartition to be found in various syntactic relational systems and suggests a new tripartition to unify them 29 ; and in my own proposal there are to be seen triple tripartitions which overlay each other 29. In each such attempt what is aimed at is the casting over language of a net of rationalisation. I do not mean this last in any pejorative sense, of course, but rather that the dual characteristic of natural

27 J E L Farradane. 'Relational indexing and new methods of concept organisation for information retrieval' (American Documentation Institute. 26th Annual Meeting. *Automation and scientific communication* (Washington, 1963), pt,ii, 135-136 (a usefully brief compendium of Farradane's several longer pieces on the subject)).
    A very interesting confirmation of Farradane's view of knowledge as arising from the overlaying of the two 'facets': 'Increasing association (mental time)' and 'Increasing clarity of perception' is to be found in R Sokolowski, *op cit,* 222:
    ... the concept of constitution presupposes, as its ultimate condition of possibility, two flows of temporality: the historicity of subjectivity and the change of reality. Both are necessary for the coming-to-be of what is real. The problem of constitution then studies how the two stream of temporality or change interact in the growth of sense and presence.
28 J-C Gardin, *Draft of final report on a general system for the treatment of documentary data,* pt i, 'Theoretical applications of Syntol' (Paris, Association Marc Bloch, 1963), 11.
29 E de Grolier, *On the theoretical basis of information retrieval systems* (AF61(052)-505) (Paris, 1965), 203-208.
30 J M Perreault, 'Categories and relators: a new schema ' (*Revue internationale de la documentation,* xxxii/4 (1965), 136-144; also, 'Transparency and Self-definition in classification',below, where a defense against some of de Grolier's arguments is attempted.

languages is that in any class of words some are superfluous
synonyms of others, while still others are unduly burdened
with multifold meanings. The rationalisation of each such
attempt consists then in substitution of *meaning* for *verbiage*.
The divergences between these systems thus rests upon more
than linguistic differences, but upon epistemological ones,
which are ultimately founded upon a view of the important
distinctions among the realities represented in the language
– ontological ones. This view of the agreement is interesting
in that, even if the agreement is only minimal, it is at least
apparent in rough outline. (It is also interesting in that we
could go on from it to a comparison between the two levels of
surrogation: the first that of reality in natural language, the
second that of natural language in rationalised documentary
language (classification).) While I cannot contend that the
following schematism is less than crude, there is enough
common basis between the various systems to justify the
conclusion that tripartition is the natural way of viewing the
classification of relationships:

DE GROLIER[31]	GARDIN[32]	PERREAULT[33]	HJELMSLEV[34]
Object in itself	Coordinative, Predicative	Subsumptive	Interdependence
Objective in active relationship	Consecutive	Determinative	Determination
Object in environment	Associative	Ordinal	Constellation

What is achieved by this admittedly imprecise matching? It
surely does not spring from a 'collective unconscious',
determining all these originators to be, in fact, merely repeaters.
Each system looks at the universe of discourse and study from a
slightly different point of view, and each may well concentrate
on something less than the u n i v e r s e; there are thus enough
differences to render them non-congruent as r e f l e c t i o n s
of that universe, but similar enough to show that the differences
are not simply the result of different regions of that universe
having been the object of each system's attention. But insofar as

31 De Grolier, *op cit*, 203.
32 Gardin, *op cit*, 11.
33 Perreault, 'Categories and relators', below.
34 L Hjelmslev, *Prolegomena to a theory of language*, tr F J Whitfield (Madison, Univ of Wisconsin Press 1961), 24ff.

what I desire to project here is an epistemological foundation — and hopefully a common one — it is the nature of their reflection-ness that interests me now.

Now Ceccato does not seem to be one whose system readily conforms to the general tripartition just given, yet I shall hope to analyse a fragment of it so as to show a strong relevance of the phenomenological epistemology given earlier — however sketchily — to the systems just now listed. (Ceccato's own tripartition — Differentiation, Figuration, Categorisation — is far from congruent.)

> Differentiation, figuration, and categorisation,
> individually or combined in composites, do not
> yet constitute any thought: they merely constitute
> the possible future contents of thought . . .
> This choosing of elements and assigning to them
> this particular temporal order constitutes *correlating*.
> Hence we can say: thinking is correlating, i.e. opening
> and closing correlations.[35]

This is quite in agreement with my own understanding of the perennial dictum that truth is in the judgment. But Ceccato has, in establishing his three major classes which are the ingredients of thought only when combined, used techniques notably close to the phenomenological reduction — despite Husserl's close connection, through Brentano, with scholastic epistemology [36]. For instance, something very like the reduction is used in establishing Differentiation:

> . . . If, in full daylight one thinks of light, one will have
> to give up the thought of light for at least one moment
> during which one must think of darkness in order then
> to be able to make the step from darkness to light. [37]

and in establishing Categorisation:

> . . . One may try to become aware of this category
> also by placing one's hand on the table, and then
> thinking of it as 'something'. One will notice that
> the hand which, before, was detached in spite of

35 S Ceccata *et aliter, Linguistic analysis and programming for mechanical Translation* (RADC-TR-60-18) (Milan, G Feltrinelli, nd), 36-37.
36 This last is a good example, I believe, of the 'cognitive' tradition of linguistic analysis (or at least of epistemology) that Ceccato's 'operationalism' is intent upon defeating.
37 Ceccato, *op cit*, 30

the contact with the table, now participates in it.[38]
Most generally of all, his definition of 'constitution' is remark-
ably close to that given by Husserl, emphasising as it does not
the causal origination of the object, but the constitution of
its object-ness [39]. Note too that in Ceccato's investigations as in
Husserl's phenomenology, there is simultaneously a movement
'to the things themselves' and an intense concern for the rectific-
ation of the s u b j e c t i v e apparatus for o b j e c t i v e knowledg

I would then conclude that the phenomenological method as a
clue to the examination of 'external' (objective) reality, coupled
with the theory of knowledge which it mediates — it stands as a
bridge between Brentano's neo-scholasticism and the existentialistic epistemology of Heidegger — can in fact be fundamental
to a balanced and scientific view of the problem of knowledge;
and since the surrogation of documents is but one form of surrogation as such, that only with such a foundation well understood
can we hope to achieve balanced and scientific classificational
theories and practices.

Epilogue

Retrieval is a function of memory — of one sort or other,
human or mechanical. So, as an uncommented-upon epilogue to
my previous (hopefully) more systematic treatment, I want to
call up whatever authority there is in the most thematically
memory-oriented work of them all: the *Remembrance of things
past* of Marcel Proust. In a passage where the Narrator is
reflecting (as he so often does) upon the explanations of her
possibly evil past actions, as given by his mistress —
. . . One of the words of the sentence that was meant to
calm us sets our suspicions running upon another trail.
The demands of our jealously and the blindness of our
credulity are greater than the women whom we love
could ever suppose.

38 *Ibidem,* 34
39 Compare *ibidem,* 28:
.. It [the table being observed] is operations inasmuch as it is obtained, not
from the transformative operations of the cabinet maker, but from the
constitutive operations of the observational type, which are, precisely, one
or several differentiations separating wood and air, . . . and then the movements
which outline the figure or form, by following the line of differentiation between
the wood and the air, etc.
1-1 with R Sokolowski, *op cit.*

When, of her own accord, she swears to us that [a
rival has been rejected, we may at first believe her.]
But presently, when we recall what she told us, we shall
ask ourselves whether her story is really true.
—he concludes with what I shall also end with:
for there is wanting, between the different things that
she said to us, t h a t l o g i c a l a n d n e c e s s a r y
c o n e x i o n w h i c h, m o r e t h a n t h e f a c t s
r e l a t e d, i s a s i g n o f t h e t r u t h.[40]

40 M Proust, *Remembrance of things past,* *tr* C K S Moncrieff & F A Blossom (New
York, Random House, 1932), v ii, 444-445; emphasis mine.

STRUCTURE OF UDC

In my own opinion the first essay here, 'Towards explication of the rules of formation in UDC', is the most important of my statements about UDC in a theoretical light (and of course I am convinced that a statement in such a light is fundamentally more important than any in a practical light, which merely follows from the former). Especially in view of the continued incursion of computing devices and techniques into the field of information retrieval, we need to see what characteristics a classificatory system such as UDC possesses or can be made to possess b e f o r e we make the attempt to use such means upon it. The work of Freeman and Atherton and of Caless, while surely not denigrated as being of both practical and theoretical value, is necessarily based on an at least i m p l i c i t theory about the rules of formation in UDC. I have tried simply to e x p l i c a t e what seems to me to be the received theory in these matters, providing thus a framework for further refinement − a refinement that can thus, hopefully, avoid a patchwork result.

The first essay in this section is intended as a wholly general treatment of the structure of UDC, and the three essays 'Transparency and self-definition in classification', 'Categories and relators', and 'Emendations to the relator-schema' all concern themselves with the inadequacy of the colon, $n:n$, to fulfill its function. The essay 'On the colon in UDC and on the Boolean operators' is accordingly a general treatment of a single structural device in UDC, to be taken as introductory to the more critical essays that follow.

Perhaps less theoretically fundamental than 'Towards explication of the rules of formation in UDC', but surely more attended to, has been the suggestion first put forward by Desiré Kervégant that there needed to be a development of the relation-sign in UDC, the $n:n$. My essay 'Categories and relators' is a further stage of the development which he initiated, and is represented here by that essay and two others, 'Transparency and self-definition in classification' and 'Emendations to the relator-schema, The first, 'Transparency and self-definition in classification', is a summary of my general theory, strongly resembling 'On the articulation of surrogates', but oriented toward more immediate support of the central proposal-statement, 'Categories and relators'. That proposal can be seen to have several flaws, the elimination of which is attempted in 'Emendations to the relator-schema'. It seemed best not to recant such flaws as could not be eliminated, though essays later in the volume suggest superior solutions.

Finally, 'Automated retranslatability of UDC codes' attempts to summarise the benefits derived from application of the rules of formation sketched earlier (benefits of the use of the relator-schema are also to be found in the essays discussing that schema).

58

V

Towards explication of the rules
of formation in UDC

Classifications can be divided (among other principles of
division) according to their use of general-categoric, mnemonic,
or faceting devices: on the one hand we have those which are
enumerative, on the other those which are synthetic. This
judgment is of course only true in terms of preponderance,
since the most nearly purely enumerative current classification,
LC, does indeed utilise a good many general-and special-
categoric devices; and even implicitly present facets can
sometimes be detected there.

But among those which are predominantly based on general-
categoric, mnemonic, or faceting devices — which includes, at
various levels of intensity, and in order of date of origin,
DC, UDC, CC, and BC — I wish to concentrate on those two
most closely related, DC and UDC; and primarily upon the
latter. Synthesis implies the juncture of elements (more or
less primitive) of meaning, into unities of higher meaning; and
it is the varieties of such junctures, and the explication of the
implicit rules for their application and interpretation, that I
propose to attempt. It will also be shown that the relatively
undeveloped state of the rules for such juncture (I shall
henceforth refer to them as 'rules of formation' — along
with the consolidation of synonyms and the explication of
homonyms they constitute the basic operations in the
construction of that type of artificial language called a
classification or an information language), as found in
DC, for example, is a great hindrance to the adequacy of
such a language to the performance of its tasks; and that even
a classification with fairly well developed rules of formation
(such as UDC), but with their operation and interpretation
still largely implicit, is hampered from a full utilisation of
the possibilities opened up by their presence.

Since the time when I was working on' my schema

'Categories and relators' [1] I have been concerned with the *formative* elements of UDC even more perhaps than with the *substantive* or vocabulary elements. I will therefore attempt here to deepen this interest along somewhat different lines than that implied by the fractioning of the UDC colon-relation; that schema was a micro-system, and there must thus be a macro-system into which it can be inserted.

The standard undeveloped rule of formation

In DC, as in general subject heading systems such as LCSH, there are to be found syntheses of relatively primitive terms, according to rules; some of these rules are general, some are special in that they apply only to one class or term. The standard subdivisions in DC have their analogues in the general form subdivisions and the direct and indirect geographical subdivisions in LCSH. And, again, the non-standard subdivisions in LCSH correspond, even though in a far less frequent way, to the direct hierarchical explication of general classes into special in DC.

I wish to emphasise the form of the last two qualifying words: n o t 'generic' and 'specific', but 'general' and 'special'. It is unfortunate that the logical terms in '−ic' have given rise to the degenerately non-logical terms in '−al'. It is of course necessary to have such terms as 'general' and 'special'; what is unfortunate, though, is that there is too easy a transfer into such terms of the logical content of the other pair − a content which should be intentionally absent from the pair in '−al'. (Classificatory hierarchies can certainly be characterised as trees organised in terms of 'generals' and 'specials'; it is not safe, though, to assume that classificatory trees are necessarily composed throughout of true 'generics' and 'specifics'.)

Such a complex term as *Magyar lyrical poetry—20th century* or its DC equivalent 894.51110409003 conforms to the standard undeveloped rule of formation that can be stated algebraically as $A > B > C > D > E$, or verbally as 'each successive term added to the previous term(s) modifies the whole previous string'. In the

1 'Categories and relators: a new schema' *(Revue internationale de la documentation,* xxxii (1965), 136-144, reprinted below; *cf* also my essays below, 'Transparency and self-definition in classification', 'Reclassification: some warnings and a proposal', (Urbana, Illinois University Graduate School of Library Science, 1967) (= its *Occasional papers,* no 87), and §10 of the FID circular letter 'C66-41 (27 October 1966)'.

case mentioned this is adequate because there is no need for a more complex articulation [2]. But such a fairly highly articulated complex as *catalogue of scientific periodicals in the libraries of Australia* or *measurement of turbulent flow in pipes, using radioactive isotopes*, cannot be successfully reduced to a one-dimensional diagram. In such cases we can see the advantage of Ranganathan's theory of rounds and levels as against Vickery's expansion of the basic formula PMEST; where Vickery's expansion simply gives greater refinement to the five more general categories, the theory of rounds and levels allows for more than a merely linear (one-dimensional) analysis.

By a linear analysis I mean this: if *Magyar lyrical poetry— 20th century* is diagrammed in a way rather like that of gradeschool grammar, we get (after opening up the telescoped term *Magyar lyrical poetry*)

Literature —Magyar—Poetry—Lyrical—20th Century   (1)

or

Literature—Magyar   (2)

poetry   20th century

lyrical

Even here we see the first hints of what will become the major problem: the non-linearity implied in the question of branches. Why, in other words, should we choose to put *poetry-lyrical* before *20th century*, and why should there not be a simple stepwise progression of added on terms? The usual answer from the Ranganathan camp (and I do not wish to discredit it, since it is after all 'postulational' in Ranganathan's own sense) is that the setting up of the citation order (facet formula) determines such results.

But a purely linear analysis can handle the situation only where there is assumed to be one major concept with a cluster of subsidiaries (or better: a string of modifiers). Such a case is exemplified in (1) and (2), though (2) reveals the presence of two strings of modifiers, one segmented and the other not:

2 *Cf* my essay 'On the articulation of surrogates: an attempt at an episte-
mological foundation' (*Proceedings,* International Symposium on Relational
Factors in Classification, College Park, 1966 Oxford, Pergamon Press, 1967)
(=*Information storage and retrieval*   iii/4 (1967)), 1-13, reprinted above.

t w o categories of modification [3], Form and Period

But the analysis of *catalog of scientific periodicals in the libraries of Australia* or of *measurement of turbulent flow in pipes, using radioactive isotopes* is not possible in such a simply linear way, even one analogous to (2):

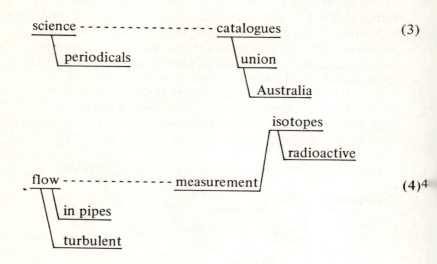

    (3)

    (4)[4]

. 3 It can well be laid down from the start, following upon the earlier discussion of 'general', 'special', 'generic', and 'specific', that *modification* is taken as the including class for all those operations that lead from the general to the special, and that the kind of modification which produces the specific (out of the generic) is called *specification;* all other types of modification are clumped together (following Metcalfe) as *qualifications.* This distinction is by dichotomy, therefore, and partakes of all the dangers of classification by dichotomy; indeed, it can be seen from figure 6 of 'Categories and relators' that the specifying modification is only one of several subsumptive relations, and that there are far more determinative and ordinal than there are subsumptive relations deduced there; *qualification* then includes far too many kinds to mean anything very precisely, but it can be assumed that a classification can be built up by *a*: isolation of all isolates, *b*: grouping of these into facets, each a tree with no relations obtaining within it but specific (foci) to genus (facet, sub-facet, *etc*), and *c*: compilation of working terms from the resulting inventory of primitive terms by means of relators, themselves arrived at by a process similar to *a* and *b* (as found in 'Categories and relators', particularly §IV.)

It is this articulate aspect of the linguistic mode of utterance which forces up to develop rules of formation (and punctuation) for our natural languages as well as for our information languages. Such development is largely unconscious; grammar is only secondarily normative, but is primarily descriptive and/or clarificatory — and classification theory, its analogue, could be much the same were it not for the lamentable state of all too many classifications, a state largely due to the unawareness of their practitioners of the clarificatory and normative advantages to be gained from grammatical/classification-theoretical examination of actual classifications.

That this is just as much the case with pseudo-natural-language classificatory systems (=subject headings, and, even more, thesauri) can be seen in the attempt — even if only half hearted - - to indicate something more than a purely linear succession of terms by the use of double dashes, commas, and parentheses as

4 I here diagram in keeping with the theory of rounds and levels: Terms depending on the central axis are either levels within the same category (PMEST) or are later categories qualifying the indicated earlier one. Terms stepped up from the central axis are new round-personalities; *isotopes* does not m o d i f y the term to which it is attached, it is only i n t r o d u c e d by it (*measurement*). Each new round can have levels and subsequent categories, as well as further new rounds, and the rounds can come in the middle of their host rounds as well as their ends; *eg*

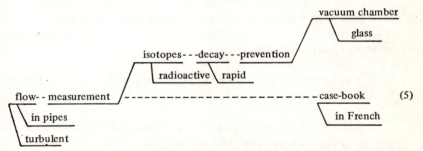

which could be phrased in English as *French case-book on the use of glass vacuum chambers in the prevention of the rapid decay of radioactive isotopes used in the measurement of turbulent flow in pipes.*

What makes such a purely linear analysis (and diagramming) impossible is the presence of multiplicity of terms in need of modification of various sorts: in (3) *Australia* must not be allowed to modify *science periodicals,* nor can *radioactive* in (4) be allowed to modify *flow,* nor is it the *radioactive* which is subjected to *measurement.*

the termini of fields and/or sub-fields [5], *eg*

HYMNS, GREEK (CLASSICAL) – DICT. & ENCYC. (6)
1-1 which could be phrased in English as *dictionary* [or
encyclopedia] *of classical Greek hymns*, and diagrammed, as
above, as

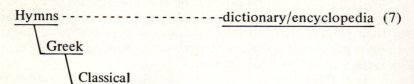

It can then be seen that the attempt to do more than string
together terms which modify each other in some fashion beyond
$A > B > C > D > E$ rests (though unconsciously) upon recognition
of the presence of a multiplicity of facets within a complex
heading. In the case of (7) and (2) the formula can be used without any discomfort or bad conscience, but a sensitive cataloger
or reference librarian should experience a degree of uncertainty
in the face of such an only pseudo-linear string as *science- -
periodicals- -catalogues- union- -Australia* as equivalent to (3),
even more with *flow- -turbulent- in pipes- -measurement-
-isotopes- -radioactive* as equivalent to (4), or (horrors!) with
*flow- -turbulent- -in pipes- -measurement- -isotopes- radioactive-
-decay- -rapid- -prevention- -vacuum chamber- -glass- -case-
book- -in French* as equivalent to (5). It is only by having
arranged such a mass of terms in some schema that goes
b e y o n d t h e l i n e a r that anyone can be sure of how to
interpret such a string.

**UDC's adherence to the standard undeveloped rule in ordinary
facet order**

A code in UDC can be composed of several elements in a
perfectly linear way, and without any possibility of misinter-

5 There is however no conscious adherence to any principle of operation or
   interpretation in this use of various punctuational junctures; *cf* my essay
   'Approaches to library filing by computer' (*Proceedings,* Clinic on Library
   Applications of Data Processing Equipment, Urbana, 1966; (Urbana Illinois
   University Graduate School of Library Sciences 1967), 47-90). I intend to consider
   the whole problem much more fully in *The idea of order: an essay in
   bibliographical systematics.*

pretation – *eg* 621.365.2.012-187.001.42 (091)=956, which can be diagrammed as above as

arc furnaces –	diagrams –	accuracy –	perform.tests –	hist.treatment in Japanese	(8)
621.365.2	621.012	621-187	- 001.42	(091) = 956	

In this example each successive term does conform to the abstract formula $A > B > C > D > E;$ *eg* the performance tests, .001.42, do not apply to the historical presentation, (091), nor to the fact that the document happens to be in Japanese, =956, but simply to the whole complex ahead of it: accuracy of diagrams of arc furnaces, 621.365.2.012-187.

This example has not displayed every possible facet that can be built together according to the standard undeveloped rule, but if such a code were actually to be built up, it might include various sub-facets of such facets as Form, (On) [7]; of place, (1/9) [8]; of Race (again unlikely in our example), (=On); and/or of Time 'n'. But even if one could locate a document in need of so much linear faceting, there would be no great problem in the placement of the codes for each facet, since the order of facet citation is generally the reverse of the order of filing, namely

X	, subject X unmodified	
X =956	, subject X in Japanese	
X (038)	, the vocabulary of subject X	
X (091)	, historical treatment of subject X	
X (1-077)	, subject X in demilitarized zones of the world	
X (254)	, subject X in farmlands	(9)
X (45)	, subject X in Italy	
X (=50)	, subject X among Italians	Continued
X "19"	, subject X in the 20th century	overleaf

6   This first term (*arc furnaces*, 621.365.2) is itself the terminus of a chain (one digit for each term, beginning at main class 6) down from *applied science, technology, mechanical and electrical engineering, electrical engineering, thermo-electricity, heat generation;* the final .2 adds *arc furnaces*. It is assumed, perhaps inaccurately (see above), that such a chain is linked generically/specifically between every pair of adjacent orders; at any rate, there surely is at least a general/special linkage.

7   For instance, a conference proceedings or a vocabulary of the historical treatment of subject *X*:*X*(091:063) or *X*(091 :038); or both: *X* (091:063:038), *vocabulary of conferences dedicated to historical treatment . . .*

8   It would be unlikely, in the context of the example, that Place would be appropriate at all, but there could be a double or even a triple use of the sub-facets of this one auxiliary, *eg* subject *X* in the context of *demilitarised Italian farmlands: X* (45: 254-077).

X "761"	, subject X considered as reversible in time
X .001.42	, performance tests on subject X
X -187	, accuracy of subject X
X .08	, measurement of subject X
X .1	, a 'specific' sort of X

Within each such filing 'chunk' (*ie*, the divisions of subject X by ,the facets which may stand next after it) there are possible a number of combinations that doubles with each new element added. For instance, if X can only be modified by =956, there are only two possible sub chunks: X and X=956; if (038) is addable, there can be twice as many: X, X=956, X(038), and X(038)=956; there can thus be 4096 combinations (inclusive) from X.1 to X.1-187.08.001.42"761:19"(=45) (45:254:1 077:091: 038)=956, and 4096+2048+1024+512+256+128+ 64+32+16+8+4+2+1+1(=8192) if we begin the series with X unmodified. The example 621.365.2.012-187.001.42 (091) =956 thus has (with its five subordinate facets) sixteen + eight + four + two + one + one (=32) possible combinations, which can be most helpfully arranged in a matrix (p 67):

This is all only a preliminary to the main argument. Even linear analysis is seen to contain a great deal of organisational complication, especially in that all we have worked out here is the number of chunks, whereas the real situation would include variable filling of each facet, *eg* =951 for documents in Chinese; (033) for pocket dictionaries; but the linear-adequate situation will be seen from what follows to be far less than universal.

621.345.2	.012	-187	.001.42	(091)	=956
1	0	0	0	0	0
1	0	0	0	0	1
1	0	0	0	1	0
1	0	0	0	1	1
1	0	0	1	0	0
1	0	0	1	0	1
1	0	0	1	1	0
1	0	0	1	1	1
1	0	1	0	0	0
1	0	1	0	0	1
1	0	1	0	1	0
1	0	1	0	1	1
1	0	1	1	0	0
1	0	1	1	0	1
1	0	1	1	1	0
1	0	1	1	1	1
1	1	0	0	0	0
1	1	0	0	0	1
1	1	0	0	1	0
1	1	0	0	1	1
1	1	0	1	0	0
1	1	0	1	0	1
1	1	0	1	1	0
1	1	0	1	1	1
1	1	1	0	0	0
1	1	1	0	0	1
1	1	1	0	1	0
1	1	1	0	1	1
1	1	1	1	0	0
1	1	1	1	0	1
1	1	1	1	1	0
1	1	1	1	1	1

(10)

The UDC symbols for variance from the standard undeveloped rule

The fact that linear facet order is richly possible in UDC is, in the minds of both pro- and opponents, largely a secondary matter—secondary, that is, in comparison to the utilisation (whether considered to be beneficial or detrimental) of the other symbols, thus far not mentioned, namely the colon $n:n$, the stroke n/n. the plus $n+n$, the apostrophe $n'n$, and the square brackets [$n...n$]. Each of these symbols, rather than i n t r'o d u c i n g general or specific linear modifications of the primary code, serves to r e l a t e codes between which they stand. (All of the codes joined to subject X in (9) have this in common, that they cannot stand at the head of a number. Their dependence is not uniform, of course: (45) means *in Italy* anywhere it ever occurs, whereas -187 means *accuracy* only if attached to a 62-code.)

Thus all of these symbols ($n:n, n/n, n+n, n'n, [n...n]$) are logical functors; their logical arguments are the codes they serve to unite. The earlier set of symbols, as shown in (9), are functors, but they do not have a relational function. They introduce what stands to their right (or which they enclose [9]), and, in comparison to the truly relational functors, would have to be considered as a species of argument.

There is the temptation to say that this relational set of functors operates on independent codes from the main tables. But they can more accurately be seen to relate any codes which are *formally equivalent*. The $n:n$ can relate two or more codes from the same auxiliary, as in X (038:091), and similar cases can be found for the others. (Such an example provides another reason for not eliminating the closing parenthesis, lest the 091 be mistaken to represent the main class for *Manuscripts; Rare and Remarkable Works*.)

The relations shown by such relational functors are multiple, ranging from the most general (the $n+n$, and the n/n) through conjunction (the $n'n$ and the $n:n$ — which last is itself highly multiple, as I have shown in 'Categories and relators'. And the $[n...n]$ are useable for one sort of conjunction, namely subordinating, according to the

9 I suggested in 'Categories and relators' that there was no absolute need for the use of closing marks such as closing parentheses, since a new symbol would always follow such a closing symbol to introduce the next linear facet. Though a code such X. 1-187"19" (1-077)=956 could thus be written X.1-187 "19 (1-077=956 without significant loss of intelligibility (at least for examination by computer), there are two reasons for not pressing for such a minimal space-savings: *a*: because it might well confuse the optical searcher of shelf and/or classed catalogue, and *b*: because it might be possible to find cases where a real ambiguity could arise (here, in the dual use of *-n*). Also, as will be shown, there could never be such a savings in the use of $[n...n]$, without certainty of ambiguity.

abridged English edition [10] of the UDC, p 11. It will be shown in what follows that these [n . . . n] should (indeed, must) be reserved for the use which K Fill shows them to fill,

10 *Universal Decimal Classification,* Abridged English Edition3 (London, British Standards Institution, 1963). *Cf,* in regards to use and interpretation of the [n...n], J Mills. *The Universal Decimal Classification* (New Brunswick, Graduate School of Library Service, Rutgers University, 1964), 57, who only shows the [n...n] to mean subordinate conjunction; R. Dubuc, *La Classification Decimale Universelle (CDU): manual practique d'utiliation* (Paris, Gauthier-Villars, 1965), 147, 212, who does not thematically discuss the [n...n], but shows them in examples and tables to mean outside of subordinate conjunction; E Jacquemin, *La Classification Decimale Universelle (CDU); description et Commentaires des regles en usage* (=FID, *Etudes de Classification,* IX =FID Publ 312 [originally published as *Revue de la documentation,* xxv (1959), 101-114]), who accepts both usages of that [n...n], as 'indice analytique' and 'pour grouper 2 notion a:b] c*' − which latter is in fact unnecessary, since it is identical with linear order; what is needed [n...n] to group the two notions as in a: [b:c] ; P Herrmann, *Praktische Anwendung der Dezimalklassifikation: Klassifizierungtechnik* 5 (Leipzig, VEB Bibliographische Insitut, 1965), 89-92, who considers the general relation of rules of formation to search tactics, but nowhere even mentions the square brackets; this last lack is also characteristic of the complete English edition (fourth international of the *Universal Decimal Classification* (London, British Standards Institution, 1943) − the relevant part is vol 1, pt 1; K Fill *Einführung in das Wesen der Dezimalklassifikation* (Berlin, Beuth, 1960), 20-21, is the only one of these authorities who does not thematically discuss the [n...n]. He calls them 'Interkalationszeichen', which word verbally conforms to the Mills-Dubuc attitude; but his examples show that He regards them, rather than as intercalators, as algebraic sub-groupers:

621.315.2:[629.113+629.13] Elektrische Kabel für Kraftwagen und Flugzeugen
016:[05+07](47) Bibliographie der russischen Zeitschriften und Zeitungen

S C Bradford, *Documentation* (London, C Lockwood, 1948), 39-40, also the discusses the general problem of rules of formation and interpretation. This , passage, in fact, is an anticipation of much of what T W Caless & D B Kirk propose in 'An application of UDC to machine searching' (*Journal of documentation* xxiii/3 (1967), 208-215); Bradford is worth quoting:

Such an expression as: 526.9:336.211.1(431)"1927"(075)=3, Guide to Prussian cadastral surveying in 1927, is justly described as "Not classification but idle jesting." The essential fact to the librarian is that the publication deals with the Survey of Prussia. It would therefore be indexed: 526.9 (431).
Exceptionally, if the librarian's clients are specially interested in the cadastral aspect of the survey, the number for this, 336.211.1, could be added as: 526.9(431):336.211.1, so that the entry would be filed also under 336.211.1.

The whole chapter (24-48) is quite stimulating, both in those points with which I can agree and those with which I cannot−and I think it is worth noting that what leads Bradford to some of these is his lack of reliance upon a theory of citation order and his lack of a theory of rules of formation and of their operation and interpretation in terms of rounds and levels.

*The closing bracket (without a corresponding opener) is intended by Jacquemin, such usage being confined to those cases where the whole expression would normally have opened with an opening bracket.

namely as an algebraic sub-grouping device; and that if the other functions of the $[n \ldots n]$ are worth retaining, they are surely of a lower level of necessity, and should be given other symbols.

Ambiguity in UDC and the use of the $[n \ldots n]$

There is thus an ambiguity in UDC caused by the uncertainty in the use of the $[n \ldots n]$. But there is even more the possibility of ambiguities in the use of codes of more than one element, where any of the junctures are effected by any of the other relational symbols, namely $n{:}n$, $n'n$, n/n, or $n{+}n$.

If this one primary use of the $[n \ldots n]$ is accepted (and not to do so is scarcely consonant with the very first problem in the construction of an information language, namely the consolidation of synonyms, and perhaps even less so with the second, namely the explication of homonyms), and if the other uses are considered important enough to retain, a binding directive should be promulgated which separates each function and assigns a separate symbol to it. The first of the classificationist's problems, therefore, must be the clear sighting of the variety of functions necessary in a classificatory language. Ranganathan and Farradane have given more help in locating these functions than almost any other classification theorists. But as I argue in 'Re classification: some warnings and a proposal'[11], such proposals as these eminent theorists make in the direction of working systems cannot be the basis for any more delay: there is an immediate need for a better answer to the common librarian's flight from DC in the face of mounting pressures, and the only answer that will prevent this flight from being towards LC seems (to me) to be UDC.

Thus the examination of the rules of formation in UDC — which rules, though well provided for in terms of raw materials (as against the paucity seen in DC and even more in LC and LCSH) are not well explicated in terms of operation and

11 Cited in footnote 1.

interpretation.

The most basic of all distinctions, though, have not yet been made in regard to the rules of formation. It is between *a*: the symbol(s) which show the extent to which the arguments can apply, and *b*: all other symbols, whether functors or arguments.

In the light of the whole foregoing matter, then, it should be predictable that the available and (according to Fill's exemplification) appropriate symbol for the first function is $[n...n]$ [12].

Consider the document coded in (3): what is to prevent the (994) which represents *Australia* from modifying the *science periodicals* represented by 5:05? The whole code comes out, if we take the citation order of (3), as

$$5:05:017.11 \ (994) \tag{11}$$

But there will be permutations of this entry, because that is what the *n:n* calls for; namely

$$05:017.11 \ (994):5 \quad \text{and} \tag{12}$$
$$017.11 \ (994): 5:05$$

The question is: is there a valid linearity to such a number, akin to that which would apply to a document-abstract which could be diagrammed without rounds and levels (or at least without rounds)? If not, which permutation shows the inadequacy of the assumption?

If there is a document that calls for a code such as 2:8 (05), who could deny that the formal auxiliary (05) did in fact modify the whole previous complex? The request for 2 (05) would be at least partially satisfied by 2:8 (05), especially if there were no document that matched such a request one-for-one. But if a code such as 2:8:05 were in a corpus (its interpretation, we shall postulate, being *religion in literary periodicals*), is there in fact also the linearly accurate interpretation 2:05, or should we insist upon a disjunctive interpretation for this :05? But since there is no non-semantic way to distinguish between these two possible interpretations, ambiguity is the functional corollary

---

12 As reported in §11 of FID circular letter 'C66-41 (27 October 1966)' Fill is now advocating the use of a double colon, *n::n*, to represent the subordinating conjunction. While the effect of this proposal is to relieve the pressure to use the $[n...n]$ for such a function, and is thus clearly admirable, there is an unfortunate aspect too, in that the line between coordinating and subordinating conjunction can be seen in Pagès', Kervégant's, Soergel's, and my tabulations to be anything but a neat or easily locatable one. (References to the first two tabulations are in 'Categories and relators'; Soergel's is in *Proc*, ISRFC, cited in footnote 2.)

of the toleration of such alternation.

What is needed, then, is a fresh look at the situation (as described above) in terms of a systematic reorganisation — one which will retain as much as possible of the language (better in terms of the implements of formation than most other classificatory languages, but poorer than CC, for instance, in terms of guidance to their operation and interpretation) that we have in UDC, merely subjecting it to a more vigorous grammatical design.

Compounds and complexes

Classificatory inscriptions, like linguistic utterances, are made up of strings of elements which, as strings, form complexes or higher unities. The primitive (or 'standard underdeveloped') complex classificatory inscription is that given above as $A > B > C > D > E$, . In such a case, each element is a member of a complex which in turn becomes an element of a still higher-level complex. Thus, while the last term to be added to the string is by definition the least, it is at the same time that very element which raises the previous complex to a higher level. This aspect can be shown by this reformulation: $[[[[A]B]C]D]E]$. But there may be need for complication of a different sort, where for instance one element is not part of the main axis but modifies only one other element—and of course also thereby indirectly modifies the whole—in such a way as $[[A[[B]C]D]E]$. which can be mapped more graphically into a tree structure as

$$[[A[[B]C]D]E]$$

(13)

as against tree-interpretation of the standard undeveloped order:

$$[[[[[A]B]C]D]E]$$

(14)

Besides the presence of internal, non-main-axis sub-complexes, we must also recognise the presence of compounds; but these are formally similar to sub-complexes, so we can simply diagram them by using a different kind of sub-tree:

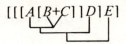

$$[[[A[B+C]][D]E]] \tag{15}$$

Compound elements differ from complex elements primarily in that their interpretation is parallel rather than simultaneous: in $[[A[[B]C]D]E]$ there is only one five-element complex idea being expressed, just as in $[[[[A]B]C]D]E]$; while the presence of a compound element such as $[B+C]$ leads to two equally valid—parallel—interpretations of (15):
$[[[[A]B]D]E]$ and $[[[[A]C]D]E]$.

UDC punctuational symbols can accordingly be classified as follows:

a: linear complicators —as in (9)
b: non-linear complicators, making possible analysis of UDC codes according to rounds an levels — $n:n$ and $n'n$
c: non-linear compounders —n/n and $n+n$
d: a symbol capable of non-linearising the string of elements, in that it indicates the compounds and sub complexes within the whole string $--[n...n]$.

Thus, while $n:n$ and $n'n$ are called non-linear complicators, making possible analysis of UDC codes according to rounds and levels, it can be seen that such a goal can be reached only if there is a symbol capable of non-linearising the string.

A proposed order of operations

From (13) - (15) it can be seen that what the $[n ... n]$ does, in its non-linearising, is to introduce an order of operations that does not proceed in the standard linear order: note that in (13) and (15), as against (14), the f i r s t operation is that which unites 'B and C. Such a formulation of (5), with *flow* represented by A, *turbulent* by B, *in pipes* by C, *measurement* by D, *isotopes* by E, *radioactive* by F, *decay* by G, *rapid* by H, *prevention* by I, *vacuum chamber* by J, *glass* by K, *case-book* by L, and *in French* by M, would run

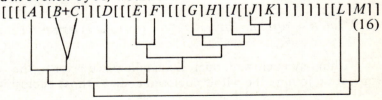

$$[[[[A][B+C]][D[[[E]F][[[G]H][I[[J]K]]]]]][[L]M]] \tag{16}$$

Or we could do the same for (3), with *science* represented by *A,* *periodicals* by *B, catalogues* by *C, union* by *D,* and *Australia* by *E:*

$$[[[A|B][[C]D]E]]$$ (17)

Thus, in UDC code elements (*A* is 5, *B* is 05, *C* is 017, *D* is 017.11, *E* is (994)), where *bibliography* and its sorts are not treatable as common auxiliaries, so that 5:05 must be coloned on to 017.11(994), we get 5:05:017.11 (994), as in (11). The code (994) must not be allowed to modify the early part of the whole, namely 5:05, and the *n:n* seems able to perform this function; it serves as a boundary to the influence of place-modifiers, though not to that of form-modifiers.

It is probably most economical if the rule be adopted that only codes which are purely documentary (which refer not to the contents of the document, but to the document as such—such as its outer form or its language) be able to penetrate the boundary set up by the *n:n*. It is doubtful whether the following example could in fact occur, but if there were a case where the outer form did not refer to the whole previous complex, brackets could be used, as for instance in 2:[8(05)], to prevent automatic (and quite correct) interpretation of 2:8(05) as [2:8](05). From this we can conclude that common-auxiliary operations are normally prior to coloning in order of operations, and that special-auxiliary operations would be even earlier; and that a linear chain of operations with common— or special— auxiliary modifiers would always be performed in a left-to-right sequence, prior to any higher-order operations involving *n'n. n+n,* or *n:n.* (Note that while *n'n* is functionally similar to *n:n,* it is a special auxiliary; and that its meaning forces it to have the earliest priority of all operations except that of direct hierarchical specification.)

A provisional tabulation of priorities of operations in UDC would then read

$$0/9.n \quad n'n \quad n/n \quad -n \quad .0n \quad .00n \quad "n" \quad (=n) \quad (1/9) \quad n+n \quad n:n \quad (0n) \quad =n$$ (18)

Within any enclosure, operations take place prior to the operation joining the whole enclosed code to those enclosing it;

thus in $(X:Y)$. OZ the $n:n$ is performed before the .On, despite the order in (18); thus the ordinal position of $[n \ldots n]$ is variable.

To test this, the codes for the elements in (5 =16) would be $[A]$ 532.5 *flow,* $[C]$ 532.54 *flow in pipes,* $[B]$ 532.542.1 *turbulent flow in pipes* [13], $[D]$ 53.08 *measurement,* $[E]$ 546.02 *isotopes,* $[F]$ 539.16 *radioactive,* $[G]$ 639.163 *decay of radioactivity,* $[H]$ (unspecifiable) *rapid* [14], $[I]$ .004.61 *prevention* [15], $[J]$ 621.52 *vacuum chambers,* $[K]$ 666.1 *glass,* $[L]$ (079.3) *casebooks* [16], $[M]$=40 *in French.* But mere linearisation, like

532.542.1.08:546.02:539.163.004.61:621.52:666.1
(079.3) = 40   (19)

will certainly not do; it is only with the aid of $[n \ldots n]$ that we can break up this pseudo-linearity so that it adequately represents the original document-abstract, thus:

[532.542.1.08:[546.02: 539.163.004.61:[621.52:666.1]]]]
(079.3) = 40   (20)

It can be seen that though it is desirable to have an established order of formation-operations, it is even more important that the $[n \ldots n]$ be available to perform their non-linearising function of algebraic sub-groupers. It must be established what sort of penetrations are allowed:

No code with $[n \ldots n]$ modifies any outside, unless the whole complex or compound content of the $[n:n]$ is the modifier.

Modifications of any code that stands after a $n:n$ or a $n+n$ apply only to that code—unless that code and the prior code joined to it by $n:n$ or $n+n$ be enclosed within $[n \ldots n]$, as $[n:n]$ or $[n+n]$

Modification of any complex or compound code containing an $n'n$ or an n/n applies to the whole complex or compound so formed.

In all such cases, of course, the use of $[n \ldots n]$ can affect a change, but only within the bounds of epistemic possibilities. For instance, it can hardly make sense to have such a code as 52/[54(994)], because while 52 and 53 are given as wholly general, 54(994) is not—and because it cannot be determined what the

13 From the complete English edition, vol 2, pt 1, 72.
14 It would seem that no classification scheme can win them all.
15 A neologistic code constructed in conformity to seminal mnemonics.
16 A rather weak or distant attempt to match the concept.

particularities in fact are which extend from 54 through 54(994). On the other hand, it is certainly possible to have two or more intelligible codes such as 52+54(994) and [52+54](994), since each is intelligible and each has a different meaning — the first being automatically interpreted as 52+[54(994)].

Permutation (for classed-catalogue added entries) is not strictly cyclical in the usual sense, because only linear complexes are really adaptable to the cyclical idea. (Linear complexes have only one central substantive with one or more modifiers; when permuted, it is assumed that their original linearity is ritually reconstitutable. This is not the case with complexes containing more than one round, nor with more than two substantives joined by $n:n$.) Such a case as (20) requires main entry on 532.542.1, and added entries on 546.02 and 621.52; other added entries might be desired on 53.08, 539.163, .004.61, 666.1, (079.3), and even =40. Lining the notational elements up A/M, retaining only the $n:n$ and the $[n...n]$ from the original notation, we get an algebraic version (with B and C assimilated to A, G to F, and J unspecifiable) like

$$[AD:[E:FI:[J:K]]]LM \tag{21}$$

We surely need entries at least on E and J, and possible on D, F, I, K, L, and M. Noting that this centers our attention primarily (after providing for the main entry) on the first element in each $[n...n]$, we can further abridge to

$$[A:[E:[J]]]LM, \tag{22}$$

— each nested $[n...n]$ corresponding to one of the rounds in (5). To get entries on E and J of (22), then, we simply pivot code positions within each $[n...n]$, giving, for E,

$$[[E:[J]]:A]LM, \tag{23}$$

and, for J,

$$[[[J]:E]:A]LM \tag{24}$$

If entry for (say) F of (21) is desired, the E permutation is carried out plus another pivoting on the $n:n$ within the E $[n...n]$, giving

Need for better citation order

As projected, then, the UDC becomes subjected to a rigorous body of rules, much the same as govern CC; it is necessary to add rules for citation order in many classes, however: for instance it is only by a sort of intuition that sub-facets are noted in many classes and in some common auxiliaries (such as Place). And the filing (the inversion of which gives the citation order [17]) is not the same in every class for the special auxiliaries -*n* and .O*n*. In class 8, the facets are listed as A/Z for author (with a dependent facet for works), common auxiliaries as applicable, *eg* (091), literary forms -1/-9, literary science and technique .0/.09, and literatures of individual languages 82/89. Thus the citation order seems to be Literature--Language--Problem--Form--Common Auxiliaries--Authors--Works. But this order is not quite satis-factory even in its more general sectors, since if there is a choice between the two orders

Literature--Frence	--Drama	(26)
Literature--French--Aesthetics		
Literature--French--Aesthetics	--Drama	

and

Literature--French	--Aesthetics	(27)
Literature--French--Drama		
Literature--French--Drama--Aesthetics		

none but would choose the second as more helpful, because we intuitively prefer to keep Literary Form more compactly together, letting Problems become (more-)distributed relatives.

And indeed we could go further and prefer a citation order Literature--Language--Form[18]--Authors--Problem--Common Auxiliaries. This would invert to create a file such as 8, 8=*n*, 8(O*n*), 8"*n*", 8.O*n*, 8-*n*, 8A/Z, 82/89.

Such a revision of the citation order in class 8 works out

---

17 See appendix III to my paper 'Approaches to library filing', cited in footnotes.
18 This citation order is more characteristic of DC than of LC, and in this instance I am willing to give LC credit for doing something the way I would like it done. Thus I would invert the order between Form and Authors, -*n* and A/Z.

easily enough[19], once it has been decided upon, but the form of the enumeration in the abridged English edition₃ of UDC does not facilitate it in any way: we have to impose our own will on it. Besides, there is the residual problem about the difference, here, of the order between -*n* and .O*n*, from that obtaining in other classes (*eg* 621, as shown in (9)). It might be advisable to exchange facet indicators in class 8 and the like, when their order is at variance with that of the majority of such usages — but that would require a ten-year wait; so it is better to have special instructions for file-order in such anomalous cases.

19 It is to be noted that there is a difference between citation orders in various classes: in some it is a framework which can be empty or full in a n y of the patterns shown in (10); in others (like class 8 and its analogs in most other classifications) there are not as many open possibilities. For instance, it is not possible to get to A/Z for authors without having gone through Language, though we can get to -*n* or .O*n* without having gone through Language or Authors or Works. Thus, to fill out what is begun in (26) and (27) we have a possible structure (ignoring everything in the class-8 filing order not special to it, since the common auxiliaries have an invariable order and structure like

Literature			
Literature–		–Problem	
Literature	–Form		
Literature–	–Form	–Problem	
Literature–Language			
Literature–Language		–Problem	
Literature–Language	–Form		
Literature–Language	–Form	–Problem	˙(28)
Literature–Language–Author			
Literature–Language–Author		–Problem	
Literature–Language–Author	–Form		
Literature–Language–Author	–Form	–Problem	
Literature–Language–Author–Work			
Literature–Language–Author–Work		–Problem	
Literature–Language–Author–Work	–Form		
Literature–Language–Author–Work	–Form	–Problem.	

What is to be noted is that a combination like Literature–Work, or Literature–Author, is impossible (except for anonymous works, *ie* where the work is in a sense identical with its author), given that we are doing *systematic* bibliography; while in many classes any combination of elements is allowed. Here we have a case of facets (Author and Work) which are (in a different sense than is usually given this term) *dependent* on the facet Language. In my paper 'The classification of philosophy' (*Libri*, xiv (1964) 32-39) I argue that in an analogous case such a dependence is undesirable —though Work would still remain dependent upon Author except where anonymous.

Rules for interpretation

To have recommended such variants is akin to programming computer-recognition of variable patterns of codes, beginning something like 'is it a class-8 code we have? — if so, do . . .; if not do as in general instruction "X".'

Operating with explicit rules of formation, accompanied by rules of citation order — namely with such rules of formation reduced to a table of priorities of operation as in (18) — is all for one purpose: adequate and ambiguous interpretation. I like to think of classificatory inscriptions as translations into one or other artificial information language of the document-abstract; and I judge the adequacy and unambiguity of this translation by its translation back into the source language. If inadequacy or ambiguity arises at this point, it is probably due to the difficulty of interpretation of the classificatory inscription; it may also of course be due to the lack either of specificity or of concreteness in the intermediary classificatory language itself.

But the largest problem with which we are faced today is that of providing a system capable of assimilation to and utilization in the computer. In the paper by Caless and Kirk cited in footnote 10 there is proposed a way to make UDC code 'intelligible' (interpretable, utilisable) for computers, pre-interpreting all the elements of the whole code which in fact modify each other. It has been largely to provide a rationale for the construction of codes which can be automatically interpreted that I have undertaken the present explication.

In the case of such a code as (19) what Caless and Kirk propose is that the cataloguer show not merelt the whole complex, but each sub-complex within it, *eg* 539.163 (079.3), since the document is a case book on (some aspect of) radioactivity — note the similarity of his proposal to Bradford's interpretation of the code 526...   I am convinced that with the rules for operation given here, a clerk or a computer could retrieve this. document at the instance of a request phrased in terms of any of the valid correlations. For instance, a request for something in a Romance language on measurement in fluid mechanics, 532.08 =4/6, would retrieve this document with the warning that it is over-specific on both counts — though this was of course hoped for in the case of the language. Or, a request for prevention of turbulence in flow through pipes, 532.542.1.004.61, which should not retrieve it because it is not the turbulence that is being prevented, but rather the isotope-decay; the lack of the appropriate pre-correlation according to the Caless-Kirk proposal would prevent retrieval, but so does the [n...n]-structure of (20).

There are a great many valid correlations in such as (19) or (20)[20]; why make the cataloguer do all of them? if it can be done at the retrieval stage, when it is needed — by clerks or reference librarians (or even patrons) in searching the classed d catalogue, by the computer in searching the electronically stored record.

(The one thing in this example that cannot be done purely clerically —‐ie as a function of the rules for manipulation of the symbols themselves — is the assignment of special auxiliaries to their superordinate classes. In this case, what is the superordinate class of .08 — 532 or 53 or 5? It turns out to be 53, but this can be determined only by examination of the schedules, not by rule. It would probably be wise, in computer installation, for the cataloguer to indicate such affiliations: if the whole code were 228.09:75.04, to write out in a prescribed place, 22.09 and 7.04. This would prevent the assumption that .09 is a special auxiliary of class 2, but will show its relation to a request for (say) 225.09.)

The interpretation of complex codes in UDC can usually best be accomplished by reading right-to-left, 'word'-by-'word'; for (20) *a (linguistically) French case-book on glass used in the vacuum chambers which are used to prevent* [rapid] *decay of the radioactive isotopes used to measure turbulent pipe flow.* While this is not particularly significant for the computer[21], it is so for the clerical creation of the secondary entries in the classed catalogue, and even more so for the adequate, unambiguous, and easy interpretation of all the entries there or in an electronically stored record.

20 More exactly, at least twenty-two: 532.542.1.08, 532.542.1:546.02, 532.542.1(079.3), 532.542.1=40, 53.08:546.02, 53.08(079.3), 53.08=40, 546.02, 546.02:539.163, 546.02(079.3), 546.02=40, 539.163.004.61, 539.163(079.3), 539.163=40, .004.61:[621.52:666.1], .004.61 (079.3) .004.61=40, 621.52:666.1, 621.52(079.3), 621.52=40, 666.1(079.3), and 666.1=40.

21 Largely because of the ambiguity within the *n:n*, which the librarian can translate into the proper relational term, but which the computer cannot; hence the value of a system of univocities like that elaborated in 'Categories and relators'.

APPENDIX I Some examples of the need for [n...n] to assure proper interpretation

1   *Hallmarks of English goldsmiths of the 15th century*

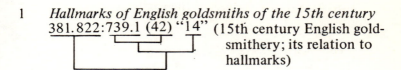

381.822:739.1 (42) "14" (15th century English goldsmithery; its relation to
hallmarks)

[381.822:739.1] (42) "14" (15th century English hallmarks in English goldsmithery)

2   *Practices involved in the pricing and sale of MSS in medieval France*

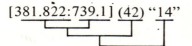

(091:658 8.031(44) "04/14" MSS on pricing and selling in
medieval France)

[091:658 8.031](44) "04/14" (medieval French pricing
and selling of MSS)

3   *The composition of the sand of the beach at Big Sur*

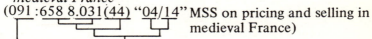

553.623:54-1/-4.(794 B: 210.5) (chemical composition
of the beach at Big Sur
in relation to sand)

[553.623:54-1/-4](794 B: 210·5) (chemical composition
of sand of Big Sur beach)

4   *The contribution to medieval learning of English scholar*

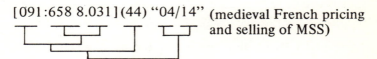

0/9.007.6(42) "04/14" (medieval English scholars in
general studies)

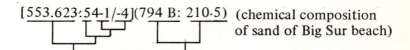

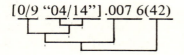

[0/9 "04/14"].007 6(42) (English scholars on general
medieval studies)

5   *Isotopes of iron and molybdenum in the core of the earth*

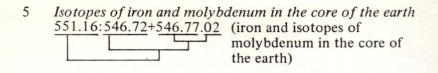

551.16:546.72+546.77.02 (iron and isotopes of
molybdenum in the core of
the earth)

551.16:[546.72+546.77].02 (isotopes of iron and molybdenum in the core of the
earth)

6   *The use of marble in altar-domes in churches of the
Protestant Episcopal Church*

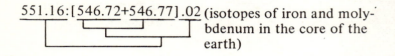

264-03:69.024 4:691.215.3:283(73)   (altar domes in
marble PEC churches)

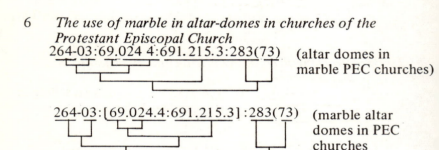

264-03:[69.024.4:691.215.3]:283(73)   (marble altar
domes in PEC
churches

APPENDIX II: Formal codes and topical codes in DC and UDC

As noted with (3) and the other codifications that flow from
it, there is an at least apparent problem in DC that arises when we
encounter a document within a formal main class like Bibliography, i f it also contains some other formal code, and
i f the elements of its concreteness cannot be successfully
change of the 011/019 into formal codes. This can more briefly
and generally be stated in the shape of a question: How many
formal codes can be applied to one document? If we have
016.5 we have one; with 016.505 still one, and not a correct
translation of the source-document; with 505.016 two — and here
the real question arises: which (or both?) of these apparent
formal codes is to be taken as such? If only one, which? If only
one, what is our interpretation of the other?

In DC there is an unfinished attempt at the setting up of main-
schedule classes to mirror formal codes: the same stricture
applies to UDC, but the latter commonly employs additional
devices, *a*: the parentheses seen in the (O*n*) and *b*: the colon in
the (O*n*:O*n*) to separate two or more formal codes. Thus in

UDC there would need to be no doubt that in the equivalent of
505.016 the 05 is a t o p i c a l -formal code; this is effected simply
by replacing (05) by :05. The purpose of abandoning 016.5 (in
DC) was that 05 could not be added except by mistranslation
of the source-document, whereas 505.016 is a correct translation by virtue of the following principle:

> *Whenever one formal code is directly followed by
> another, the first is automatically to be interpreted
> as a topical-formal code.* (29)

In UDC it would seem that this point is unnecessary, since we
can put this as 5:05:016 or 016:5:05. But there still remain
troublesome cases, both in DC and in UDC. In DC, we can
encounter documents wherein the two (or more) formal
concepts remain that, as in *a periodical-form bibliography of
science.* If (29) is accepted as binding, to leave the three
elementary codes 5, 016, and 05 in that order, since they
cannot but be interpreted linearly, as

$$5 \quad 01.6 \quad 05 \qquad\qquad (30)$$

cannot match the source-document, but inevitably means *a
periodical about the bibliography of science.* What is needed is
something like the [*n...n*] in UDC, giving

$$500 \quad [016.05] \qquad\qquad (31)$$

or the like. But such a device is precluded by the pure-
numerical notation of DC; we must either *a*: accept (28) as
universally binding, *b*: accept the precise opposite, namely

> *Whenever one formal code is directly followed by
> another, both are to be interpreted as formal codes*[22], (32)

or *c*: accept the confusion and ambiguity resulting from the
lack of either rule.

In UDC the two possibilities ((3) and *a periodical-form
bibliography of science*) using the same three concepts, in one
case taking bibliography as topical-form, in the other as form,

---

22 This results in additional difficulties, since purely topical elements are given
along with formal and topical-formal codes in the DC 'standard subdivisions',
eg 01 *philosophy and theory,* which can surely be modified by such as
05, to give 501.05 for *a periodical on the philosophy of science.* The
answer of course is to have a different table for such entirely non-formal
standard subdivisions.

are effected either by an evasion, namely the replacement of
016, which can only be a form, by 01, which can only be a
topic, giving

> 5:01 (05) and
>
> 5:016 (05),   (33)

or by attaching to 016 a point-of-view code like .001.8 'methodology', giving

> 5:016.001.8 (05) and
>
> 5:016 (05)   (34)

But a serious difficulty remains in UDC, stemming from the
combination of two points, a: the principle enunciated in the
main text, namely that operations within (On) or $[n...n]$ are
prior to all between the contents of the enclosure and any code-
elements external to them, and b: the fact that there is no
perfect mirror-relation between the form-tables and the main
schedule in cases where the same concept may be alternatively topical or topical-formal. In footnote 7, for instance, the
standard instruction was followed in constructing numbers like
$X(091:063)$, $X(091:038)$, and $X(091:063:038)$. It follows from
what has just been said that the first is diagrammed

> X $(091:063)$ (35)

which corresponds to (31), making the two formal codes that
and nothing else — precluding, therefore, the interpretation
conference proceedings on the historical aspects of X, except
that (09), like 01 in DC, is n o t a form to start with. A better
example, then would be the variant articulation of such a set
of elementary concepts as *economics, vocabulary,* and
serial, giving either

> 33 (038 : 05) or   (36)
>
> 33:030.8 (05)

denoting respectively *a periodical-form vocabulary* [a pure form]
of economics and *a periodical on the vocabulary of economics.*
In such a case there i s a mirror-relation between formal code and
topical-formal code. But where there is n·o t, and when the first
is to be taken as a formal code rather than as a topical-formal code
the two form-codes must be left unconnected by $n:n$, *scil,* in
their own individual (On)s. An example would be *a serial on*

histograms used in economics, as against *a serial set of histograms on economics,* coded respectively as

33 (083.58) (05) and

$$(37)$$

33 (083.58 : 05)

Another solution for this second case (though one never suggested in standard instructions) would be

33 (083.58 + 05)

$$(38)$$

which may indeed be the most logically adequate of all.

It follows that 33(6-77), *economics of the undeveloped parts of Africa,* is allowable, while 33(6:05)[23] is not, since the order of operations would prevent the desired interpretation.

Until a considerable sample of literature is examined it would appear that this principle is of greater importance in DC, which has no way of joining topical-formal elements to a primary element except as standard sub-divisions (and hence could make no use of a complete mirror-relation between formal standard subdivisions and topical-formal codes from the main schedules), than in UDC. However, since my purpose is the raising of the rigor of UDC input for the sake of clerical (perhaps computerized) interpretation of the corresponding output, even this minor point is worth settling.

23 Attempted is *a periodical on the economics of Africa*: but the (...:05) code is prevented from modifying the basic substantive 33 by the enclosure of (6:...) with it in the parentheses.

VI

On the colon in UDC and on
the Boolean operators

It was pointed out during R.R. Freeman's presentation that
aside from subordinating facet indicators such as (On),"$\overline{n}$", $(=n)$,
(n), .OOn, -n, and .On, the CFSS system for storing and retrieving
UDC surrogates did not attempt to take advantage of syntactical
devices such as $n+n$ (co-occurrence), n/n (span) and (most of all)
$n:n$ (conjunction).

It was observed, however, that the Boolean operators AND, OR,
and NOT were allowed during the search. From this contiguity of
argument can (and did) arise the impression that the Boolean
operators serve as syntactical symbols. This is at least all too
easy to agree with especially in that $n:n$ and $n+n$ seem close
(resp) to AND and to OR.

This conclusion is somewhat reinforced by the fact that while
a search for a AND b would retrieve $a:b$; and one for a OR b
would retrieve $a+c$, $b+c$, or $a+b$, this last search would also
retrieve $a:c$, $b:c$, or $a:b$; and lastly the first search (for a AND
b) would retrieve not only $a:b$ but also $a+b$. The point at issue
is whether the a AND b stipulation implies anything of the
relationality of $a:b$; the answer, at least in some minds, is
y e s.

I disagree with this answer; my inclination is toward the
strong retention, even the further development, of syntactical
devices in UDC, especially the $n:n$, arguing that without at least
this last UDC has been emasculated into little more than a notationally complicated DC. This inclination is easy to see in my
involvement in T Caless' project[2], with its stressing of the
linkage between elements of each surrogate. If this argument is
not trivial, then the Boolean operators must be demonstrated
to be inadequate to the task of syntactical linkage.

1 At the Seminar on UDC in a Mechanised Retrieval System, Copenhagen, 1968 –
   to be published as FID/CR Report No 9.
2 *Cf eg* T Caless, 'Subject analysis matrices for classification with UDC' also
   presented at the Copenhagen seminar, to which the present essay is an appendix.

Syntax is definable either as the orderedness of what is present together or as the coupledness of the structured; I choose here to emphasise the first aspect. But *a* AND *b* is precisely the same in meaning as is *b* AND *a*. AND, accordingly, exhibits no specific syntactical orderedness. This is of course true *a fortiori* of OR. NOT, on the other hand, shows no inclination to be syntactical for a wholly different reason; it, unlike AND and OR, is no connective at all.

Now as to the UDC devices *n+n* and *n/n,* I will admit that they do not order the terms 'joined' by them anymore than do AND or OR, except in the sense that the left-hand *n* is always lower in numerical value than the right-hand one — especially in the case of *n/n* which calls for no permutation such as is appropriate to *n+n*.

It is commonly argued too that *n:n* does not impose order between the terms joined by it, since it is normally to be expected that the substantive following (n_2 in $n_1:n_2$) will be a sought term, calling for permutation of $n1:n2$ into $n2:n1$. And such an example as 016:33 would seem to prove the point, since surely 33:016 is just as much needed, if not more so.

The orderedness that characterises syntax, though, is clearly enough seen in such codes as 026:05 and 05:026, the first conveying *Special libraries dealing with the subject: periodicals* and the second *Periodicals dealing with the subject: special libraries*[3] People, some of them librarians, do speak of the syntactical sense of *n:n* in UDC; what else can they mean but such variant meaning as a function of variant order, just as arises in natural-language syntax? But, if permuted entry ntry of 026:05 is allowed or even insisted upon, how can anything but confusion arise? It is to the elimination of such confusion, and therefore to the strengthening of the chances of UDC to become dominant in implementation of such proposals as the World Information Network, that my own relator-schema is dedicated.

The feature of syntax that is primary in the discussion above is that of orientation, whereby the meaning 026   05 can be permuted into 05   026 without such change as inevitably as accompanies 026:05 becoming 05:026 — but without use of any such exotic symbolism.

3   This at least seems what the meanings must be in terms of the instruction on p 28 of BS1000:A, 1961, (026:61 Medical libraries) though the citation order seems precisely backwards to me.

To return to the Boolean operators, then, we can see them as analysable into the intersection of two tiny facets: one we shall call Strictness, and it shall contain just two foci, Must and May; the other we shall call Accompanance, with two foci as well, Presence and Absence. The resulting matrix is

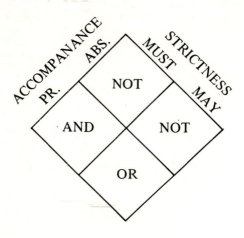

Obviously, not both NOTs are to be used, and when we realise this we see that AND, OR, and NOT are not even junctures between terms at all, for otherwise they would not belong to the same set of terms at all. Taken as stipulations about the presence or absence of terms 'may be present' is no different from 'may be absent' ; but the first is naturally to be preferred, resulting in the following translations of AND, OR, and NOT, now seen as term-modifiers rather than as junctures:

AND = must be present
OR = may be present (or absent)
NOT = must be absent

Accordingly, it is not only true that the Boolean operators are inappropriate to use in documentation, since analysis of them in such use is wholly foreign to their origin in symbolic logic (as junctures in propositions), but even that their use in verbal equivalence of Venn-diagrams is suspect.

The function of $n:n$ in UDC is seen then to be a wholly different sort of thing. Searching for 32 AND 37 is similar neither to 32+37, 32/37, nor 32:37, though there is at least some similarity between 32 OR 37 and 32+37. But to n/n or $n:n$ there is entirely no similarity in AND. But since n/n is merely a shorthand way of showing $n+n \ldots +n$, the only inter-equal-codes symbol in UDC that is truly syntactical is $n:n$; and the conclusion must be that its exclusion is a serious defection from the ideal image of UDC that we must always keep in view when we think of its use in the real world of documentation or libraries.

VII

Transparency and self-definition
in classification

Die Synthesis eines Mannigfaltigen aber (es sei empirisch oder *a priori* gegeben) bringst zuerst eine Erkenntniss hervor. [1]

The outward face of speech is thus: it is like solid blocks of lava erupted from the surface of silence, lying scattered about and connected one with another by the surface of silence. [2]

0 PRELUDE
0.1 OCCASION AND NEED

The time available for the presentation of a detailed paper at a congress is seldom sufficient; nor was it in the case of my paper 'Categories and relators: a new schema'[3] (referred to henceforth as C/R). Thus, in the last desperate moments before the presentation, I sought to identify the primordia from which the schema had arisen, in order to have not merely a string of results to present in the brief available time, but the philosophical arguments that were not more than barely mentioned in the text itself. It is from further reflection on these primordia that the present paper has arisen.

0.2 'CLASSIFICATION' AND LIBRARY CLASSIFICATION

It is likewise a response, here, that I wish to make to a comment made even during the congress, as well as subsequently[4], that classification as we know it is soon to be a thing of the past. I do not plan to attempt to demonstrate (as I think would not be too difficult a matter) that classification in some sense is basic to all our mental operations. In any case this would not be much of a defense of library classification. What i s more intended is an affirmative answer to S Artandi's question *Is the intellectual* [*ie,* non-automatic] *organisation of knowledge* [*viz*, in libraries] *still valid*? and more:

I intend to show how the hope of a thoughoroughly transparent classification for library use can be (even if only in one part of it) achieved, and how this achievement must be linked to the ubiquitous classification that is the common possession of all mind; and to show the limits of transparency and the necessary value of what lies outside it, namely enumeration.

1 CONTEXT AND TRANSPARENCY

1   I Kant, *Kritik der reinen Vernunft*, §10 (*ed* Hartenstein, III, 98)
2   M Picard, *The world of silence, tr* S Godman (Chicago, H Regnery, 1952), 29.
3   J M Perreault,'Categories and relators: a new schema' (*Revue internationale de la documentation,* xxxii/4 (1965), 136-144; presented at the 1965 Congress of the International Federation for Documentation, Washington DC), reprinted below.
4   By (resp) B Markuson and R Bregzis.

90

1.1 CONTEXT AND THE-LANGUAGE-AS-A-WHOLE
1.11 CONTEXT AND DEFINITION

In all discourse, and especially in that which aims at definition, there is the ineluctable need for context. 'The' language as a whole, we can postulate, must be 'present' for a definition to be attempted, since definition is 'by definition' the use of other (known) words or concepts to make more known any particular less known word or concept.

Thus it can be concluded that there could be nothing such as 'this' concept without other concepts; these others make possible the one, in one of two ways: *a:* by being used in a discursive definition, or *b:* by setting a limit to the extension of the one concept. Thus there are two senses of 'definition', but for our purposes the distinction need not be more deeply examined nor kept in mind throughout this paper.

Though there could not be 'this' concept without 'those', there might of course be 'this' word with no others 'present' – but only in the trivial sense of words as phonemic. We shall confine ourselves mainly to considering concepts, and shall use 'words' only as bearers (adequate or inadequate) or concepts, whenever they do enter in.

The general rule for definition is that no definition may make use of that which is being defined, at the risk of begging the question. When asked, for instance, what is 'this', the answer must be in terms of 'that' or 'those'. However, it cannot be denied that, even if this rule be obeyed in each particular case, there is a sort of begging of the question involved when all the definitions within one language are apprehended together. This is not a criticism, of course; it is really only to say that a language is an organic whole, each cell within which is in some analogous manner dependent upon the whole, or at least upon some other cell(s).

1.12 DEFINITION AS *CIRCULUS VITIOSUS*

Thus, if each 'new' word must be defined by reference to some 'old' word, that old word must, when new, have been defined by reference to a yet older.

Even if we do not view the concatenation of words as 'new', and 'old' ones, we still see that (say) *a* is defined by *k,k* by *p,p* by *y*, and finally *y* by *a*. Though the actual fact of the situation may not be as clear as this, and though quite surely the fact is that each word is defined by reference to a syntactical group of words (that is, definition is a more complex process than the mere finding of synonyms), the picture as a whole looks very much like a *circulus vitiosus* (which is, in fact, merely an expression for a concealed non-linear begging of the question[5]).

Definition, then, despite our prohibition of using the term defined in its own definition, seems necessarily to involve begging the question.

5 *Cf* for instance Aristotle, *Posterior analytics*, cap 3, and G W F Hegel, *Wissenschaft der Logik*, bk II, sect 3, §A, (a)-(b).

1.2 THE *CIRCULUS VITIOSUS* AND THE PROCESS OF LEARNING
1.21 CONTEXT AS MEDIUM OF LEARNING

First, though, let us try to see why there should be the prohibition of the *circulus vitiosus*. We seek n e w knowledge, and our minds necessarily go from old to new, known to unknown. Thus we start with what is already known and move thence to what we do not (yet) know. At least the mental process of the learner can be pictured thus –he to whom the new is unknown until the definer defines it to him. And the definer much necessarily do so in terms of what the learner knows already. But how is this process possible unless we postulate teacher-definers who know everything already; and, indeed, how does the learner have the first 'old' concept with which to build forward to 'new' ones? The epistemological is thus seen as radically distinct from the pedagogical, though standing in an originative and foundational relation to it.

Not wishing to enter into this problem-area here, however much light it might cast on the problems of mechanical information storage and retrieval and mechanical translation, we shall concentrate on definition as circular instead of as linear, accepting as our epistemological basis the following:

1.22 THE *CIRCULUS VITIOSUS* AND ANALYSIS

There is a profound passage to be read on the problems of the *circulus vitiosus* in § 32, 'Verstehen und Auslegen' , of Martin Heidegger's *Sein und Zeit* [6]. I shall briefly resume his argument, insofar as it is relevant to our present purpose:

Analysis (Auslegung) is grounded in understanding (Verstehen), which is the human response to the externalities presented to it in its circumspection (Umsicht) of its environment. These externalities are the world as adaptable (Zuhandenes = at-hand), and are understood as 'in order to . . .' (um-zu); each of them is something as s o m e t h i n g (else?). What is this 'something'? It is something-in-order-to . . . The 'as' is what constitutes analysis: understanding erects a world for itself in which all these 'as's' fit together into an articulated picture of adaptability as such, and this articulation is carried over and strengthened in analysis. It is this picture which we call 'world'. It is this a l r e a d y -understood world which enables analysis.

Textual analysis relies upon this phenomenon: it explicates 'what is right there'– and that is 'nothing other than the self-evident, undiscussed pre-judgment of the analyst' . Heidegger then asks whether the 'right there' of understanding and the 'as' of analysis are grounded together in the project (Entwurf) basic to man's whole stand. Such a structure, implicit in analysis, seems to obviate any truly scientific proof: 'Scientific proof must not already presuppose that which it is its task to substantiate.'

6 M Heidegger, *Sein und Zeit,* 7. unveränd Aufl (Tübingen, M Niemeyer, 1953) 148-153; translated (by J Macquarrie and E Robinson) as *Being and time* (London, SCM; New York, Harper, 1962), 188-195. Quotations, however, are given in my own version.

The historical 'sciences', dealing as they do with what is 'right there already', are apparently excluded from truly scientific methodology. There is thus a compensating tendency to replace these all-too-given data with their spiritual significances, so as to free history from the point of view of the observer.

But to imagine that understanding and analysis fail in comparison to some · abstract ideal of knowledge, as if they represent some merely derivative type of knowledge, is to misunderstand the whole stand of man, out of which springs the only mode of knowledge he can attain to: 'This circle . . . is the expression of the existential p r e - s t r u c t u r e o f m a n (Dasein) himself.'

Though there is a kind of circle present in human knowledge as a whole, it would be unfortunate to imagine that some circumscribed sector of it (such as the apparently tight logic of mathematics) is of a higher type than that of which it is merely one part.

1.3 CONTEXT IN AUTOMATIC DOCUMENTATION

In the sphere of documentation this need for context can be seen at work too, even among those who appeal to statistical methods as the opening wedge in the noble project which will eventuate (it is hoped) in fully automatic processing of natural-language text for storage and retrieval, without need for such human intermediation as is evidenced in library classification as we now know it.

1.31 KEY WORDS IN CONTEXT

For instance, one of the most widespread and economical techniques for automatic storage-processing is that known as KWIC — key words in context. Key words as such (without context, that is) could of course be used with equal or greater economy, but there is (apparently) recognition of the danger that the words of title or abstract would, each by itself, be apt to produce deformations (either 'noise' or 'silence') in the retrieval process.

The technique is familiar to most, so I shall describe it only sketchily: A list of words presumed to be of no significance is used as a filter to reduce the bulk of the text to be input to the computer. Each remaining word is used as the alphabetizing element for the title or abstract from which it stems, and is stated in its alphabetical position along with the context from which it has been noted. The basic assumptions are a: that either i: all authors will use word A to signify concept or that ii: at least the future querist will use A or $A_1 \ldots A_n$ in his retrieval; or b: that if the word A is only partial in its signification of concept ϕ, its verbal context will supply the defect. That in fact this contextual presence does assist in the retrieval of truly relevant (as against merely verbally-apparently relevant) documents can be seen by the briefest look at an actual KWIC index. Such an examination will disclose two rather antithetical facts: a: the presence of the context will place the word (say, *crane*) in its proper conceptual environment (either transportation techniques or water-birds but *b*: even this improvement of relevance is dependent on the ability of the querist (or his delegate) to exclude from the output those titles or abstracts which even so are irrelevant (or inappropriate). The question is, *Can the computer, or any other purely clerical system, do the same?* If not, an a u t o m a t i c retrieval system has not been achieved, even though the storage itself may have been[7].

1.32 THE NEED FOR GREATER AUTOMATIZATION

This is not, however, the only or necessarily the most promising area of statistical work towards fully automatic storage and retrieval. (As we see from the above, there can easily enough be fully automatic storage without their being correspondingly automatic retrieval; if the gap is due to the KWIC system having been set up in such a way as to store automatically what could be retrieved only 'manually', we must conclude that the way to retrieve automatically can only be enabled by the way in which the storage is made to take place. *Ergo*, back to the drawing-board.) If the context of the keywords is capable of revealing their correct conceptual environments, as we see in the case of the KWIC index – even though only to the human querist – there may be a way of enabling the computer or its analogs to do the same at both ends. Two of these attempts are *a*: the thesaurus and *b*: associative techniques.

1.33 THE THESAURUS

The thesaurus is a development of the subject-heading technique of indexing – in particular of its syndetic structure[8], by which latter a more or less implicit subsumptive organisation is broken up and as it were fragmentarily reflected in each node of what 'was' the underlying total organisation.

From a sector of classification, such as

the subject-heading or thesaurus listing of *A* shows only the words/concepts including, included in, and coordinate to *A*:

But through this fragmentary reflection of the underlying systematic organisation is what characterises the syndesis of subject-headings, it is not, strictly speaking, what makes a thesaurus.

7   The classic texts on the KWIC index are H P Luhn 'Potentialities of auto-encoding of scientific literature' (Yorktown Heights, IBM Research Center, 1959 (=RC-101), and 'Keyword-in-Context index for technical literature (KWIC index)' (Yorktown Heights, IBM Advanced Systems Development Division, 1959 (=RC-127) – also reprinted in periodicals.

8   See also § 1.37 .

The central and original characteristic of Roget's thesaurus is a d u a l structure *a*: the tree-structured classification of the whole vocabulary, plus *b*: the alphabetical (relative) index.

And characteristic of the classified part is the attemp to group together all · all equivalences; if word *B* is equivalent (synonymous) to words *b* and β, it will be placed in each of these classified environments, and the index will indicate both placements. This dual placement can be of two sorts, *a*: that where the conceptual content of the s a m e word is capable of equivocal meanings, and *b*: that where the a p p a r e n t l y same word is assigned to its two (or more) univocal meanings. (An example of the first sort of *form*, = *human form* 245.4, and = *musical form* 462.11; of the second, *can*,= *receptacle* 192.5.11, and = *be able* 156.10 [9].)

1.34 THE THESAURUS AND THE LINEARITY OF CONTEXT

But the thesaurus, though it can be used in what may be claimed to be a fully automatic storage and retrieval system, in that it allows the computer to assign each word of natural-language text input to a context where its conceptual content is revealed, by having compared the incoming word a n d i t s n a t u r a l c o n t e x t with the contextual structure of the thesaurus; and in that it allows the same for the query [10]; – still it does not in fact satisfy the strict sense of 'automatic', since the organisation of the thesaurus is the result of intellectual effort, and is ultimately based on a classificatory mapping.

The second attempt at a fully automatic system of information storage a s w e l l a s retrieval is that represented above as 'associative', and is cited in connection with the names Borko, Bernick, Doyle, and Stiles[11]. These experimenters are attempting to be fully automatic, with the computer constructing the context for each word in the input from all (or a selected span) of the other words in the input.

9 From *Roget's international thesaurus₃* (New York, Crowell, 1962).

10 *Cf* G London, 'A classed thesaurus as an intermediary between textual, indexing and searching languages' (*Revue internationale de la documentation,* xxxii/4 (1965), 145-149):her later works with similar titles have taken a different turn.

11 (As examples:) H Borko & M D Bernick, *Toward the establishment of a computer based classification system for scientific documentation* (Santa Monica, System Development Corp., 1964 (=TM-1763); 'Automatic document classification' (*Journal of the Association for Computing Machinery,* x/2 (1964), 151-162+); H E Stiles, 'The association factor in information retrieval' (*Journal of the Association for Computing Machinery,* viii/2 (1961), 271-279); 'Progress in the use of the association factor in information retrieval' (*Proceedings,* Symposium on Materials Information, Wright Patterson AFB (=Rpt no ASD-TDR-63-445, May 1963)); I B Doyle, *Is automatic classification a reasonable application of statistical analysis of text?* (Santa Monica, System Development Corp, 1964 (=SO-1753)):*Some compromises between word grouping and document grouping* (Santa Monica, System Development Corp, 1964 (=SP-1481)).

The results of these experiments have been encouraging but not spectacular [12]; what I wish to make clearly visible, from these results is the fundamental fact that language, the basis of all literature and the bearer of information, is d i s c u r s i v e: it flows on from known to unknown; and that the unknown becomes known in the light of the just-past discourse.

C o n t e x t, in a word, i s t h e c r e a t o r o f m e a n i n g. Without context no word could mean anything, and this context is of two types: *a*: the context constituted by the place of the conceptual 'load' of the word in the midst of other words equivalent, partially equivalent, and not equivalent to it; and *b*: the context created in the discursive enunciation of the one word among others.

These new contextualities correspond to the bifurcations *paradigmatic* and *syntagmatic* (Gardin), *semantemes* and *morphemes* (Bèrnier), *lexical* and *syntactic* (Elsinore Conference), *arguments* and *functors* (mathematical logic).

An analogy can be seen in music, where a single pitch cannot be taken as defining what we might call 'proto-tonality', but can do so only insofar as it is preceded or followed by others; and where the duration of a tone does not define a rhythm, but can do so only insofar as it is preceded or followed by others. And these two together are required to define a melody. That this is true is easy enough to realise from the ambiguous (equivocal) effect of the first, or even the first several, notes of a melody (especially if there is only a single line of tone, since concomitance tends to provide a context for the definition of rythm). Take the opening of Buxtehude's Toccata and Fugue (organ, F m ajor; Keller I/7), where the whole first two measures are open to misinterpretation:

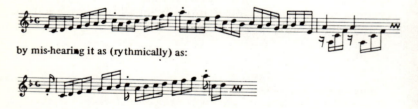

by mis-hearing it as (rythmically) as:

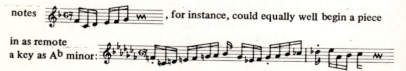

It is only when we get to the quarter-notes and their accompanying arpeggios (measure 3) that we are on sure ground. The same can apply to tonality; the first six

notes ♩♩♩ , for instance, could equally well begin a piece

in as remote
a key as A♭ minor: 𝄞♭♭♭♭ ,

12 *Cf* E de Grolier, *On the theoretical basis of information retrieval systems* (Paris, 1965 (=AF 61 (052) - 505)), 2-3.

— where a direct statement of the real tonality comes only with the last four notes quoted.

We are accustomed to imagining such 'neutrals' as musical notes to be far more functional than words; to be less burdened with semantic ambiguities. And so they may be; but in either case, context is supreme — and is likely to be even more crucial when the semantic factor is strongly present, as in words.

1.35 CONTEXT IN UNITERMIC SDI

The total-statistical, all-computer approach of the 'associative' group of investigators contrasts sharply with that of the proponents of all-computer approaches such as the uniterm system of M Taube[13]. But even here it is not impossible to detect a recognition of the need for context — though this recognition did not eventuate in large-scale modifications of the working systems[14]. Recognition for the need for context is embodied, rather, in the use of the abstract as a corollary of the unitermic index. (Abstracts have of course had a long and honorable existence independent of the computer; what is being focussed on here is rather the absolute need for them to back up unitermic— thoroughly non-contextual — indexing.)

In a uniterm-organized SDI (selective dissemination of information[15]) system, for instance, it is not the fact that a new document labelled x is now available that is the trigger which sets the researcher's (intellectual) mouth to watering, but rather that the uniterm x arouses in this researcher a hope which is either strengthened or squelched by the abstract itself. This strengthening may be illuory: the document has to be read to see if so; and anyway, the abstracter has his own axes to grind, and may mislead — because not everyone's total context is the same. The squelching may also be illusory, but is irreparable, since the document will not be read because hope was killed at the outset.

Another contextual aspect of SDI system is the user- profile as a systematic unity. The researcher who is to be notified is allowed to stipulate more than isolated uniterms as criteria for notification: he hopes for documents on concepts α β γ and therefore must ask for words (uniterms) a, a_1, a_2, b, b_1, c, c_1, c_2, etc. And he can weight each lable the a's (say) 5, the b's 3, the c's only 1, and the total weight of the document must be such as to cross a threshold (say 6) to qualify it for being brought to the researcher's attention[16]. Thus, a document labelled a, b ($5 + 3 = 8$)

13 See *eg* his 'Storage and retrieval of information by means of the association of ideas' (*American documentation*, vi/1 (1955), 1-18); 'Some notes on logical products and associations' (*ibid*, vi/4 (1955), 239-242); 'Classification today — shadow or substance" (Illinois University. Graduate School of Library Science. *The role of classification in the modern american library* (Urbana Illini Union Bookstore, 1960), 31-41).

14 I am not referring to the somewhat half-hearted allowances for pseudo-or quasi-syntagmata (*eg*, roles and/or links) that Taube was making in such papers as 'Extensive relations as the necessary condition for the significance of 'The-sauri' for mechanical indexing' (*Journal of chemical documentation*, iii/3 (1963), 177-180) and 'Notes on the use of roles and links in coordinate indexing' (*American documentation*, iii/2 (1961), 98-100)— though these are significant indeed.

15 See H P Luhn, 'A business intelligence system' (*IBM journal of research and development*, ii/4 (1958), 314-319) for the originating source of the idea.

16 We might well put *qualify* in quotes, since what is really meant here is a criterion for notification constituted of quality (presence of terms a n d quantity (the weights).

would be brought to his attention, as would one labelled b, b_1, or one a, c but not one labelled b,c etc.

The point here is that what the researcher is demanding of the SDI system, by means of this weighting-strategy, is a m i n i m a l l e v e l o f c o n t e x t u a l c o h e r e n c e; by insisting on certain overlapped labels, he is demanding paradigmatic contextuality, much in the same way that is secured by the use of the KWIC index.

And when we remember that even all this apparatus is only a more elaborate way of preventing the unwarranted arousal of hope, and that it is finally the abstract itself which will set off a demand for the original text, we can see the overwhelming part that context is called upon to play—even within indexing techniques supposedly opposed to classification, whether intellectual or statistical-associative.

1.36 FROM THE LINEAR TO THE 'MAP'

The users (cataloger, reference librarian, patron) who makes use of subject headings may not be strongly set against classification, at least not in libraries (as against 'information centers', where a certain degree of unreasoned prejudice in this regard may be found); but they too are often unaware a: of the extent to which subject headings do depend on an underlying classification, even if, as at the Library of Congress, b: subject-headings and classification are consciously promulgated as two independent systems[17]. It has been argued that this independence is beneficial as well as intentional, that the verbal access mechanism (subject headings) is intended as a means of s u p p l e m e n t a t i o n of the shelf-classification, especially in cases where a new subject is called for to indicate a concept n o t coterminous[18] with any previous or present document. Whether or not this justifies the present divorce of one (public) classification system from another (the hidden one underlying the subject headings), both at work on the same collection, it must be granted that each must be able to work independently: if we aim at strategizing browsing at the shelf we must lay out a conceptual structure in terms of an ordinal code capable of guiding the searchers from concept to concept, whether one contains or is contained by the other generically, as congeries, as organism, or whether the two be related in some determinative or ordinal manner—and the same must of course be equally possible at the catalogue.[19]

17 Examination of my paper 'The conceptual level in bibliography' (*Libri*, xv/4 (1965), 302-310) will disclose that a classification can indeed be seen to underlie LC subject headings, even though it is notably inferior to the actual shelf-classification embodied in the schedules; see also E J Coates, *Subject catalogues: headings and structure* (London, Library Association, 1960 [repr 1963], 69-79.

18 For my use of this term, see my essay 'Coterminous or specific; a rejoinder to *Headings and canons*' (*Journal of documentation*, xxii (1966), 319-328; also my essay 'Documentary relevance and structural hierarchy'(*Information storage and retrieval*, iii/1 (1966), 13-18; and *American documentation*, xvii (1966), 136-139), reprinted above.

19 Whether or not the two strategisations are congruent, that is. This reservation must not be taken invidiously, since there are collections strategised o n l y in the catalogue.

1.37 VERBAL STRATEGY: SYNDESIS

How is such strategisation actualised in a subject-heading catalogue? In a word, by syndesis.

Syndesis [20] is that which sets up a binding network, as of ligaments, such that a strategy is provided for manipulation of classes in a non-classified (alphabetical) file: alternative possibilities, in brief, are suggested when the results of the first search are too broad, too narrow, too complex, too simple, *etc.*

We saw above how this strategy is the embodiment of an unseen classification, but an embodiment seen only in fragmentary reflections. The primary differences between it and either a thesaurus (in G London's sense; see footnote 10) or a classification, then, is that it focusses on one word/concept at a time; and, between it and a classification, that it does not provide an ordinal mechanism manifestative of the underlying structure [21]. Yet, despite this apparently lower-grade strategisation, what can be seen in such a subject-heading structure is that its words/concepts are defined (at least in part) by the context into which they fall. *a*: For instance, a heading such as *Bibliography* is capable of two major connotations, depending on whether it is the first, or second ...*n*th element in a subject heading. As a first element it names the major c o n c e p t u a l aspect of the documents grouped by it, whereas as second ... *n*th it names a f o r m a l aspect, since the firstness of the rest of the heading implies the major aspect — which is presumed always to be conceptual (at least in normal L C practice). Again, *History* as a first element must indicate a broad conceptual orientation present in the documents grouped by it, whereas as second ... nth it names a mode of approach to the concept(s) named prior to it. *b*: A heading such as *Abitibi Indians* is defined as belonging to the broader class *Indians of North America* by the *xx* and *sa* references (resp) which bring out the syndetic relation.

This does not deny, of course, that recourse must be had to scope-notes in some cases, especially where the terminology of two member-classes of a single higher class is not capable, by itself, of thoroughly clear differentiation. But even here we see the intrusion of context as strategising clarifier: the relation between a heading and its scope-note is congruent to that between an SDI uniterm and its accompanying abstract, except that it points at some other concept as having been 'defined-off', from the first sought, whereas the abstract casts no light beyond the document and the uniterms descriptive of it.

1.4 DEFINITION, LINEAR AND MULTIDIMENSIONAL

1.41 DEFINITION BY DICHOTOMY

The familiary Porphyrian tree is an example of (partial) definition by context. In what is at least commonly taken to be

20 From the Greek δυν δέω,to bind together; whence the old term *syndesmology* for the study of the ligaments.

21 *Cf* M Scheele's approval (*Punched card methods in research and documentation, with special reference to biology, tr* J E Holmstrom (New York, Interscience, 1961), 123-125) of a plan for the transformation of biological nomenclature into such an ordinal structure.

true Aristotelian fashion, the neo-Platonist Porphyrios [22] begins with an including genus and applies to it a *differentia specifica* which assigns part of the beings within the generic extension to one species, the rest to the other.

Since it is difficult to assure oneself of totally exhaustic enumeration of species, it is safer to divide the genus along the lines of a strict yes/no dichotomy, such as: (genus) material being, (sentient? yes) animate ≠ (sentient? no) inanimate. There is of course the danger that such a procedure will provide far too few classes to be of use in the arrangement of ideas, since it is at least probably that the 'no'-classes contain all-too-many undetected *differentiae*, as in

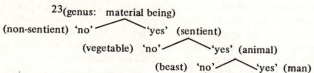

[23](genus: material being)

(non-sentient) 'no' — 'yes' (sentient)

(vegetable) 'no' — 'yes' (animal)

(beast) 'no' — 'yes' (man)

Since the probability is that the membership of 'no' is numerically equal to that of 'yes' at any level, we see that our differences, which can lead us down from 'material being' to 'man', is of no help at all in dividing up the residual 'no' - classes.)

Nonetheless, a clear enough formal congruence can be seen between this 'tree' and Gardin's derivation of paradigmata and syntagmata; see for instance that of the relations:

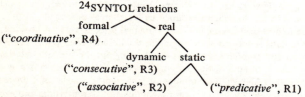

[24]SYNTOL relations

formal — real

("*coordinative*", R4)

dynamic   static

("*consecutive*", R3)

("*associative*", R2)   ("*predicative*", R1)

1.42 BEYOND DICHOTOMY

When we overlay this Porphyrian organisation of knowledge on the process of learning/defining as sketched above, a very real difficulty occurs: if what is now known is 'animal', and if we must add the conceptual note 'rational? yes' to this knownness to arrive at a definition of 'man', how can this be accomplished unless we already know what 'rational' means?

The question could of course be answered easily enough merely by presupposing that 'rational' is already known from

22 *Cf* for instance A Lalande, *Vocabulaire technique et critique de la philosophie* (Paris, Presses Universitaires de France, 1960), 76 *sv* 'Arbre de Porphyre'.

23 It must of course be remembered that *genus* here does not prevent *material being* from being specific to some higher generality.

24 J-C Gardin, *Draft of final report on a general system for the treatment of documentary data*, I: 'Theoretical applications of SYNTOL' (Paris, Association Marc Bloch, 1963), 11.

some other area of the language-organism; then all that is necessary for definition of 'man' is the indicating to the learner who comprehends each note separately but has not previously synthesised them, that they are intersected or conjoined in the previously undefined term 'man'. This is an adequate enough explanation, mechanistically, but it is somewhat less than profound at the epistemological level.

As superficial as this mechanisticism may be epistemologically, it does clearly offer something helpful to the psychology of learning (insofar as this latter contributes to the theory of classification) in that the idea of facets certainly cannot explain the origin or acquisition of knowledge, but is highly helpful in our attempt to track it down for the sake of more adequate and retrievable strategisations. There is of course the phenomenon of radically new ideas – in classification there is at the very least the constant arisal of new personalities (in Scheele's vocabulary we can put this: though 'terminology' remains fairly constant, 'nomenclature' is ever growing). And there may even be new terminological concepts. But the major type of growth to which the maker of classifications must give attention is that brought forth by new syntheses – and our example above gives just such an example. For the idea of rationality, as much as its primal locus may be in the specification of man as over against the rest of animal nature, does apply throughout the whole universe of knowledge.

1.43 FACET ANALYSIS AS THE WAY BEYOND

As a brief and very simple example of what facet analysis can accomplish in classification, let us imagine a tree-structured classification of some subfield of the universe of study, say the stringed/bowed musical instruments. Such a tree might, at its very crudest, look like

But there is also need, if our classification is to be capable of any real proficiency in the trailing of developing (or developed, but less obvious) concepts, that we be capable of distinguishing different periods of provenance in each pitch-range. We could accordingly expand our tree to

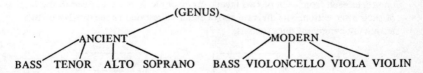

But now we see a difficulty in providing for treatments of each pitch-range where both periods of provenance are exemplified, unless we expand again to a tree such as

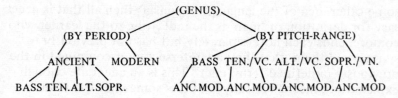

If, however, we go back to the beginning, we can represent the whole subfield as an enclosed plane, divided in one direction by one facet (period of provenance) and in the other by other (pitch-range), thus

ANCIENT	MODERN	
		LOWEST RANGE
		LOWER-INTERMEDIATE RANGE
		UPPER-INTERMEDIATE RANGE
		HIGHEST RANGE

From combinations of these facets and their foci we can extract every specification so much more cumbersomely built into the tree-structure. And, more important, we can imagine other facets intersecting with our basic two-dimensional model, to form *n*-dimensional models of the complexity of concepts (as with facets such as Parts, Materials, Construction and maintenance, Artistic utilization, *etc*). With this sort of flexibility available, chimerical combinations are indeed possible, but, more important, all r e a l complexes are made allowance for − in additional to some unreal ones.

By this device, the over-simplified one-dimensional model of the process of learning and of classification is shown to be inadequate, withour our ever having to enter into substantive arguments.

1.44 THE RELATIONS IMPLIED IN FACETS

However, even this *n*-dimensional model of conceptual intersections is unable to recommend itself as absolutely adequate, because the m o d e of the intersection of one focus each from each of two facets, for example, is n o t implied in the fact of their intersection. The diagram above could be restated as the overlay of two terminally congruent ones such as

and

Viewed thus, it is clear that there is no necessarily single relation between either of the vertical with any of the horizontal ones – especially if we take the diagram in a more generalised sense (that is, as not representing any determinate subfield).

1.50 FACET ANALYSIS AND TRANSPARENCY
1.51 FROM FACET-RELATIONS TO SYNTAX

It is to the construction of a generalized syntax by which to enable complex (semi-discursive, contextual) 'propositions' made up of n intersected foci that Gardin, Farradane, and several other investigators have devoted much of their attention[25].

Gardin's, Farradane's, and my own attempts to realise this ideal can all be characterised, in opposition to the others, as being based upon some inner principle of organisation; the rest are more aptly characterised as enumerative. The old arguments against enumerative classifications – in favor of faceted – are postulated as having been repeated here. The facet-analytic nature of Farradane's system is quite apparent. His two overlaid diagrams[26] each represent a single facet and its foci; their intersection gives rise to nine *operators,* each symbolised by a two-digit symbol and thus capable of reversible linearity. Gardin's *syntagmata* are, as pointed out above, congruent with the Porphyrian dichotomies. Facet analysis is present in SYNTOL mainly in the attempt to group *words* (paradigmata) according to another diagram, itself congruent to that for the syntagmata.

1.52 THE AMBIGUITY OF SYNTAX

This intersection is assumed, by the way, to be entirely univocal, despite the postulated lack of such a univocity in the

25 *Cf* C/R, especially the numerous examples of previous attempts tabulated in Figure 3; also D Soergel, 'Some remarks on information languages, their analysis and comparison' (*Proceedings,* International Symposium on Relational Factors in Classification, College Park, 1966 (Oxford, Pergamon, (1967) (=*Information storage and Retrieval*, iii/4 (1967), 43-115.
26 Given in 'Relational indexing and new methods of concept organisation for information retrieval' (American Documentation Institute. 26th Annual Meeting. *Automation and scientific communication* (Washington, 1963), pt 2, 135-136), 136:

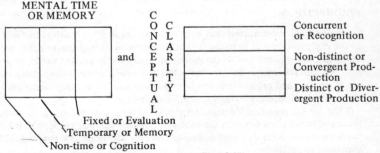

This diagram is to be found in several of Farradane's papers; this particular one is cited because it is a usefully brief compend of Farradane's several longer pieces on the subject of relational factors in classification.)

intersection of substantive elements of the classificatory vocabulary §1.44) The mind boggles, of course, at any other resolution, lest we become lost in a bewildering infinity of regress of relations between relations between . . .

Perhaps there is even more similarity to the Augustinian-Franciscan philosophical doctrine of intermediary forms, such as that form of matter which allows it to receive the vegetative form; but then there may be needed a form intermediate between this first intermediary form and its (vegetative) perfection, *ad inf.* The question, nonetheless, cannot be turned aside by mere reference to such a 'horror'; an answer should be given, and no one has yet attempted it – nor shall I just here.

1.53 FACET ANALYSIS OF SYNTAX

In these cases there is the attempt to create a sort of artificial syntax–rather than simply enumerating the relations seen to be useful in natural language, as in the 'others' tabulated in C/R (which enumerations may or may not be articulated into classes of relations – or of roles – as well as into single arrays). In terms of the diagram above, this represents a thematic concentration upon the mode of overlay (represented by the dotted lines) between facets (represented by the solid lines):

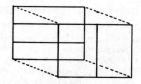

In contrast to the tree-structured classification, what has been accomplished here is to make the ordering of classes of concepts in a classification *transparent* – as against the *opacity* of pure enumeration.

It should be remembered that an additional, corollary, advantage of facet analysis in the real procedure of indexing is that enumerative strategisations tend, out of deference to economy and to the reality of momentarily present needs, to provide only for those concepts – and, in particular, those conceptual intersections – which are of obvious and present use; but facet analysis and the accompanying preparation of facet classifications provide for this a n d m o r e.

What faceted classification does n o t provide for is any systematic variability in the modes of connection between the foci; as Farradane summarised it, 'the relations between concepts (in different facets, or however otherwise ordered) should be expressed explicitly.'[27]

27 J E L Farradane, 'The challenge of information retrieval' (*Journal of documentation*, xvii/4 (1961), 233-244), 238.

1.54 THE LIMITS OF TRANSPARENCY

The phenomenon which I have characterised as *transparency* is not simply equivalent to deductivity. What Ranganathan in particular attempted was to render transparent, by the aid of the super-general facets Personality, Matter, Energy, Space, Time, the organisation of conceptual complexes. But the attempt could at best only achieve a partial success, since the setting-up of facets, however transparent, does not render the organisation (within each facet) of the foci equally transparent. In each such case what is necessary is the same sort of enumeration which characterised the non-faceted classifications. But we are not thematically concerned with these perhaps unavoidable deficiencies of classification; what i s our thematic concern is the e x t e n t o f and means to the e x p a n s i o n o f transparency in classification.

I submit that, besides the unquestioned contribution of facet analysis to transparency in classification, the cardinal characteristic is *self-definition* — and that the idea of *context*, elaborated at some pains above, is a first approximation to what will be proposed as the content and function of self-definition.

1.60 TRANSPARENCY AND TWO PHILOSOPHERS

A glance into two of the most respected of the systems of categories[28] will demonstrate the difference, in a context not normally within the daily conspectus of the librarian or the classificationist, between opaque enumeration and transparent self-definition — in the categorial systems of Aristotle and of Kant. Without in any way taking sides in terms of the merits of these respective results, the intention is simply to compare the methods of arriving at these results, and to compare the resultant clarity or obscurity (as resulting from transparency and opacity, resp) in the lists themselves.

1.61 THE CATEGORIES OF KANT AND ARISTOTLE

Kant, first of all, was concerned with something other than was Aristotle (though he did not seem to be fully aware of it); namely, with that which makes judgment possible: 'these functions [the pure concepts of the understanding] specify the understanding completely, and yield an exhaustive inventory of its powers. These concepts we shall, with Aristotle, call *categories*' [29] — whereas Aristotle was concerned instead with differences between beings, and between the characteristics of beings[30]. After listing the categories — 'Expressions which are in no way composite signify substance, quantity, quality, relation, place, time, position, state, action, or

---

28 At this point it is not at all intended to go into the ontological status of categories; some hints were given in C/R.

29 I Kant, *Critique of pure reason, tr* N K Smith (London, Macmillan, 1933 [repr 1950]), 113.

30 *Cf* the famous paper of E Benveniste, 'Catégories de pensée et catégories de langue' (*Les etudes philosophiques*, ns , xiii/4 (1958), 419-429; also repr in his collection of essays *Problemes de linguistique générale* (Paris, Gallimard, 1966)), which would prove something still different, that the categories are neither ontological nor epistemological, but merely linguistic.

affection'[31] – and giving examples of each, Aristotle concludes that: 'No one of these terms, in and by itself, involves an affirmation; it is by the combination of such terms that positive or negative statements arise. For every assertion must, as is admitted, be either true or false, whereas expressions which are in no way composite, such as 'man' 'white', 'runs', 'wins', cannot be either true or false.'[32] The modes of combination of non-composite terms is reserved for other works, notably the *On interpretation, Posterior analytics*, and *Topics*. Nevertheless, however much support for our own argument about the need for context can be seen here, Kant's criticism seems valid that Aristotle 'merely picked them [the fundamental coneepts] up as they came his way, and at first procured ten of them, which he called categories'[33], whereas Kant's own purpose was (and ours must be) to 'furnish an exact classification of the concepts which compose that totality [*ie*, of a science], exhibiting their *interconnection in a system*'[34].

Kant's arrangement of the categories (no attempt will be made to digest the full deductive argument, as given on 102-175 of the cited version) is in four sets of three elements each, each set exhibiting a similar structure(113),based on the 'ancient' transcendental triadism: *Every being is one, true, and good.* Again, each set of categories has standing behind it a congruent set of forms of judgment (107); whether, however, these forms can be accepted as more than merely enumerated I will not attempt to say[35], but it seems to me fair to conclude that in this case (as against Aristotle) we have a strongly self-defining system of concepts, on two

31 Aristotle, *Categories,* tr Edghill (*The works of Aristotle translated into English under the editorship of WD Ross* (Oxford Univ Press, 1928 [repr 1963])),ı), i[Bekker p] 1ª [line] 25-26. Aristotle could also be quoted – perhaps somewhat less seriously – against those who rail at t h e c l a s s i f i c a t i o n o f d o c u m e n t s as against the apparently more desirable c l a s s i f i c a t i o n o f k n o w l e d g e, thus: 'If genera are different and coordinate, their differentiae are themselves different in kind. Take as an instance the genus "animal" and the genus "knowledge". "With feet", "two footed", "winged", "aquatic", are differentiae of "animal"; the species of knowledge are not distinguished by the same differentiae. One species of knowledge does not differ from another in being "two footed"'.' [1ᵇ 16-19]

32 *Ibidem*, 2ª4-10.

33 Kant, *tr cit*, 114; Kant goes on to propose that the predicables were later added, as if coordinate, to these predicaments – thus opening himself up to serious criticism at not havıng grasped Aristotle's intention at all; still, his methodological strictures are valid from the point of vantage of our present-day approval of *systematics*.

34 *Ibidem*, 102. For a much fuller discussion of the nature of a science as a *system*, see E Husserl, *Logische untersuchungen*, I: 'Prolegomena zur reinen Logik' (Halle ad S, M Niemeyer, 1928).

35 Though Hegel, by his expansion of this methodological clue taken from Kant, and, through him, from the 'ancients', into the metaphysical basis of his system, was led by his apparent success to conclude that: 'The syllogism, and the threefold generally, has always been recognised as the general torm of reason; but it was considered as a wholly external form which did not determine the nature of the content.. . . . Formalists have seized upon this triplicity, and have held fast to its skeleton; and this form has been rendered tedious and of ill-repute by the shallow misuse and the barrenness of modern so-called philosophic *construction*, which consists simply in attaching the formal framework without concept and immanent determination to all sorts of matter and employing it for external arrangement.' [*Science of logic*, tr W H Johnston and L G Struthers (London, Allen & Unwin, 1929), ii, 479ı].

grounds: *a*: the quasi-facet structure implicit in the table of categories (iteratively based on *unum, verum, bonum*); and *b*: the overlaying of the table of categories on the table of judgments.

In the case of Aristotle we have a contextual system only insofar as the examples of each category tend to self-definition of each including category, but this context seems far more fluid at its 'edge': it evinces no internal structure (whether or not we agree with Hegel on structure as metaphysically important), and leads to the question *What else could we add?* Kant's diagram, on the other hand, is well-defined at its 'edges'; we are moved only to seek for the source of the similarity between the groups of terms; and when we discover it (whether or not it is correct) we are led to s e e t h r o u g h their structure to their structural p r i n c i p l e. This, indeed, is just what Hegel did, and just what gave him the basis on which to mount his system.

1.62 A (PROVISIONAL) DEFINITION OF TRANSPARENCY

Transparency, then, is provisionally definable as that characteristic of a conceptual composite (a proposition, a diagram, *etc*) which, by virtue of self-defining characteristics, allows a clear view through to the underlying principles upon which the composite has been grounded.

2   SYNTAX IN CLASSIFICATION
2.1   SYNTAX AND DOCUMENTARY CONTEXT
2.11 SYNTAX AND JUDGMENT

What, aside from these philosophical considerations, is the use of *operators* (Farradane), *syntagmata* (Gardin), *roles and links* (EJC), *semantic indicators* (WRU), *relators* (C/R)? In other words, in what situations do such ideas take on value? What ends do these ideas serve as means?

Either we *a*scribe or *de*scribe documents, or else we *in*scribe them into a *pre*scribed system of concept-bearing notations[36]; in any of these cases we have a choice of placing the individual '(-) scriptive' notes over against the documents they represent in free-floating or associated clusters: the current terminology for this set of alternative is 'post-coordinate' *vs* 'pre-coordinate'.

The need for context, as outlined in §§1-1.37, leads to the need— lest we be all too willing to accept a meaning-destroying fragmentation[37]— for 'pre-coordination'. (This particular terminology, however, is not to be tolerated any longer. 'Coordination' is by no means identical with 'intersection' or 'conjunction'; its related terms are 'subordinate' and 'superordinate', and the only frame of reference within which it is significant is therefore that of hierarchy. Hierarchy,

---

36 *Cf* J M Perreault 'Documentary relevance and structural hierarchy.'

37 Here too, in his theory of meaning as *sammeln* (to collect), Heidegger can offer us a philosophical guiding clue — but this one I leave for the reader to seek out for himself.

of course, can be either explicit, as in a *pre*scribed system, or implicit, as in most *a*scriptive and *de*scriptive ones.)

Articulation in (-) scription leads either to thesaural method (see § 1.30) or to explicit (hierarchical) classification. And these structures that are the result of the articulation of the articulated, are themselves organised, either by tree structures (with all their inherent deficiencies), or by facet analysis.

Even a hierarchy, rendered *n*-dimensional by faceting, cannot cope with the actual complexity of documents, because the reduction of documents to surrogates must, to preserve the informativeness which is after all the primary intention of the documents, preserve the j u d g m e n t a l implications of the document as well as the 'raw' c o n c e p t u a l implications. This is the basis of the distinction between (resp) the *informative* and the *indicative* abstract, as well as between (monadic) categories and (dyadic) relators.

2.12 INDICATION AND INFORMATION

We must accept J Mills' terminological suggestion – that all forms of conceptual bibliography be characterised as 'indexing' – *ie*, that whether we *a*scribe, *de*scribe or *in*scribe, we are i n d i c a t i n g the conceptual content or orientation of the document. Facet analysis is the most adequate means to this end, and is accordingly seen by Mills as the basic investigation preliminary to any classificatory process. But it stops short precisely with i n d i c a t i o n, when what we really require is i n f o r m a t i o n. And this last is conveyable only in propositions: not merely semantics (concepts), but semantics articulated by s y n t a x.

It requires only brief consideration of the etymological and intellectual-historical status of the two words *indication* and *information* to see how this distinction is, as it were *a priori,* justified. The root of the one is *indicare,* to point out (as in 'index-finger'), of the other *informare,* to give shape.

In this latter case a rather wide range of connotations is subsumed, from the scholastic-philosophical usage for the informing of 'matter' by its 'form', to the current sense of that which is transposed from mind to mind through some medium such as speech; yet the basic sense persists even in this current connotation, in that information informs (in the current sense) by informing (in the scholastic sense) the recipient mind with a new 'form' which transforms its materiality (=receptivity = ignorance) into formality (=knowledge).

I n f o r m a t i o n, a c c o r d i n g l y, i s a m a t t e r o f k n o w l e d g e a s s u c h i n a k n o w i n g *s u b j e c t*; i n d i c a t i o n, o n t h e o t h e r h a n d, i s a m a t t e r o f e l e m e n t s w i t h i n *o b j e c t s*, c a p a b l e o f t o l e a d i n g t o j u d g e m e n t s.

2.13 THE CONTEXT OF CONTEXT

The articulation of the conceptual system is what Gardin characterises as *paradigmatic;* but the real burden of his attempt to go beyond faceted classification rests upon another, far further, articulation, the *syntagmatic.* And it is this articulation, capable of carrying along another articulation within itself, which is the context of context.

2.2 CYBERNETIC BALANCE AND SURROGATION

2.21 BALANCE AND INFORMATION

This idea of the context of context will be returned to. But I wish to digress momentarily into an allied field, that of mechanical translation, which requires (as does totally automatic mechanical storage and retrieval of information) the cybernetic background of self-organising systems. Such systems are similar to living organisms in at least one respect: they are (or are striven to be made) self-moving. Plato's idea that this is perhaps the most basic indication of life may be true, but we can see that it is true of cybernetic self-organising systems only in a qualified manner[38]. Yet it is certainly true that no cybernetic apparatus can do more than it has been prepared to do; this is true of all machines. What is striven for, then, to make possible a self-organising system capable of mechanically translating, for instance, is to make its responses not merely determinate but what we could call 'balanced'. E von Glasersfeld, in a report entitled 'Multistore–a procedure for correlational analysis'[39], points out that a sentence such as 'I like green and blue bottles' can be reduced to a correlational formula that would make possible, by reverse transformation, its translation into another language, but that its obvious meaning (*green* and *blue* as modifiers of *bottles,* all of which is object of a transitive verb and its subject) could be mistakenly formulated as 'I like green (the abstract color) and (I also like) blue bottles'[40]. He then goes on to say that: 'If the human reader rules this second understanding our (or does not even become aware of the ambiguity) it is because his understanding of linguistic expressions is guided by probability values computed, consciously or unconsciously, on the basis of the entire linguistic experience he has had previously.'[41]

---

38 Even the subtleties of the multi-valued logic – intended specifically for the freeing of cybernetic machines from over-rigidity, and hence for the enabling of 'balance' for them–G Gunther ('Cybernetic ontology and transjunctional operations' (*Self-organising systems, 1962* (Washington, Spartan, 1962), 313-392)] seems poor when compared with the flexibility of truly human reaction and evaluations – of which my favourite examples are the dialectics of the Narrator of Proust's *Remembrance of things past* and Husserl's *Ideen.*

39 E von Glaserfeld, *'Multistore' – a procedure for correlational analysis* (Milano, Instituto Documentazione della Associazione Meccanica Italiana, 1965 (=Grant AF EOAR 64-54)), 9-11.

40 He misses a third possible misunderstanding, which could be paraphrased 'I like bottles each of which is both green and blue' – as against liking bottles which are each one coloured, either (disjunctly) green o r blue.

41 *Ibidem,* 10.

The avoidance of such misunderstandings would be, in my opinion, the result of the truly cybernetic ability to move itself (insofar as this is possible to a machine); if the machine could do so (even if it could not make good coffee or sneeze when damp) it is as 'alive' as it need be, for our purpose. Life, outside this cybernetic frame, implies self-motion for the sake of the assimilation of the needed environment, or, more briefly, for self-preservation; a self-organising system need not go quite that far. Von Glasersfeld does not propose to enable his machines to do even the more circumscribed task, at least not in this phase of his work, but he does not despair of the possibility – nor do I. What I want to make forceful from this example, though, is this:

a: The 'entire linguistic experience' is the context within which such decisions can be made. No person has so wide an experience as to rule out a l l such mistakes, so machines cannot be expected to do much better; but without such a context nothing at all could be achieved. *b*: Syntagmata (called by von Glasersfeld *correlators*, either explicit or implicit) are the major means whereby we implant context between concepts; it is the organisation of concepts into phrases, clauses, sentences, paragraphs, chapters, whole works, the entire educative process, and finally the whole of one person's experience with i n f o r m - a t i o n which is made possible, structurally, by syntagmata. It is syntagmata which act so as to make language more than just determinate, but 'balanced'; it is the presence and full comprehension of syntagmata that makes a system (living or life-simulating) self-moving in the region of information: capable of 'balanced' rather than merely determinate (one-for-one) response.

2.22 BALANCE AND INFORMATION-SURROGATES

Thus, returning to the main argument, we can see that something as fluent, balanced, articulable as natural language is needed for a truly adequate surrogation of documentary conceptual orientations. The stiffness of enumerative classifications has led many documentalists astray into imagining that a mere piling upon one another of the indicative elements of information can serve the purpose, but they have been gradually driven back to the need for some sort of syntagmatic substitutes, such as roles and/or links.

The real-world need is for a surrogational model capable of leading to documents from a point of view of context within contex – for such is the world of thought of the researcher himself. These layers of context can be summarised as RELEVANCE, APPROPRIATENESS, and 'SUPRA-SYNTAX'.

2.23 THREE LEVELS OF ARTICULATION

RELEVANCE we recognise as essential, but the role of s t r a t -
e g y as provided in the paradigmatic organisation of the classification is too little recognised:we must be able to seek including
and included classes easily, because when we seek i n f o r m -
a t i o n (not mere f a c t s) we cannot afford to be satisfied
at a low 'noise'-level, but must demand a low 'silence'-level as
well[42]. APPROPRIATENESS is not as well recognised as
essential, except when we are looking something up ourselves
and must suffer the deluge of items relevant but too old, too
brief, not properly illustrated, in the wrong language, *etc.*
And what I have called 'SUPRA-SYNTAX' (along with the
already formidable paradigmatic-syntagmatic apparatus that
is necessary for a machine to be capable of allowing for full
discriminations of relevance and appropriateness) must be
available to allow the interiorisation of the records of interior-
ised documents.

To show this point (very sketchily), let us imagine a surrogate such that Roman
letters indicate the paradigmatic elements of conceptual bibliography, Arabic
numerals the syntagmata, Greek letters the formalities of appropriateness, and
punctuation the supra-syntax; and that we want an adequate surrogate to inform us
that the document is partly by γ , who writes in German (δ) and publishes in
1902 (ϵ) that cultures (A) are manifested in (1) their attitudes (**B**) with regard to
(2) war (C); and that this is exemplified (1) in Assyria (D) attacking, and the response
to it (3) of Israel (E); a supplementary section, by η and θ , joint authors, in
French (ι) and published in 1904 (κ), is in two parts: one giving archaeological
evidence (F) that substantiates (4) Assyria's (D5) superiority (G) with regard to
(2) military strength (H) with regard to (2) the whole fertile crescent (I); the other
(/) giving a secondary bibliography (ζ) on the concepts symbolised above as
D3E; the whole document being oversized (β) and not requiring security clearance
for use (α). A formulary statement of all these aspects, in a way that makes
possible contextual judgements on the part of the machine that will be doing the
searching, would look like

$$\alpha,\beta[\gamma,\delta, [[A1[B2C]]1[D3E]] : [[F4[D5[G2[H21]]]] / [\zeta[D3E]]]\eta,\theta,\iota,\kappa$$

No such scheme, so far as I know, now exists; but none other could adequately
represent the complex context-within-context of real documents in such a way as to
retrieve them in more than a simple-minded determinate way. Even our present
schemes of classification are such as to stultify the efforts of reference librarians
to retrieve adequately — and such persons can make good guesses, usually, at what is
not explicated on the catalogue-entry. How can a machine be expected to do so,
unless we have recorded the surrogates it must examine in a way such as to allow the
use of cybernetic techniques in a self-organising way?

42 See my essay 'Documentary relevance', cited in footnote 18 .

2.3 TRANSPARENCY AS THE GOAL IN CLASSIFICATION

2.31 THE CONTRIBUTION OF RANGANATHAN

Finally, then, we return to examine the methodological basis of transparency in classification – namely, self-definition. And here self-definition is meant as that which renders the entire structure of complex concepts clear. This, it seems to me, is the motivation for the work of that most significant classification-theorist of our time, S R Ranganathan. In all the successive modifications which have been undertaken in regard to the Colon Classification, there has been a continual attempt to increase its transparency. But this has in all cases consisted in improvements in the analysis, order, or indication of facets. The foci within these facets have not been able to be subjected to similar treatment; they are all still merely enumerated – and surely we know by now that if anything is anathema in our search for transparency, it is mere enumeration. It is this unavoidable lack that has stimulated many improvements, though, so that we cannot legitimately derogate it entirely, yet we cannot help wanting to eliminate it. And it is to be noted that it was partly because of Ranganathan's non-distinction of the areas of classification to which transparency in its fullest sense is appropriate that led to his salutary attempt to make it apply to library classification at all.

2.32 THE TRIADISM OF C/R

In the course of attempting to arrive at a highly economical means of classifying the relators revealed in the preliminary stages of C/R I came upon a means of organising the whole manifold by the successive overlaying and intersection of three triadic 'facets'.

There was no explicit attempt to produce a final version after the triadic pattern of the Kantian or Hegelian systems, or of the scholastic transcendentals, but there does seem to be justification for agreeing with Hegel's estimation of the basic structural significance of the triad, insofar as we see it evidenced in such profusion in the (physical as well as intentional) world about us. Whether or not this significance is either evident or provable, the classificatory effort as such (*ie*, that part of conceptual bibliography which is directly complementary to the deductive effort that is also necessary in the real task of classifying), applied to the classificanda at hand, does yield at least a majority of cases wherein triadism is evident.

2.33 THE PROBLEM OF EXHAUSTIVE DEDUCTION

The basic problem in passing beyond mere enumeration is that of knowing when the limits of exhaustivity have been reached; this is the first apparent benefit of the use of a schematism such as that used for the relators, that it helps avoid this problem. But this may be only an illusory advantage, since as a matter of fact there is no limit, however systematic the deduction, to the number of levels that a tree structure may have, nor to the number of intersecting dimensions available in a faceted classification [43]. This may be taken as a less-than-perfect conclusion, but

43 J E L Farradane has pointed this out in a private communication (1965/iv/20) referring to C/R: 'In working out your list of relations, how can you be sure you have reached the limit (logically or just practically useful)?'

there is another major desideratum of classificatory structures which is revealed in the relator-schema. It is that of self-definition, as against that of such seminal principles as the triad.

2.4 SELF-DEFINITION AS THE MEANS TO TRANSPARENCY
2.41 SELF-DEFINITION AS A PERMANENT FEATURE OF CLASSIFICATION

The ordinary (but by no means insignificant) phenomenon of self-definition in classification is implicit in the very nature of hierarchy. There are three major ways in which it can enter in: a: by comparison of an array with its including class, b: by comparison of an including class with its included array-members, and c: by analysis of an isolate into its including class and its intersecting (sub ordinating, therefore coordinate with the super-ordinate) facet(s).

This last may be the only form of definition recognised as meaningful by the scholastically inclined, but the others, which can be characterised as definition by extension as against definition by intension, can be of great use in the real world of subject cataloging – as well as in the construction of schedules. For instance, there can easily be arrays clearly not extending to the limits of their including classes, and without any sort of standardised names, but nevertheless forming some sort of unity[44]. This unity may have no common name, but there is nonetheless no difficulty at all in defining it precisely by the extension of its subordinate array taken as a whole. Similarly, it is of common occurrence in practical work that a particular term is not of itself revelatory of the nature of the concept intended (for instance, as in our thesaural example above, the term *can*, which can be defined by reference to the alternative including classes *receptacle* and *be able*). It is comparison to this including class which gives the mere w o r d its c o n c e p t u a l content.

All this tends, of course, to confirm the earlier arguments in favour of the need for context in the creation of surrogates. But it is really nothing new, except to those who are busily inventing all sorts of wheels. If it is at all new, it is so in that it allows classification of concepts for which we barely have verbalisms at all. It was the unfortunate fate of one of the pioneers in relational-factors research, Ruvinschii[45], to attempt to establish a repertory of relations by means of classification of the prepositions of a particular natural language. This effort could not but come to a sorry fate, precisely because of the unavoidable ambiguity in language – the very thing which intellectual (as against statistical) classification attempts to overcome. (That it is unavoidable can be ascertained from the utterances of all those hoping to enable mechanical translation, such as von Glasèrfeld

44 *Cf* J M Perreault, 'Coterminous or specific'   cited in footnote 18 .
45 Reported in E de Grolier, *A study of general categories applicable to classification and coding in documentation* (Paris UNESCO, 1962), and note 26 (176).

and the others in the group centered on Silvio Ceccato; it is the fact that a single word can generate entirely different syntactical structures which prevents pure dictionary-based determinism from enabling mechanical translation.)

2.42 NATURAL LANGUAGE AS *NON*-SELF-DEFINING

This fact of ambiguity is what brings about the need for 'balanced' or 'self-organising' systems for automatic mechanical translation and/or storage and retrieval of documentary information. But at the same time it forces upon us the need to resort to a plurality of verbalisms to replace the old single one. As an example, think of the variety of relational connotations involved in the simple English *of*: at a quick survey we can name *forth from, belonging to, concerning, character-ised by* ... And to name these different relations adjectivally, so as to free the resulting relator-scheme from an unwieldy burden of examples, some times results in serious neologisms. But the fact that these terms are *a*: embedded in a tree-structured hierarchy (though originating in a facet-principle of which they are only the enumeration), so that reference to including, included, and coordinate classes can quickly clarify them; and that they are each *b*: defined by the symbol indicated for them, with each element of each symbol itself defined in terms of the order of application of the particular triads used in building them up – can, when thoughtfully considered, render their meaning, and hence their use, unambiguous. The characteristics noted here are those mentioned previously: the transparency of this schema depends on context and on the clear awareness of the engendering structural principles underlying it.

2.43 A CONTESTED EXAMPLE

One example given in C/R (130) was of how I could code de Grolier's *Study of general categories*: 161.1 eihe [002 ded [025.3 + 003.6]]. In de Grolier's more recent report *On the theoretical basis of information retrieval systems* [46], question is raised *a*: over the implications of the code ded, which gives *classification and coding* as *organs* of *documentation*, and *b*: over the conversity of active and passive relators. On *a*, I would of course agree with M de Grolier's right to question my interpretation of his understanding of the a c t u a l relation between *documentation* and *classification and coding*. What I would not agree with is the idea that such a relation as *organism/organ* is conceivable only in living nature, and not at any higher level. Indeed the theory of integrative levels as propounded by J K Feibleman[47] strongly supports my contention here, I think. On *b*, I would point out that, besides the systematic completeness which would not be present without the listing of both *active* and *passive*, there is an operative need for allowing all notations to be writeable and readable linearly, *ie*, always in the same direction. Now if there be a pair of paradigmata *A* and *B*, in such a relation as to have (say) *A curing B*, there can arise cases where that order of linearity applies, but there can also arise cases where *B*, because of its relation to some term necessarily earlier in the surrogate, or because

46 E de Grolier, *On the theoretical basis* ... (cited in footnote 12), 207-208.
47 J K Feibleman, 'Theory of integrative levels' (*British journal for the philosophy of science*, v (1954/55), 59-66; *cf* D J Foskett, *Classification and indexing in the social sciences* (London, Butterworth, 1963), 132-145; J E L Farradane, 'Concept organisation for information retrieval' (*Proceedings*, International Symposium of Relational Factors in Classification, College Park 1966 (Oxford, Pergamon, 1967) (= *Information storage and retrieval*, iii/4.(1967), 121-135)).

of A's relation to some term necessarily later, must come first. Therefore an arrangement must be provided whereby we can notate B *cured by* A. (And, in use of such notation with computers there must be programmed recognition of the identity of these variant configurations –and it is provided for by the notation itself, in that a pair of relators where g (positive) and i (negative) are exchanged, and in which the paradigmata have been exchanged, is such an identity variantly stated. Thus $A \ldots g\, B = B \ldots i\, A,$ and $A \ldots i\, B = B \ldots g\, A.$

2.5 CONCLUSION/SUMMARY
2.51 INDUCTION, DEDUCTION, AND CONTEXT

Classification (in the sense of conceptual bibliography, not of the mere preparatory creation of a systematic conceptual organisation) strictly speaking is inductive, not deductive, and to this extent the proponents of all computer mechanical translation and mechanical storage and retrieval of documentary information are on a track we can agree is right. But, at the same time, perhaps unnoticed by the conceptual bibliographer, deductive processes are at work as well. Even purely inductive classification would be impossible without that preliminary   presence of context which makes definition possible[48].

It is to the artificial creation of context that the most promising of all computer experiments are directed. But such attempts seem scarcely more than evanescent compared with the capability of the human mind – which, after all, has framed the documents we seek to control, and which also poses the queries we seek to respond to, and whose tendencies we must accordingly respect, however well we could do the whole job over with electronic logic machines. This all helps reveal to us, through epistemology and the psychology of learning, the extent to which classification (both inductive and deductive) is part of the process of thought.

2.52 CONTEXT AND NATURE

But even beyond the problems of definition, we must conquer those of adequate surrogational representation; and this calls for the capability to represent documents syntagmatically as well as paradigmatically.

There are two polar attitudes toward the (systematic conceptual) arrangement of syntagmata:a: the enumerative, inductive, natural-language-bound, and b: the systematic, deductive, artificial-language-oriented. But between these poles we can envision a systematic natural-language-oriented schema, one in which variations from accepted terminology does not have to be

48 *Cf* R Sokolowski, *The formation of Husserl's concept of constitution* (The Hague, M Nijhoff, 1964, 172: 'It is important to note, finally, that a full-grown sense or meaning can be present only *after* a judgment is made. A fixed sense which has the consistency and solidity to reappear in different acts as the same ideal entity appears for the first time in judgments. We might say that "concepts" arise only in judgments . . . There is no crystallised meaning in pre-predicative encounter.'

explained, but is self-defining in the same way that every classification tends to define its member nodes. It was at this solution that C/R was aimed.

All systematic conceptual organisation, in that it attempts to avoid mere enumeration, aims at the erection of contextual self-definition. This cannot be a totally successful operation, though, as long as there are extra-mental beings, since these cannot be totally defined either by the intersection of facets or by the spreading out of discursion. But in the realm of relation, I submit, such a totally transparent operation i s possible.

2.53 CLASSIFICATION, LANGUAGE, AND THOUGHT

Classification, though, is definable not only as an *artificial language of ordinal symbols* (Ranganathan), but (as I would prefer) as a *systematic conceptual organisation*. It must resemble natural language — so that information as well as indication can be sought from it — primarily in that it needs to have two structures: paradigmata and syntagmata. But it need not resemble natural language in much else. It need have no rich store of synonyms, no possibilities for ellipses, no rythym nor imagery to assist in the mnemonic function. It is drier and more compressed, then, than natural language, for the sake of t h e e l i m i n a t i o n of b o t h i m p l i c a t i o n a n d e q u i v o c a t i o n.

It is admitted that natural language does not need only to be compressed to eliminate implication and equivocation, though this is assuredly the most frequent need when the paradigmatic part of the systematic conceptual organisation is being worked up. And the reductionist attempts of Farradane and Gardin show the same attitude of mind at work in the syntagmatic sphere as well. But, I think, not necessarily beneficially.

Words, the basic 'raw' material of the paradigmatic sphere, form an enormous population, partly for the sake of synonymous redundancy and reinforcement, imagery, *etc;* the systematic conceptual organisation, on the other hand, wants to reduce this population to that point at which each concept is respected, but in which no two signs may signify the same concept nor any one sign remain equivocally pointed toward two or more concepts. This reduction is accomplished by the thesaurus. But the rest of the language (word-signs too, but not such as relate to an independent reality; relating rather to the articulation of other signs into judgments) is, despite its crucial function in allowing us to pass from intuition to judgment, from indication to information, not a large population. Indeed, it is so small that such of its elements as *is, of,* and the comma (,), are extremely overworked, being forced to signify far more than one concept each.

What is needed, then, along with c o m p r e s s i o n of the bulk of the language into a systematic *paradigmatic* conceptual organisation, is e x p a n s i o n of the residue of the language into a systematic *syntagmatic* conceptual organisation.

2.54 SELF-DEFINITION IN C̄/R̄

When such an expansion is attempted there is an opposite problem to that of paradigmatic compression. In the latter case, a *circulus vitiosus* is required in many cases, as well as the functional role of the organisation itself; that is to say, the inclusion of concepts as a means to self-definition. In the former, since natural language has been getting on fairly well with all its burden of equivocity, there is a lack of concepts (or, perhaps better, 'terms') ready-made for sorting out the various senses, for instance, of *of*.

The fact that the syntagmatic sphere of the total systematic conceptual organisation is itself systematic is a boon in that it provides for functional (inclusional) self-definition. Thus, in C/R there are a good many terms that must be admitted to be neologisms; but the functional hierarchic structure makes it possible to see from inclusions and/or includednesses what each such term intends.

(Such a brief statement is not to be taken by itself as indicating the intention of C/R; it must be understood in conjunction with the rest of the present text.)

2.55 TRANSPARENCY IN C/R

Transparency is the antithesis of the opacity of nature. The phenomena of nature can be lifted somewhat from their opacity by the functional self-definition of hierarchic classification, but only in the classification of relationships themselves does it seem possible to achieve full transparency, whether in the intersection of two facets as in Farradane's operators, in the Porphyrian deduction of Gardin's syntagmata (and of classes of paradigmata), or in the iterative superposition of the three triads of relational principles in C/R.

But these are only structural or formal characterisations of transparency in the classification of relationships; after all, this supposes no real advance over the transparency of any faceted classification of nature. What does mark an advance would be that, *a*: given the idea of the universe-class, and then that of the facet-principles that could potentially explicate it into its *infimae species*, that *b*: such an explication can take place by a motion of the mind unfettered by any of the constraints of the enumeration of non-essential realities, and hence *c*: can give to a product whose features are intelligible f r o m   t h e   i d e a a n d   i t s   e x p l i c a t i o n   a l o n e,   w i t h   n o   r e f e r - e n c e   t o   e n u m e r a t e d   e x p e r i e n c e. We have come some distance from the provisional definition given in §1.62.

2.56 ENUMERATION AND TRANSPARENCY

Transparency is not enough, then: it would do nothing to help us in the library, because we must classify the phenomena not of *a priori* relationship, but of *a posteriori* experience. We must enumerate, then, too, if we are to get beyond purely *a priori* classification as a philosophical exercise, and self-definition helps out here. But we must not forget that it is such transparent classification of the *a priori* that makes possible the transformation of *a posteriori* paradigmata from indication into information. (This is what is meant by 'the context of context', mentioned in §2.13, and of 'supra-syntax' in §2.23.) Nor must we forget that paradigmata are most nearly transparently organised by facet analysis, which is a sort of transparent classification that does not go beyond the first step—but without which opacity must remain our lot, hindering our work at both the storage and the retrieval stage.

3.00 EPILOGUE

In the very helpful, though sometimes mystifying work of Max Picard from which the second motto was chosen, there is a citation from Wilhelm von Humboldt which very nearly summarises all that is proposed above:

'In order truly to understand one single word, not as a merely physical stimulant but as an articulated sound describing a concept, language must reside in man as a whole and as a coherent structure. [49]

We must constantly remind ourselves of this truth, whether we propose to expand the use of intellectually based classification, or to enable the computer to take over the task of storage and/or retrieval of documentary information entirely.

49 M Picard, *op cit*, 55.

VIII

Categories and relators:
a new schema

I   If the (major) premise is accepted, that fully effective
machine stragesation of a retrieval system depends upon the use
of a (hierarchically) structual (but highly flexible) notation as the
equivalent for the verbal access provided by either unitermic or
articulated conceptual indicators, a faceted [1] classification
logically emerges as the desideratum[2].

The two aspects of a structual notation most determinative
here are hierarchicality and uniform use of general categories[3]
(the latter, not merely for the sake of uniformity as such, but as
the means to a heightened flexibility). These desiderata could
of course be present on the idea plane alone; but without their
being present notationally they do not furnish, to a mechanical
retrieval system, the type of assistance it requires for optimal
functioning.

The second (minor) premise ought to be that the Universal
Decimal Classification, being both hierarchical and general-
categoric, provides the desired structurality. But the melancholy
fact is that this desideratum is not always satisfied, for instance
when UDC uses direct division of a hierarchy when division by
general category would be equally appropriate [4].

However, research by Ranganathan, Perry-Kent-Berry-Melton,

---

1   Taking this term in the broadest sense, to include all the structures
    comprehended in the various types 'analytico-synthetic', 'faceted',
    and 'free' – principally to avoid the strictures of J C Gardin's paper.
    'Free classifications and faceted classifications; their exploitation with
    computers' *(Classification research: proceedings,* International Study
    Conference on Classification Research, Elsinore, 1964, ed P Atherton
    (Copenhagen, Munksgaard, 1965), 161-176).
2   *Cf* 'The need for a faceted classification as the basis of all methods of
    information retrieval', reprinted in *Proceedings,* International Study
    Conference on Classification for Information Retrieval, Dorking, 1957
    (London, ASLIB, 1957), 137-147.
3   *Cf* E de Grolier; *A study of general categories applicable to classification and
    coding in documentation* (Paris, UNESCO, 1962).
4   *Ibidem,* 18-42 (sect 11).

the US Patent Office, the Engineers Joint Council, Pagès, Farradane, Gardin, and several others, leads inevitably to the
conclusion that even if the desired lexical and relational aspects
within the substantive elements of the classification are
provided for in a way to enable strategisation of mechanical
searching, there is need for many relations not provided by
hierarchy and general categories — relations, in fact
b e t w e e n rather than w i t h i n the classifying terms
themselves. B. C Vickery points out[5] that
    A second defect of the UDC, from the standpoint
of faceted classification, is that the symbol for general
relationship, the colon, gives no guidance as to the
specific relation existing between the terms linked.
Recently, Dr.Kervegant has studied the matter, on the
grounds that the indexing of periodical articles makes
the indication of relationship practically indispensable[6]
    M Kervegant's tabulation[7] is included in the comparative
enumeration that follows (Figure 3).

II My intention to embark upon the construction of a philoso-
phically adequate schema of relators was not as precisely focussed
as the foregoing would seem to indicate — to begin with.
However, considerations of the means for increasing the
applicability of UDC to mechanised retrieval were present from
the first. The original starting point, rather than inter-classificatory

5   B C Vickery, *Classification and indexing in science* (London, Butterworth,
    1959), 186.

6   There is a fairly commonly held opinion that only in a truly enormous
    collection of documents does the need arise for relational terms (see for
    instance the comments by R A Fairthorne, *Proc* ISCCIR (cited in footnote 2)
    107); and by F W Lancaster, 'Some observations on the performance of
    EJC role indicators in a mechanised retrieval system' (*Special libraries,*
    1v/10 (1964), 696-701).

    However, the Itek Laboratories' *Summary of project activities* (Program
    of Research on Information Searching Systems) (=IL-4000-17; NSF-C88),
    13, states that: 'Experiments were conducted where syntactic features of
    subject entries were ignored, and search was made only for co-occurrence of
    pertinent words within an entry. Results of searches made gave useful data.
    For example, [in one search] 60 percent of the responses were invalid. [In
    another] some 24 percent of the responses were invalid.'
    J-C Gardin states also (*SYNTOL* (New Brunswick, Rutgers University
    Graduate School Library Service, 1965), 54), that: 'an earlier experiment
    showed that retrieval with unrelated descriptors in this same field leads to an
    appreciable percentage of false drops, *ie,* to a substantial fall in the relevance
    ratio. 'He also cites R C Cros, J C Gardin, & F Lèvy, *L'automatisation des
    recherches documentaires* (Paris, Gauthiers-Villars, 1964), capp 5 and B, 3.1.

7   D Kervègant,'Developpement de l'analyse des relations dans la CDU'
    (*Quarterly bulletin* of the IAALD), iii (1958), 111-116.

relationships, was the suspicion that the symbols at present in use in the UDC were not actually all members of the same class.

The *differentia specifica* which I applied was:'Does this symbol refer to the conceptual structure as such? — or to the particular document being classified?' If the former, it is characterised as logical, if the latter, as documentary [8]. The symbols are accordingly distributed as in figure 1

	LOGICAL	DOCUMENTARY
conjunction, 'product'	$n{:}n$	
disjunction, 'sum'	$n{+}n$	$n{+}n$
span	n/n	
compounder	$n'n$	
sub-grouper		$[n \ldots n]$
language	$=n$	$=n$
form		(On)
place	(n)	
race	$(=n)$	
time	$"n"$	
point of view	$.OOn$	
auxiliary aspects	$\begin{cases} .On \\ -n \end{cases}$	

Figure 1

There are several points here that could be improved upon (for instance, use of the comma to replace the period in $.On$ and OOn[9]; elimination of closing quote and closing parentheses — or their use in some other connection; use of the compounding

---

8   There is a good deal of similarity beween this distinction and that of W C B Sayers between 'inner' and 'outer' 'forms' (see J Mills, *A modern outline of library classification* (London, Chapman & Hall, 1960), 35).

9   See J M Perreault's essay 'A new device for achieving hospitality in array' (*Américan documentation*, xvi/3 (1965), 245-246), reprinted below.

apostrophe in wider connections than chemical compounds 10;
elimination of the confusion arising from the dual use of any sign)
– but the most important improvement would be the substitution,
for the colon, of a larger gamut of relational indicators, as called
for in the quotation from Vickery.

The various categorical and relational tabulations consulted
proved intractable to collation at first – until it was noted that,
though some belonged to the general group, 'attributes of beings',
others belonged to the general group 'relations between beings'11,
and some had features (or even terms) belonging to both groups.
In general, however, a broad pattern revealed itself – it looks a
a different sort of vicious circle (figure 2).

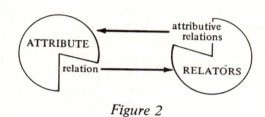

Figure 2

10 In J Mills, *The universal decimal classification* (New Brunswick, Rutgers
University Graduate School of Library Service, 1964), 61, an example is
given of a four-element number representing 'Supersonic flow: Cones: Pressure
gradient: Shear flow' —533.696.4:533.6.011.5:539.386:533.69.048.3—
comprising thirty numerical digits and twelve marks of punctaution. By use
of the compounding apostrophe this could be reduced to twenty-three
digits and ten marks —533.6'964.4'011.5'9.048.3:539.386. The fact that
the order of the original elements (a:b:c:d) had been changed (to a:b:d:c)
would make no difference in a mechanized search of a linear file, as long as
the citation order was one determined by convenience alone and not by
exigencies of meaning. (This device, of course, would be all the more likely
to be suggested in the absence of a developed repertory of relators, since if
several relators are appropriate to replace each of the colons in the original
expression, it is wholly evident that the apostrophe could not replace them.)

11 The two types are analogous to the two fashionable words 'roles' and 'links'.
J C Gardin, commenting on the deficiencies arising in the use of simple roles,
says (*SYNTOL*, 27) that: 'A better answer is to do without roles altogether,
and amplify links so that they convey the same information as roles and links
taken together...' The cited passage came to my attention after the elaboration
of the final form of the schema (figures 6-8), but it quite clearly expresses
intentions identical to those that guided me.

Enumeration of the categorical and relational tabulations studies gives figure 3 (this enumeration constituting the f i r s t s t e p toward the final relator-schema).

III   If, instead of assuming that a relator can be categoric (= capable of a variety of meanings, thus avoiding the need for explicit enumeration of a near-totality of the appropriate and useful relations – as is the case with Farradane's operators [25] or Gardin's syntagmata [26] – which, however, may be less successful in a machine scanned searching system that in an optically scanned one), a general outline of these tabulations is attempted, the following seem to me to comprise the major types present (with examples);

- *a:* ordinal (earlier than . . ., less than . . ., smaller than. . .)
- *b:* determinative (causing. . ., giving rise to . . ., limiting. . .)
- *c:* attributive (with characteristic . . .)
- *d:* interactive (differing from. . ., in concord with . . ., imitating. . .)
- *e:* subsumptive (with kind such as . . ., with parts such as . . .)
- *f:* logical (negation of . . ., reciprocal with . . ., converse to . . .)

In each of these cases a generally applicable line of division can be seen:

a: mean + extremes, in several sub-types (time: *simultaneous, prior, posterior;* size: *equal, smaller, larger;* degree: *equivalent, inferior, superior;* position: *lateral, axial, vertical* – each with its own tripartition)

b: a triadic movement from favourable to unfavourable: *production, limitation, destruction*

c: (the categories of *attribution* here become part of the

25 *Cf ibidem,* 135: 'Since each operator is in effect a category, each may express varieties of meaning.'
26 See Gardin, *SYNTOL* (New Brunswick, 1965); and his and R C Cros' *Final report on a general system for the treatment of documentary data,* i (Paris, Association Marc Bloch, 1963).

ARISTOTLE	LULL 12, 13,	KANT14		MILLS15	COSTELLO-WALL16	EJC17
substance	*general*	*relative*	*quantity*	whole	2, application	1, matte
accident	*questions*	*principles*	unity	thing	2, cause	2, prod
quantity	possibility	difference	plurality	kind	3, matter	3, by-p
quality	definition	concord	totality	parts	4, means	4, appli
relation	materiality	contrariety		materials	5, medium	5, envir
place	formality	beginning	*quality*	processes	6, by-product	6, cause
time	size	middle	reality	properties	7, product	7, effec
position	quality	end	negation	agents	8, research	8, majo
state	temporality	majority	limitation	operations	9, dependent	9, passi
action	locality	equality			variable	loca
passion	modality	minority	*relation*		10, design	10, mean
	instrumentality		inherence/		11, processed	0, bibli
			subsistence		(passive)	data
			causality/			
			dependence			
			community			

modality
possibility/
impossibility
existence/
non-existence
necessity/
contingency

12 This tabulation of *quaestiones generales* is freely translated from T & J Carreras y Artau, *Filosofia Cristiana de los siglos XIII al XV* (Madrid, Real Academia de Ciencies Exactas, Fisicas y Naturales, 1939), i, 425, citing Lull's *Logica nova.*

13 This tabulation of relative principles is freely translated from *ibidem*, i, 430. Lull, however, is hardly the most representative thinker between Aristotle and Kant, so R J Deferrari's *Lexicon of St.Thomas Aquinas* (Washington, Catholic University of America Press, 1948) was examined as well, without all of St Thomas' relational terms being listed in figure 3; but the only relations given in the *Lexicon* and not included in figures 5-8 are *master/slave, principle/ procession,* and *relatio personalis.* The first of these can be assimilated to the relations of *degree,* the second (which Deferrari equates with that of filiation) to *origin/derivation,* and the third is, I feel, entirely peculiar to theology.

14 From *Critique of pure reason, tr* N K Smith (London, Macmillan, 1950), 113.

15 From *Guide to the Universal Decimal Classification (UDC)* (London, British Standards Institution, 1963).

· 16 From B C Vickery, *On retrieval system theory,* (London, Butterworth, 1961), 49, citing J C Costello & E Wall, *Recent improvements in techniques for storing and retrieving information* (Wilmington, DuPont, 1959). *Cf* J C Costello, 'A basic theory of roles as syntactical control devices in coordinate indexes' (*Journal of chemical documentation* iv/2 (1964), 116-124).

17 From the Engineering Joint Council's *Thesaurus of engineering terms* (New York, author, 1964), XVII.

18 From Vickery, *On retrieval system theory,* 27-28, 36.

19 From deGrolier, *op cit ,* 72-74, citing several publications of Pagès' listed on 174 (note 11).

20 From *ibidem,* 80, citing P Braffort, 'Strategies optimales pour la recherche automatique des informations' (*Automatic documentation in action* (Frankfurt/ Main, Nachrichten für Dokumentation, 1961), 154-163).

	PAGES[19]	LEROY-BRAFFORT[20]	KERVEGANT[21]	GARDIN[22,23]	FARRADANE[24]
tegoric/	a, *order in*	action	:, *relation in*	subject	concurrence
insic	*general*	A, relation	*general*	object	comparison
lusive/	ab, equal	to	→ 1——→ , appurtenance	qualifier	association
egate	ac, prior	B, for the	→ 11——→ , inclusion;	location	equivalence
ted	ad, intermediate	purpose	implication	instrument	state;
luctive	af, first	L, location	→ 12——→ , parts; organs	*SYNTOL*	dimension
umental	ag, last	M, by means	→ 13——→ , constituents	*words*	appurtenance
tive	e, *determin-*	of	→ 14——→ , properties	predicates	distinctness
butive	*ative*	R, results in	→ 141—→ , physical pr.	entities	reaction
lative	eb, cause		→ 142→ , chemical pr.	states	causation
	ec, influence		→ 143→ , biological pro.	actions	
	ed, source; origin		→ 15——→ , aptitudes; pre-dispositions		
	ef, suppression; injury		→ 2 ——→ , process	*SYNTOL*	
	eg. frame of reference		→ 21—→ , action	*relations*	
	i, *concrete*		→ 211→ , favourable ac.	coordinative	
	ib, simultaneous		→ 212→ , unfavourable ac.	consecutive	
	ic, means		→2121→ , retardation	associative	
	id, barrier		→2122→ , inhibition	predicative	
	if, aiding		→2123→ , destruction		
	ig, supply; transfer		→ 21←— , interaction		
	ij, competition		→ 21k— , favourable i.a.		
	il, aggression		→ 212←— , unfavourable i.a.		
	im, attack		→ 22——→ , operation; product		
	in, resistance		→ 3 ——→ , dependence		
	o, *capacity*		→ 31——→ , causality		
	ob, high cap,		→ 32——→ , origin		
	oc, average cap,		→ 33——→ , conditions		
	od, low cap.		→ 31←— , correlation		
	u, *reciprocity*		→ 32←— , association		
	ü, *converse*		→ 33←— , combination		
			→ 4 ——→ , orientation		
			→ 41——→ , aspect		
			→ 42——→ , application		
			→ 43——→ , utilisation		
			→ 5 ——→ , comparison		
			→ 51——→ , resemblance		
			→ 511—→ , analogy		
			→ 512→ , equality; identity		
			→ 52——→ , non-resemblance		
			→ 521→ , difference		
			→ 522→ , opposition		
			→ O ——→ , negation of the relation		

≥ 3

21 From Vickery, *Classification and indexing in science* 2, 186; and from Kervégant, *art cit* (footnote 7). The fullest statement is in Kervégant's mimeographed note 'Subdivisions communes de relation; exposé des motifs'.

22 From J-C Gardin, 'On the coding of geometrical shapes and other representations, with reference to archaeological documents' (*Proceedings,* international Conference on Scientific Information, Washington, 1958 (Washington, National Academy of Sciences, 1959), ii, 889-901), 900.

23 From J-C Gardin & F Lévy, 'Le SYNTOL (Syntagmatic Organisation Language)' (*Information processing 1962* (Amsterdam, North Holland, 1963), 279-283).

24 From J E L Farradane, 'Relational indexing and new methods of concept organisation for information retrieval' (*Automation and scientific communication* (Washington, American Documentation Institute, 1963), II, 135-136).

relational 'sphere' , just as at *relation* the converse occurs; *cf* Figure 2)

d: a triadic movement from favourable to unfavourable: *concord, difference, contrariety*

e: intersection of the two aspects 'subsumed' and 'intrinsic/extrinsic' give rise to the triangle and the resultant relations in figure 4.

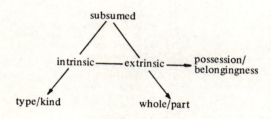

Figure 4

f: aside from the triadic (and rather arbitrary) division of 'capacity for . . .' there is the more legitimate triad *reciprocal, converse,* and *negative,* which could perhaps be shown to be the basic structure holding all the sub-types together into types — as will be attempted in § IV.

Thus, while not wishing on the one hand to denigrate Pagès' or Kervégant's careful divisions nor, on the other, Farradane's and Gardin's stimulating variable-context methods, I would conclude to the need for a more universal and more systematic deduction of relations. But first, as the s e c o n d s t e p toward the final arrangement, I exposit a semi-systematic version (figure 5) of the tabulations previously simply enumerated (figure 3), abstracting from all of them all distinct relations.

Figure 5

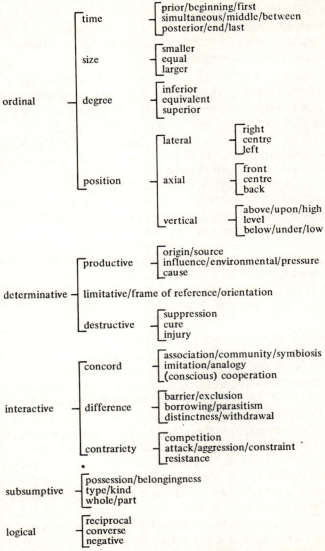

IV Particular deficiencies in this preparatory scheme can be seen with relatively little trouble, though the systematic correction of the arrangement as a whole is by no means so obvious. It seemed to me, while seeking for the path to such a systematic corrective, that the tripartite relation (for instance, as most fundamentally embodied in the three interactive terms — *concord, difference,* and *contrariety* – taken from Ramon Lull's relative principles) was characteristic of the tabulation as a whole. The same has been already mentioned of the logical terms — *reciprocal, converse,* and *negative.*

There seemed no way of having this general-categoric ideal cover the whole extent of the schema, until it was noticed that the tripartition under *determinative* consists of terms all of which are a c t i v e, as are the further tripartitions. If p a s s i v e determination is also to be included, the tripartition of *determinative* can be seen to require i n t e r a c t i v e as well. Our main member classes then have become *ordinal, determinative, subsumptive,* and *logical.* And if any one of these four can be seen as congruent to the other three taken together, a perfect tripartition-schema might become possible. This new attempt is not abstractive (like that embodied in figure 5) nor tabulative (like that in figure 3) but systematising, and constitutes the t h i r d a n d f i n a l s t e p toward the desired schema.

The logical relations are the first choice for the task of matching all the others, and can be seen to fulfil the need thus:

The relation *reciprocity* is a true relation (though *affirmation* would be merely an attribute), and when seen in correlation with the three residual members, clearly shares many characteristics with *subsumptive:* they both refer to a relation in which a t o t a l i t y i s p r e s e n t e d a s a t o t a l i t y, including its elements.

The relation *converse,* on the other hand, is one in which a t o t a l i t y i s p r e s e n t e d a s e l e m e n t s - i n - r e l a t i o n; this corresponds to the relational type *determinative,* which implies action/reaction/passion.

The relation *contradictory* (or the attribute *negative*) corresponds to the type *ordinal,* in that w h a t - i s - o r d e r e d i s c o n t r a d i c t o r y t o (or at least farthest from) t h e s u b s u m p t i v e i d e a o f t o t a l i t y.

---

27 **A** more general statement of this tripartition might be *affirmative, contrary,* and *contradictory;* but *affirmative* is not actually a relation, but rather an attribute — and the same can be said of *negative.*

The categories (*attributive*), not discussed since §II, are included here wherever they can be seen to be appropriate. In general, any relational codification can be transformed into an attribute (category) by the prefixation of (say) a semi-colon[28]. It should be noted that the notational radix is 9, so that, while I have used letters (as the most appropriate symbolisation to combine with the predominantly numerical UDC[29]), these notations could be easily transformed into numbers for use with a verbal classificational system. Also note that the derivational factor is shown with each tripartition. The characteristic of a thoroughgoingly systematic deduction (as of a literal translation) is the possibility of retranslation back into the source language. This characteristic, it is hoped, is to be found in figure 6.

Note that though this schema absorbs almost all of the concepts enumerated in figure 3, treating even pure attributes as left-to-right relations, *quality* and *quantity* are not included in the vast ramificative enumeration of which they are capable, but only generally — in Ranganathan's terms, only the facets are shown, not all the foci. figure 7 gives a systematic tabulation, and figure 8 is an alphabetical chain-index to the schema.

V A few examples of how such coding could be used in conjunction with UDC numbers in the classification/indexing of articles, chapters, and books follow. (Note that the relators, though designed for use with UDC, and for incorporation into mechanised retrieval, can also be used with any substantive classificatory vocabulary.)

'Clouds prior to the hurricane' would be
551.576 fffa 551.55 [30]

28 A convention must establish the position of such attributive usages with reference to the substantive code being modified; the examples given below, however, will refrain from such usage and hence from the need to establish such a convention.

29 As mentioned above, this schema was intended as the basis for a structural notation capable of forming complex classifications from a compound classificatory schedule, and the notating of it offered at least three choices: *a:* punctuation symbols, *b:* letters, *c:* numbers. The first was attempted, but the results were so bizarre as to make optical scanning highly difficult. Letter — or number-combinations of the radix a-i or 1-9 are therefore recommended.

30 The UDC numbers used here are from the Trilingual Abridged Edition.

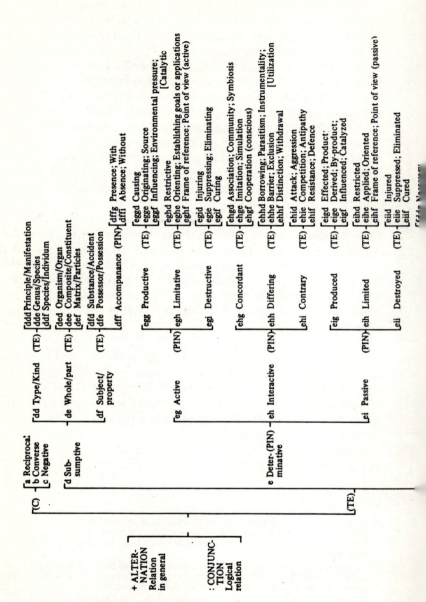

Figure 6

+ ALTER-
NATION
Relation
in general

: CONJUNC-
TION
Logical
relation

130

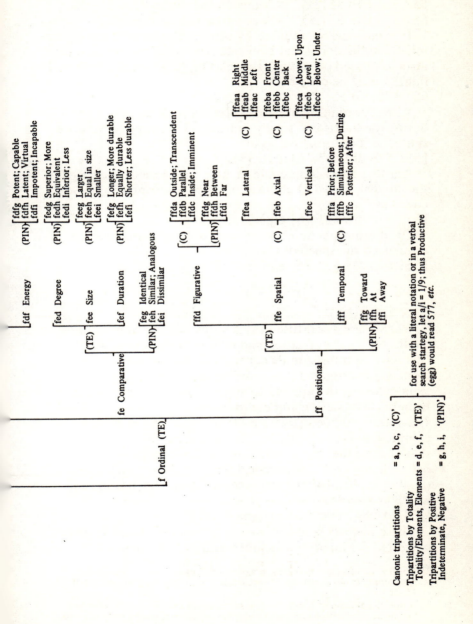

Canonic tripartitions = a, b, c, '(C)'
Tripartitions by Totality
Totality/Elements, Elements = d, e, f, '(TE)'
Tripartitions by Positive
Indeterminate, Negative = g, h, i, '(PIN)'

for use with a literal notation or in a verbal search startegy, let a/i = 1/9; thus Productive (egg) would read 577, *etc.*

131

Two other temporal relationships could be similarly expressed
551.576 **fffb** 551.55   'Clouds during the hurricane',
551.576 **fffc** 551.55   'Clouds after the hurricane'.

If 'clouds' were modified by some sort of accidental characteristic in the document being reduced to its surrogate — for
instance 'speed of clouds', the relation (always read from left to
right) would be coded as
551.576 **dfd** 531.76.

When forming a complex expression such as 'speed of clouds
during the hurricane' square brackets[31] are used to indicate
syntactic subordination, as in
[551.576 **dfd** 531.76] **fffb** 551.55.

Another expression could include the cause of the speed of
the clouds: 'Speed of clouds caused by atmospheric pressure',
coded as
[551.576 **dfd** 531.76] **eigd** 551.54.

Or, if atmospheric pressure were not the cause, but somehow
influenced the speed of the clouds, as
[551.576 **dfd** 531.761 **eigf** 551.54.

When using a real title like 'A study of general categories
applicable to classification and coding in documentation' we will
first have to transform its conceptual content into an order
from which assignment of numbers and relators is possible:
'general categories applied to areas within documentation,
namely classification and codification':
161.1 **ehe** [002 **ded** [025.3 + 003.61]][32]. An even more
complex real title would be 'On the coding of geometrical
shapes and other representations, with reference to archaeological documents' (geometrical shapes and pictorial elements
(coding applied to), in reference to the documentation for
which archaeology sets the goals):
[[515 + 084] **eihe** 003.6] **eghe** 930.26]

These relators (and other punctuation modifications) are
suggested for incorporation into a large scale (perhaps

31 For the use of square brackets (as against the English usage), see K Fill,
   Einführung in das Wesen der Dezimalklassifikation 2(Berlin, Beuth, 1960),
   20-21.
32 A questionable point is whether it is necessary to specify classification and
   coding as areas within documentation; this inclusion is fairly nearly obvious.

centralized or cooperative) mechanization of classification/ indexing and retrieval activities, especially if such an activity were intended to supply a variety of levels of institutions with documents classified/indexed, at correspondingly differing levels of richness and depth, in terms of UDC[33]. The computerised mechanism of such supply could of course confound all of these relators into the colon for print-out of surrogates in the form of catalog-cards, or could (say) use the colon for all relations except the *determinative,* or for all except the *subsumptive* and the *conditional,* or could use the notation as a whole only up to two digits — for any of the institutions needing such variations.

To summarise, then the following revised tabulation of UDC punctuation is suggested figure 9).

Figure 7

+	ALTERNATION, Relation in General
:	CONJUNCTION, Logical Relation
a	Reciprocal
b	Converse
c	Negative
d	Subsumptive
dd	Type/Kind
ddd	Principle/Manifestation
dde	Genus/Species
ddf	Species/Individuum
de	Whole/Part
ded	Organism/Organ
dee	Composite/Constituent
def	Matrix/Particles
df	Subject/Property
dfd	Substance/Accident
dfe	Possessor/Possession
dff	Accompanance
dffg	Presence; With
dffi	Absence; Without; Lack
e	Determinative
eg	Active
egg	Productive
eggd	Causing
egge	Originating; Source
eggf	Influencing; Environmental pressure; Catalytic
egh	Limitative
eghd	Restrictive
eghe	Orienting; Establishing goals or applications
eghf	Frame of Reference; Point of view (active)

33 See (as general background) J M Perreauit s papers 'On bibliography and automation; or how to reinvent the catalog' (*Libri,* xv/3 (1965), 287-339) for a proposal oriented toward such a centralized activity.

egi		Destructive
egid		Injuring
egie		Suppressing; Eliminating
egif		Curing
eh	Interactive	
ehg		Concordant
ehgd		Association; Community; Symbiosis
ehge		Imitation; Simulation
ehgf		Cooperation (conscious)
ehh		Differing
ehhd		Borrowing; Parasitism; Instrumentality; Utilization
ehhe		Barrier; Exclusion
ehhf		Distinction; Withdrawal
ehi		Contrary
ehid		Attack; Aggression
ehie		Competition; Antipathy
ehif		Resistance; Defence
ei .	Passive	
eig		Produced
eigd		Effected; Product;
eige		Derived; By-product
eigf		Influenced; Catalyzed
eih		Limited
eihd		Restricted
eihe		Applied; Oriented
eihf		Frame of reference; Point of view (passive)
eii		Destroyed
eiid		Injured
eiie		Suppressed; Eliminated
eiif		Cured
f	Ordinal	
fd	Conditional	
fdd		State
fddg		Necessary
fddh		Contingent
fddi		Arbitrary
fde		Attitude
fdeg		Favourable
fdeh		Indifferent
fdei		Unfavourable
fdf		Energy
fdfg		Potent; Capable
fdfh		Latent; Virtual
fdfi		Impotent; Incapable
fe	Comparative	
fed		Degree
fedg		Superior; More
fedh		Equivalent
fedi		Inferior; Less
fee		Size
feeg		Larger
feeh		Equal in size
feei		Smaller
fef		Duration
fefg		Longer; More Durable
fefh		Equally Durable
fefi		Shorter; Less Durable
feg		Identical

134

feh	Similar; Analogous
fei	Dissimilar
ff	Positional
ffd	Figurative
ffda	Outside; Transcendent
ffdb	Parallel
ffde	Inside; Immanent
ffdg	Near
ffdh	Between
ffdi	Far
ffe	Spatial
ffea	Lateral
ffeaa	Right
ffeab	Middle
ffeac	Left
ffeb	Axial
ffeba	Front
ffebb	Center
ffebc	Back
ffec	Vertical
ffeca	Above; Upon
ffecb	Level
ffecc	Below; Under
fff	Temporal
fffa	Prior; Before
fffb	Simultaneous; During
fffc	Posterior; After
ffg	Toward
ffh	At
ffi	Away

Figure 8

Above [Vertical: Spatial: Positional: Ordinal] .. ffeca
Absence [Accompanance: Subject/Property:
    Subsumptive] .... dffi
Accident, Substance/ [Subject/Property:
    Subsumptive] .... dfd
Accompanance [Subject/Property: Subsumptive] dff
Active [Determinative] .... eg
After [Temporal: Positional: Ordinal] .... fffc
Aggression [Contrary: Interactive: Determinative] ehid
ALTERNATION, Relation in general .... +
Analogous [Comparative: Ordinal] .... feh
Antipathy [Contrary: Interactive: Determina-
    tive] .... ehie
Applications, Establishing goals or [Limitative:
    Active: Determinative] .... eghe
Applied [Limited: Passive: Determinative] .... eihe
Arbitrary [State: Conditional: Ordinal] .... fddi
Association [Concordant: Interactive: Determi-
    native] .... ehgd
At [Positional: Ordinal] .... ffh
Attack [Contrary: Interactive: Determinative] .. ehid
Attitude [Conditional: Ordinal] .... fde
Axial [Spatial: Positional: Ordinal] .... ffeb

Back [Axial: Spatial; Positional: Ordinal] .... ffebc
Barrier [Differing: Interactive: Determinative] ehhe
Before [Temporal: Positional: Ordinal] .... fffa
Below [Vertical: Spatial: Positional: Ordinal] ... ffecc

tive]	ehge
Simultaneous [Temporal: Positional: Ordinal]	fffb
Size [Comparative: Ordinal]................	fee
Smaller [Size: Comparative: Ordinal]	feei
Source [Productive: Active: Determinative]	egge
Spatial [Positional: Ordinal]	ffe
Species, Genus/ [Type/Kind: Subsumptive]	dde
Species/Individuum [Type/Kind: Subsumptive]	ddf
State [Conditional: Ordinal]	fdd
Subject/Property [Subsumptive]	df
Substance/Accident [Subject/Property; Subsumptive]	dfd
Subsumptive	d
Superior [Degree: Comparative: Ordinal]	fedg
Suppressed [Destroyed: Passive: Determinative]	eiie
Suppressing [Destructive: Active: Determinative	egie
Symbiosis [Concordant: Interactive: Determinative]................................	ehgd
Temporal [Positional: Ordinal]..............	fff

TOTALITY, TOTALITY/ELEMENTS, ELEMENTS; TRIPARTITION BY .... (TE)⎰ . d . .
. e . .
. f . .

Toward [Positional: Ordinal]	ffg
Transcendent [Figurative: Positional: Ordinal]..	ffda
Type/Kind [Subsumptive]	dd
Under [Vertical: Spatial: Positional: Ordinal]	ffecc
Unfavourable [Attitude: Conditional: Ordinal]	fdei
Upon [Vertical: Spatial: Positional: Ordinal]	ffeca
Utilisation [Differing: Interactive: Determinative]	ehhd
Vertical [Spatial: Positional: Ordinal]........	ffec
View, Point of (active) [Limitative: Active: Determinative]	eghf
View, Point of (passive) [Limited: Passive: Determinative]	eihf
Virtual [Energy: Conditional: Ordinal].......	fdfh
Whole/Part [Subsumptive]	de
With [Accompanance: Subject/Property: Subsumptive]...........................	dffg
Withdrawal [Differing: Interactive: Determinative]	ehhf
Without [Accompanance: Subject/Property: Subsumptive]	dffi

Figure 9

LOGICAL			DOCUMENTARY	
conjunction, 'product'	*n:n*	(=a/ffi)	*n:n :: n:n*	to join complex interrelated groups one of which already contains a colon or a/ffi)
disjunction, 'sum'	*n+n*		*n. . .!n. . .*	to join complex but non-related groups sharing the same bibliographical matrix.

span	*n/n*		
compounder	*n'n*	to be used wherever applicable	
sub-grouper		[*n. . .n*]	to be used wherever applicable
language	*=n*	*= = n*	
form		(O*n*	without closing mark
place	(*n*	without closing mark	
race	(=*n*	without closing mark	
time	"*n*	without closing mark	
point of view	,OO*n*	comma replaces period	
auxiliary aspects	,O*n*	comma replaces period	
	−*n*		

IX
Emendations to the relator-schema

1. Investigation and experimental use has led to the discovery of a serious but not uncorrectable lapse in my schema of relators[1]. The origin of the problem was an uncritical use of the (PIN) relator-elements **g**, **h**, **i** to mean both *a*: positive, indeterminate, and negative i n t e r m s o f c o n t e n t, and *b*: normal (*ie*, left/right), bi-directional, and reversed (*ie*, right/left) i n t e r m s o f o r i e n t a t i o n. Thus there resulted several relators whose orientation could not be reversed, since only **g**, **i** digits represent positive and negative in terms of content, as in **fdeg**, **fdei** (favourable, unfavourable). But *A*-**fdeg**-*B* is not properly reversible into *B*-**fdeli**-*A* (*A* is favourable to *B* ≠ *B* is unfavourable to *A*). Another possible origin of the problem is that the (C) relators subsumed under **ff** are b o t h positive, indeterminate, and negative in terms of content a n d normal, bi-directional, and reversed in terms of orientation, for example *A*-**fffa**-*B* = *B*-**fffc**-*A* (*A* prior to *B* = *B* posterior to *A*).

But reversible orientation is available (without change of content from positive to negative or vice versa) under **e**, and is successfully shown by the **g**, **i** transposition. How to preserve this advantage while not tampering with the apparently correct formulations under **ff**?

2. A theoretical/practical problem[2] in the use of UDC demands such a reversibility. Such code as 820:22 could well translate *English literature influenced by the Bible*: 22:820 could well

---

1 'Categories and relators: a new schema' [presented to the 1965 FID Congress] (*Revue internationale de la documentation*, xxxii (1965), 136-144); reprinted in *On the Perreault schema of relators and the rules of formation in UDC* (Copenhagen, 1966 = FID/CR Report no 4) and above; translated into Russian in *Razrabotka i primenenie Universal' noi desiatichnoi klassifikacii* (Moscow, VINITI , 1967).

2 The abstracts/codes used here to exemplify this problem were suggested by C David Batty.

translate *Bible influenced* [*stylistically*] *by English literature.*
Permutation of such entries would therefore almost inevitably
result in misapprehension. Thus only *Bible and English
literature in mutual influence* should be permutable; only for
this meaning does no misapprehension result. It was partly in
order to remedy this unfortunate situation (namely, that
permutation is allowed to occur even when misapprehension
inevitably follows) that the schema was constructed – but as has
been seen, the intention was not fulfilled throughout.

3. A solution seems available by substitution of **a, b, c** for **g, h,
i** when the orientation-reversibility is necessary. This gives **ea,
eb, ec** for **eg, eh, ei**, which percolates down to the lower levels
of **e**, thus **eag** for **egg**, *etc ,* and **eagd** for **eggd**, *etc.*

This solution leaves all determinative relations reversible [3],
but does not make those ordinal relations which need
reversibility reversible, since their **g, h, i** elements are (PIN) in
the content sense only. Nor does it make subsumptive relations
reversible, since they have no **g, h, i** elements except for **dffg,
dffh**[4], **dffi** (which do not require reversibility, being no less
symmetrical than the *n:n* properly used).

3.1   As elements that can be employed in solving this
problem, I would mention the following: Each subsumptive
relation is possible only in the left/right and right/left orientations; if *A* is whole and *B* is part, then *B* is part and *A*
is whole; but there can be no intermediacy of orientation (bi-
directionality). Each determinative relation is possible in left/
right, bi-directional, and right/left orientations, and (PIN)
relations are present here under **e** as they were not under **d**.
Ordinal relations do not form such a homogeneous mass as do
either the subsumptive or the determinative ones; but all that
was available in **e** over **d** is present in **f**, plus the mentioned
factor of the occasional mutual assimilation of orientational
indeterminacy and content indeterminacy.

3.2   Each relation that requires reversibility (*ie* each one
that is oriented, not symmetrical like *A*-fe-*B* = *B*-fe-*A* = *A*
compared to B), either has or lacks **a, b, c** element(s); if it has

3   Note that *A*-e-*B* may be taken to be properly permutable, since it means
only that *A* and *B* are in some (indeterminate, in terms of content) relation,
whereas *A*-ea-*B* is reversible into *B*-ec-*A*, and *A*-eb-*B* indicates that *A* and
B are interactive (*ie*, indeterminate in the orientational sense) relation (mutual,
therefore symmetrical).

4   This code should be added, as suggested by J C G Wesseling in *On the
Perreault schema,* cited in footnote 1, to mean 'passive presence'.

reversibility is made possible by transposition (*eg*, from
A-. . . **a** . . . -*B* to *B*- . . . **c** . . . -*A*); if it has not, reversibility is
made possible by addition at the end of the relational notation
of **a** or **c** as called for. Thus a document concerned with the
principle/manifestation relation between topics *A* and *B*, but
not coming to any conclusion as to their orientation (*eg*, *A* =
criminality, *B* = drug addiction) would be coded *A*-**ddd**-*B* = *B***ddd***A*
one arguing for an orientation with *A* as principle and *B* as
manifestation would be coded *A*-**ddda**-*B* = *B*-**dddc**-*A;* one
arguing for the opposite orientation would be coded *B*-**ddda**-*A*
= *A*-**dddc**-*B*.

3.3   The addition of **a, c** to those codes which lack them effects
reversibility quite adequately in **d**; **e** has the necessary reversibility
from the presence of reversible elements within each code (if the
notation is changed as suggested in §3.0); we are left then with
the ordinal relations, **f**, where there is occasional mutual
assimilation of orientational and content indeterminacy.*A*-**fd**-*B*
means that *A* and *B* are conditionally related, and must therefore
(if *A* is taken as the condition for *B*) be made reversible without
giving *B*-**fd**-*A*, since that would mean that *B* is the condition for
A, not (as is desired) that *B* is conditional upon *A;* so the solution
in 3.2 applies here, giving *A*-**fda**-*B* = *B*-**fdc**-*A*, but also giving
A-**fdb**-*B* for the document thematically concerned with the bi-
conditionality of *A* and *B*, leaving *A*-**fd**-*B* for those for which
permutation causes no change in meaning.

   Comparative and positional relations at the general levels are
properly permutable: *A*-**fe**-*B* = *A* and *B* are being compared;
A-**ffe**-*B* = *B*-**ffe**-*A* = *A* and *B* are in spatial relation to each other.
3.4   In addition to the extension of reversible relations by
a, b, c,some substitutions of **a, b, c** for **g, h, i** need to be made in
the lower levels of **fd** and **fe**, namely under **fdd, fed, fee**, and **fef**;
these changes are shown in the revised schedule given below in
§ 5.
3.5   Spatial relations, **ffe**, should not be partitioned **a, b, c**, for
the terms *lateral, axial, vertical*, since this would imply that the
lateral is the reversé of the vertical; the ideal solution would seem
to be to change **ffea, ffeb, ffec** to some triad of elements not
previously used at all,as being incommensurable with any of the
three original triads. Assuredly we could not substitute **d, e,
f**, so a weak solution (one that might not cause irrelevant
retrievals and would not go beyond the desired nonal radix)

143

would be to use the (PIN) elements **g, h, i.**

4. With these changes, we can be assured that any code reading
A-. . . **a** . . .-*B* can be permuted, without change of meaning, to
B-. . . **c**. . . -*A* ; and that any code reading *A*- . . . **g** . . . *B*
has as its opposite in terms of the relational content *A*-. . **i** . . -*B*.

5. A revised schedule, replacing Figure 7 of the original schema,
is given here (additional relations are shown by +, change of
terminology by #, change of notation by *):

[(O) #Tripartition by Orientation: **a, b, c**]

. [(TE) Tripartition by Totality, Totality/Elements, Elements: **d, e, f**]

[(PIN) Tripartition by Positive, Indeterminate, Negative: **g, h, i**]

a # Normal; Left/right
b # Bi-directional
c # Reverse; Right/left
d Subsumptive

+**da** *A* subsumes *B*
+**dc** *B* is subsumed by *A*

dd Type/Kind
+**dda** Type〉Kind
+**ddc** Kind〈Type

ddd Principle/Manifestation
+**dda** Principle〉Manifestation
+**ddc** Manifestation〈Principle

dde Genus/Species
+**ddea** Genus〉Species
+**ddec** Species〈Genus

ddf Species/Individuum
+**ddfa** Species〉Individuum
+**ddfc** Individuum〈Species

de Whole/Part
+**dea** Whole〉Part
+**dec** Part〈Whole

ded Organism/Organ
+**deda** Organism〉Organ
+**dedc** Organ〈Organism

dee Composite/Constituent
+**deea** Composite〉Constituent
+**deec** Constituent〈Composite

def Matrix/Particles
+**defa** Matrix〉Particles

```
        +defc   Particles ⟨Matrix
 df   Subject/Property
        +dfa    Subject ⟩Property
        +dfc    Property ⟨Subject
      dfd   Substance/Accident
        +dfda   Substance ⟩Accident
        +dfdc   Accident ⟨Substance
      dfe   Possessor/Possession
        +dfea   Possessor ⟩Possession
        +dfec   Possession ⟨Possessor

      dff   Accompanance
                +dffa A accompanies B
                +dffc B is accompanied by A
        dffg    Presence; With
        +dffh   Passive presence
        dffi    Absence; Without
 e  Determinative
      *ea  Active
        *eag    Productive
        *eagd   Causing
        *eage   Originating; Source
        *eagf   Influencing; Environmental pressure, Catalytic
      *eah Limitative
        *eahd   Restrictive
        *eahe   Orienting; Establishing goals or applications
        *eahf   Frame of reference; Point of view (active)
      *eai Destructive
        *eaid   Injuring
        *eaie   Suppressing; Eliminating
        *eaif   Curing

   *eb  Interactive
      *ebg Concordant
        *ebgd   Association; Community; Symbiosis
        *ebge   Imitation; Simulation
        *ebgf   Cooperation (conscious)
      *ebh  Differing
        *ebhd   Borrowing; Parasitism; Instrumentality; Utilization
        *ebhe   Barrier; Exclusion
        *ebhf   Distinction; Withdrawal
      *ebi  Contrary
        *ebid   Attack; Aggression
```

                    *ebie   Competition; Antipathy
                    *ebif   Resistance; Defence
      *ec   Passive
      *ecg   Produced
                    *ecgd   # Effected; Product
                    *ecge   # Derived; By-product
                    *ecgf   Influenced; Catalyzed
      *ech   Limited
                    *echd   Restricted
                    *eche   Applied; Oriented
                    *echf   Frame of reference; Point of view (passive)
      *eci   Destroyed
                    *ecid   Injured
                    *ecie   Suppressed; Eliminated
                    *ecif   Cured
f   Ordinal
   fd   Conditional
                    +fda A conditions B
                    +fdb A and B are mutually conditioned
                    +fdc B is conditioned by A
      fdd   State
                    *fdda   Necessary
                    *fddb   # Arbitrary
                    *fddc   # Contingent
         fde   Attitude
            fdeg   Favourable
                       +fedga A favours B
                       +fedgb A and B mutually favourable
                       +fedgc B favoured by A
            fdeh   Indifferent
                       +fdeha A indifferent to B
                       +fdehb A and B mutually indifferent
                       +fdehc B 'indifferented' by A
            fdei   Unfavourable
                       +fdeia A unfavourable to B
                       +fdeib A and B mutually unfavourable
                       +fdeic B 'unfavoured' by A
         fdf   Energy
            fdfg   Potent; Capable

                       +fdfga A capable of B
                       +fdfgb A and B mutually capable

                    +fdfgc *B* 'capabled' by *A*
        fdfh Latent, Virtual
                    +fdfha *A* latent in *B*
                    +fdfhb *A* and *B* mutually latent
                    +fdfhc *B* latent with *A*
        fdfi Impotent; Incapable
                    +fdfia *A* incapable of *B*
                    +fdfib *A* and *B* mutually incapable
                    +fdfic *B* 'incapabled' by *A*
fe Comparative
  fed Degree
                    *feda Superior; More
                    *fedb Equivalent
                    *fedc Inferior; Less
        fee Size
                    *feea Larger
                    *feeb Equal in size
                    *feec Smaller
        fef Duration
                    *fefa Longer; More durable
                    *fefb Equally durable
                    *fefc Shorter; Less durable

        feg Identical
        feh Similar; Analogous
        fei Dissimilar
ff Positional
        ffd Figurative
                    ffda Outside; Transcendent
                    ffdb Parallel
                    ffdc Inside; Immanent
                    ffdg Near
                    ffdh Between
                    ffdi Far
        ffe Spatial
                    *ffeg Lateral
                                *ffega Right
                                *ffegb Middle
                                *ffegc Left
                    *ffeh Axial
                                *ffeha Front
                                *ffehb Center

147

	*ffehc	Back
*ffei	Vertical	
	*ffeia	Above; Upon
	*ffeib	Level
	*ffeic	Below; Under
fff	Temporal	
fffa	Prior; Before	
ffab	Simultaneous; During	
fffc	Posterior; After	
ffg	Toward	
ffh	At	
ffi	Away	

The revision of the chain-index (figure 8 of the original schem
is a simple enough matter not to need attention here.

X

Automatized retranslatability of
UDC codes

Epistemology, or at least semiology, however doubtful its
grand function in documentation system design, enters opera-
tively at least in the principle 'The conceptual surrogate for the
document must l e a d to the document by (in some way)
m e a n i n g what the documents does' ; or, negatively stated:
'The conceptual surrogate must not be allowed to be found to
mean what the document does only a f t e r the document
has been (accidentally) located' .

I postulate that such *meaning* is possible only in an information language characterised by a high degree of *concreteness*
or precision[1], and have undertaken to provide the means for
the improvement of UDC in this regard [2].

This can be put another way: concordance, total or partial, is
not the essential intention of a document-surrogation system; it
is, rather, the surpassing of words by meanings or relevances[3].
This intention is attempted, though not necessarily achieved, by
every systematic search strategy; this latter is taken to include
everything from the simplest controlled vocabulary to the Colon

1   *Cf* in particular my *Reclassification: some warnings and a proposal* (=Illinois.
University. Graduate School of Library Science. *Occasional papers*, no 87),
reprinted above, §2.1.

2   See *On the Perreault schema of relators and the rules of formation in UDC*
(=F I D/C R Report no. 4), which contains *a*: a reprinting of my 'Categories
and relators: a new schema' from *Revue internationale de la documentation*,
xxxii/4 (1965), 136-144, reprinted above; *b*: 'The Universal Decimal Classification and the Perreault system' by J C G Wesseling; and *c*: my 'Towards
explication of the rules of formation in UDC' reprinted above. The last of
these is the essential item as background to the present paper.

3   *Cf* for instance J Belzer & W Goffman, 'Theoretical considerations in
information retrieval systems' (*Communications* of the A C M, vii (1964),
439-442), 440:
   In information retrieval, if the user is interested in information rather than
a quotation, the question posed to the system must be in metalanguage.
   – and K C & M Rothkirch-Trach, 'Erfahrungen und Erkenntnisse bei der
Aufstellung von Thesauren' (*Nachrichten für Dokumentation,* xv (1964),
118-121, 119 (my version):
   It is not the word as lowest element of speech which is decisive, but the
concept as basic element of thought.

Classification. The systematicity of all these search strategies tries to go beyond *discreteness* and towards *concreteness*[4]; and classification, particularly analytico-synthetic classification, attempts this. The majority of classifications attempt concreteness in a pattern I call *linear*[5]. Good examples of this can be seen in the majority of DC codes involving standard sub-divisions of form of presentation and/or place; these can be linearly diagrammed as [[[A]B]C], or better, to show the order in which the concreteness is made to arise as,

A B C

But such a simple pattern is unable to cope with the type of conceptual concreteness to be found in sophisticated research embodied in periodical articles, research reports, book-chapters, and many whole books. For the purpose of creating adequate surrogates of such complex or (conceptually) compound documents[6] we must have access to a supra-linear pattern. I postulate that the fullest statement of such a pattern in the bibliographical-documentary frame of reference can be found in Ranganthan's theory of *rounds and levels*[7]. This theory, obviously, is foundational in C C; my paper 'Towards Explication of the Rules of Formation in UDC' is an attempt to put something

---

4 This is true in two ways, both *a*: as a result of the tendency od such a vocabulary to be self-defining as a whole (*cf* the essay above, 'Transparency and self-definition in classification' and *b*: as a result of that surpassing of mere vocabulary − no matter how considerable an accomplishment the establishment of such a v o c a b u l a r y may be − which is made possible by the syntax which constitutes an information l a n g u a g e on the basis of a 'mere' searching vocabulary.

5 *Cf* 'Towards explication of the rules of formation in UDC', cited in footnote 2.

6 By the phrase '(conceptually) compound' I mean to exclude the simple case of an apparently unitary document which is in reality a group of micro-documents, such as can be diagrammed A B + C D E, and refer

instead to one diagrammable as A B + .C D + E, or the like. Note the introduction of a different order of operations than the linear; this can be made possible only by the use of a sub-grouping device of some sort, analogous (as explained later in the main text) to Ranganathan's rounds and levels.

There is a non-trivial opposition to the whole idea of the '(conceptually) compound' in C Petersen, 'Zur Problematik von Pluszeichen und Schrägstrich in der D K' (*D K Mitteilungen,* xi (1966), 29-31), but if (which I neither accept nor argue against, here) he is right there is no difficulty in transforming from the notation I propose to that he proposes, along the familiar lines A (B + C) = (A B) + (A C).

7 *Cf* S R Ranganthan, *Prolegomena to library classification*2 (London, Library Association, 1957), §46 'Rounds, Levels, and Phases' (pp 270-277).

very like it in the same position relative to UDC, and attempts to do so by the eliciting of an *order of operations* from the rather disunified and non-theoretical practice and discussion of UDC by its proponents [8], and as the means of providing a macrosystem into which the micro-system displayed in 'Categories and relators' can advantageously be fitted.

I postulate that the impetus to the development of so-called 'coordinate' indexing has been *a*: the difficulty of locating subordinate aspects of complex and (conceptually) compound subjects, and *b*: the difficulty of verifying the presence of meaningful alternative sub-complexes within the total complex. (These two problems can be referred to respectively as *distributed relatives* and *partial relevance*.) However, the alleged solution by means of 'coordinate' indexing is not what it claims to be, in either case. In regard to *a,* the nature of information languages which do not clearly reveal the various facets within their codes (especially L C S H, D C, and L C) is what has forced the attempt at such a solution; but such a force would not have arisen if the starting point were UDC or CC, or even BC. In regard to *b,* the freedom of combination that results from the splintering of the whole into unarticulated ('coordinate') index terms is in fact the destruction of meaning and thus the condition for error.

What is needed — which the splintered approach recognised, without accomplishing it — is a means of making *sense* without sacrificing *fact.* Indexed fact is simple, it is not subtle; indexed sense though is just the opposite, it i s subtlety and mutual internal modification. The theory—the hope—was that subtlety could be infused into a conglomeration of facts, merely by virtue of their conglomeration. And whether this hope could succeed, it is certain that the sense to be found in L C S H, DC or LC could not easily enough reveal its constituent facts. So the mold had to be broken.

But the splinters were not put back together.

The task of an articulated, analytico-synthetic classification is to take sense apart into constituent fact and then to reassemble them so that both fact and sense are retained. What does this metaphor mean for mechanised information storage and retrieval?

---

8 I shall only mention, without citing their works, some of the principal persons: S C Bradford, F Donker-Duyvis, R Dubuc, K Fill, O Frank, C D Gull, P Herrmann, E Jacquemin, G A Lloyd, G Lorphèvre, J Mills, M Schuchmann.

This: that if a structure can be found which reveals sense while letting factual elements be recognisable within the complex, electronic devices can be amployed to abstract from such a code all its *implicit* and all its *virtual* relevances, in addition to that single relevance which would be found if there were an *explicit* one-for-one match between it and the query. Of the candidate systems, UDC or CC or BC, CC is the most satisfactory in terms of the syntax that enables subtlety. B C is the factually least up to date, and UDC is factually most nearly satisfactory. The need is either to infuse factual adequacy into CC, or syntactic elegance into UDC. My attempt has been the latter – primarily because it's easier and quicker.

The theory of rounds and levels, borrowed from CC, applies to UDC in the form of tightened rules for citation order, of restriction of the use of the square brackets $-[n...n]$ – to the function of phrase-markers 9, and of a strict order in which the various punctional facet-indicators and compounders and complexers are to be made operative in the interpretation of a total code. With this additional strictness – and with the factual inadequacies of UDC hopefully to be corrected at least no less soon than they will be in any other system – UDC becomes thoroughly adaptable to computer use. Thus, in a complex code like

[532.542.1.08: [546.02:539.163.004.61: [621.52:666.1]]] (079.3)=40

(pipe flow   isotopes,   prevention,   case-book
      turbulent,   radioactive,   vacuum chambers,   French)
      measurement,   decaying,   glass,

the brackets mark off the limits of influence of the modifying facts (*levels*); the order of operation is strictly controlled so that appropriate sub-complexes, not even envisioned by author and/or indexer, can be retrieved – and inappropriate ones prevented –; and permutation is made possible on a purely ritual basis, if desired. (It is admitted that chain-indexing is not so easily made automatic, at least without undesired retention of implied

9   This restriction is at least partially accomplished by tne substitution of the
double colon $-n :: n$ – for the square brackets used as subordinating (non-permutabl
colon; see 'Draft P-note 1967:15'.

generic and/or unsought links.)

The point made at the beginning, that the conceptual surrogate must not be allowed to be found to mean what the document does not a f t e r the document has been (accidentally) located, can now be satisfied. The interpretation of the complex is now accurate both as to its concrete wholeness and as to its discrete factualities.

The crucial point in this reform, after strict citation order for each main class, is the rigorous order of operations, as worked out in 'Toward explication of the rules of formation in UDC', ' , namely: *n, .n, 'n, n/n, -n, .On, .OOn, "n" (=n), (n), n+n, n:n, (On), =n.* This results, in regard to the mentioned complex code, in the following analysis:

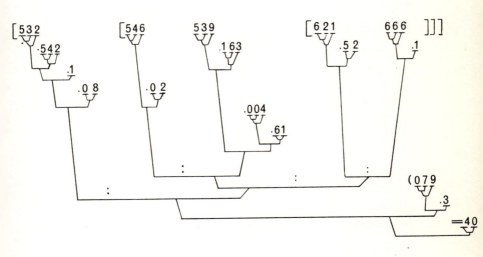

This is, in regard to the influence of the *.n* not entirely satisfactory: a better solution would exclude the *'n'* from the operational order entirely except where it is more than a courtesy (as in DC), namely except where it precedes O*n* or OO*n*. It might then be retained as a courtesy, and the comma used in its place in ,O*n* and ,OO*n*. Thus we get:

153

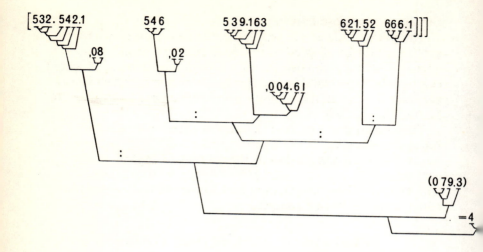

PROBLEMS OF DISPLAY (NOTATION)

A classificatory search-strategic system is necessarily less familiar than a verbal search strategy. Its notation is its manifestation, the way it displays itself. Accordingly, the adoption of a new classification in place of an old one entails the use of a less familiar notation, and the adoption of a n y classification entails the use of a system of display less familiar than a verbal search strategy. But there can be advantages, especially if we are concerned with international use, use with computers, *etc.*

Yet it is not to be denied that there is much to be improved in the notation of UDC, even if it has notable points of superiority over competitor-systems.

The opening essay here, 'On the ideal form of UDC schedules', attempts first of all to lay down the froundworks of any theory of notation; but again much is left out of a presentation designed for committee consumption. Still, it is to be hoped that this and the subsequent two essays can demonstrate the non-*ad hoc* possibilities of intelligibility and structural improvement that a theory can generate.

The essay 'A new notational device for achieving hospitality in array' is not very specifically oriented to UDC, though its motivation was a reaction against the move of class 4 to 8.07, seen as a means of opening up an additional class for science. It should be taken as something of an appendix to 'On the ideal form of UDC schedules'.

Yet another appendage to 'On the ideal form of UDC schedules' is the essay 'A new notational device to replace the apostrophe in UDC'. It is a slight thing, and is as unlikely as is the preceding essay to result in action; but it should be seen as part of what is entailed by many of the more substantial discussions earlier on. What is needed to come to the conclusion argued here is a systematic, transparent, theoretical view of UDC. Such a view is necessary in an age of increased reliance on logic and on logical machines, not just in order to capitalise on such techniques or to prevent their supporters from rejecting UDC as archaic, but even more to clarify our own processes of thought about what we are trying to accomplish as librarians and by means of libraries.

The last essay here, 'On the classification of multiple-attribute events and event-like documents', settles on deficiencies in the means of display of every search strategy with which I am familiar, and should be read along with 'Reflections on the relation between *general* and *special* in verbal search strategies'. Together they reflect a perhaps somewhat unfortunately Leibnizian view of information retrieval; but even so an improvement along these lines seems possible − the lines, that is, of making the elements of a conceptual complex the threads along which the searcher can grope when he is in the dark about just what he wants. (Note that the elements suggested here are elements i m m a n e n t to the concepts themselves, even to the conceptual e l e m e n t s; I am not suggesting the dissolution of the conceptual complex as the constituent item of the file itself.) Again, much further investigation is needed to see clearly where the suggestion put forth might lead us.[1]

1 A strikingly similar (though quite undeveloped) point is made in the just-received book by D Soergel, *Klassifikationssysteme und Thesauri; eine Anleitung zur Herstellung von Klassifikationssystemen und Thesauri im Bereich der Dokumentation*(Frankfurt am Main, Deutsche Gesellschaft fur Dokumentation, 1969), 58: 'Es ist meist so, dass eine durch einen Eigennamen gekenn zeichnete Dokumenta-

tionseinheit vermöge dieses Eigennamens bei der Suche nach verschiedenen allgemeineren Deskriptoren gefunden werden muss. ... *Diese Koppelung der Eigennamen mit allgemeineren Deskriptoren* muss in jedem Fall gerwährleistet sein. Sie lässt sich auf zwei Weisen erreichen: Entweder fügt der Aufschliesser die entsprechenden Deskriptoren hinzu [generic posting], oder (und diese Möglichkeit ist in Computer-Systemen vorzuziehen) man legt eine Liste der verwendeten Eigennamen an, der die entsprechenden Beziehungen zu allgemeineren Deskriptoren angegeben werden. Diese Liste bildet dann einen Anhang zum Klassifikationssystem ...'

157

XI

On the ideal form of UDC schedules

What needs to be said about the schedules of a system of
classification is not something substantive but rather something
formal. But the contents of the form of a classificatory schedule
is the substance of that classification. The relation of the two
elements is therefore not trivial — nor is it obvious

What should the relation between form and substance of a
classificatory schedule accomplish?

I

Formality is not the same as abstraction, just because it stands
over against substantiveness; formality too has its own independent manifestation[1]. This manifestation has two directions:
more nearly material is that of n o t a t i o n, more nearly
abstract is that of o r d e r.

As regards n o t a t i o n, there is a classification among
notations in terms of the syntactical levels on which they
operate. An ideal language would require several such levels if
a classificatory system is seen as an artificial language. At the
highest level is needed a: a set of phrase-openers and -closers,
either of various levels themselves, or capable of showing these
levels by being nested. At perhaps the lowest level is needed b:
a set of symbols indicating the function of the terms thus
introduced — their function within the expression, that is —
though clearly enough an even lower level is inhabited by the
terms thus introduced, though to discuss this is to enter into
entirely non-formal aspects of the classification. Between
levels a and b there may need to be several levels; in U D C we
find there the intermediate level c: these could be
called *combining functors.*

---

1 Thus we can see that the relation between formality and substantiveness is not
the same as that between form and matter as in scholastic philosophy.

In UDC level a includes $[n \ldots n]$, $(n \ldots n)$, and $"n \ldots n"$

In UDC level b includes $=n$, (On), $.OOn$, $-n$, $.On$, $"n"$, $(=n)$, (n), and $0/9$.

In UDC level c includes $n:n$, $n'n$, $n+n$, and n/n.

It is of interest to note the varying formalities: level a has symmetrical opening and closing marks around a partially symmetrical core; level c has partially symmetrical terms around a combining functor; level b has in some cases an unnecessary symmetry which could be eliminated by use of enclosing signs in wider variety, along with use of non-enclosing signs as b-level symbols [2].

As regards o r d e r, the formal order of the schedules can be seen as a paradigm of the orderliness of the resulting file, an orderliness that can lead to the predictability of searching for items in that file. In what does that orderliness consist?

Looking for instance at another classification's schedules, that of the Library of Congress Classification, a layout emerges characterisable as *general-before-special*, with groups of subdividing terms roughly of the same sort. Look for instance at class M_2 (1963), pp 99-111: HISTORY AND CRITICISM of VOCAL MUSIC is divided first by periods, then by countries, and then by problems (only one, VOCAL TECHNIQUE, appears); then comes CHORAL MUSIC (SACRED *AND* SECULAR); with the same sub-arrangement as for VOCAL MUSIC in general; then SECULAR VOCAL MUSIC, here with periods, places, and then KINDS AND FORMS; of these the first is DRAMATIC MUSIC, sub-arranged as before, coming down (p 103) to a second level of KINDS AND FORMS, without period and place sub-arrangement; then, coordinate with DRAMATIC MUSIC, comes SONGS (PART *AND* SOLO), sub-arranged by periods and places; then a second level of KINDS AND FORMS, namely first PART-SONGS (same sub-arrangement), then SOLO SONGS (same sub-arrangement); then, coordinate with SECULAR VOCAL MUSIC, comes SACRED VOCAL MUSIC, sub-arranged the same; as its special divisions are given various deneminational groups (each sub-arranged by periods and places), finally arriving at FORMS, the first only of which (ORATORIOS) is sub-arranged the same.

2 It does need to be noted that wherever an auxiliary code such as (43) could have attached to it an affix such as in (43-5) there is need for the enclosing terminal sign, lest the -5 be taken erroneously as a special auxiliary of the code preceding the (43).

159

A clear picture of faceting emerges within the general-before-special layout: *general* is the first, capable of being divided by form of presentation (though not actuated), *periods* is next most general, then *places,* then *media,* with, dependent on it, *musical forms;* and in such cases as require it, *users* (between media and musical forms). Problems arise often, because of lack of synthetic possibilities; in this regard UDC is notably superior to LC. But there are instances where the layout of UDC schedules could profit from a resemblance to those of LC, if at the same time the excessive repetition of the LC enumeration were pared away, leaving the fill-in to be accomplished by bringing auxiliaries into play.

782/784 in the abridged UDC English edition (BS 1000A: 1961) is arranged somewhat differently than is the LC example (ML1400-ML3275), and occupies only about a third of a page; yet it is capable of nearly the same specificity as is LC, though at the cost of some difficulty to the classifier; and it allows superior synthesis as well, though at some cost in difficulty of application.

To convey SACRED VOCAL MUSIC (=for chorus, in general) is simple in both cases, ML3200 in LC, 783.3 in UDC, both listed in their respective schedules. But in LC it is not easy to make a further specification by adding, say, 'in the Catholic liturgy'; this last concept puts us into ML3002- ML3051, but does not allow combination, so a choice would have to be made, a choice likely not to be followed in the next such case. In UDC we are lucky to be able to divide by :282. Again, the same primary subject should be divided by place in both classifications, but ML3200 in LC cannot be so divided though its special divisions can be.

This cannot legitimately lead to the conclusion that UDC is ideal in its schedule form, though it is handy and terse as compared with LC. For instance, programmatic tendencies can be the subject of discussion as regards any form of music; but the only place for PROGRAMME MUSIC in the UDC schedules is as a form of INSTRUMENTAL MUSIC; surely the whole topic of 'madrigalism' is an example of such an intersection of concepts. In UDC a rather forced solution might be to draw upon the special auxiliary ICONOLOGY, 7.04. A better solution, though, would be to more carefully analyse the possibility of concept synthesis within the discipline itself,

isolating facets of concepts (medium, style use, *etc*),and.
then laying out the schedule in such a way as to facilitate their
synthesis into codes representing the entities and/or subjects so
coded. Thus PROGRAMME MUSIC may be in various musical
forms: Strauss' *Don Quixote* is a theme-and-variations — again,
it is unusually *besetzt,* as a double concerto for viola and violon-
cello and orchestra. Each such level of concept is part of a clear
facet. It is the purpose of a classification to see these facets
(as even LC does), to arrange them in a general-before-special
order (as LC again does), and to provide the means of synthesising
them (as LC does not, and as UDC does — sometimes rather less
than elegantly).

To take a final example: in UDC 551.5 there has been an
attempt to isolate groups of concepts (those related to the
means of doing meteorology, to the *structure* of the atmosphere,
to *temperature, pressure, movement,* and *content* of the
atmosphere); but there is no particular order of these quasi-facets
such that complex codes can arise easily from their combination.
Again (as similar to the clumsiness of misleadingness of 784.1:
785.4 for 'madrigalism', or to the vagueness and exoticness of
784.1.04 for the same), the notation does not encourage
combination of codes to represent such a subject as 'influence of
atmospheric impurities on formation of rain during hurricanes',
which might come out such as 551.578.1:551.510.4:551.515—
which, if nothing else, is ridiculously redundant, as well as being
likely to be organised in several different patterns because of
lack of clear guidance from the schedule layout.

II

A notation can consist *a*: of a single radix, so segmented as
to represent its facets; *b*: of several radices, each representing a
separate facet; or *c*: of at least two radices, one representing the
substantive elements, the other the formal.

UDC is an example of a compromise between *a* and *c*, though
most would probably say that *c* predominates. A clearer schedule
layout would result from the thoroughgoing application of *c*
alone. Such a proposal would require (1) a better division of
the schedule of each discipline in terms of its constituent facets,
and a better general-before-special order thereto, leading to
easier rules for synthesis of complex codes; and (2) a wider
gamut of introductory signs such as .O*n* and–*n*. Probably a
superior solution would be to use alphabetic digits as the introductory signs, since they have the advantageous characteristic of

order a characteristic lacking in a punctuational radix as now used in UDC

Thus if the purely semantic element of UDC is represented by the decimal-numerical radix, and the functional element (facet indicators) by letters, the punctuational radix exclusive of enclosing signs can be used for combining functors, leaving the enclosing signs for purely syntactical use ('phrases' , 'sentences' , 'paragraphs' as in WRU telegraphic abstracts). It is also to be noted that this analysis leads to a separation between the classification *per se* (the systematic ordering of concepts) and documentary classification (the construction of expressions representing documents); this second operation and i t a l o n e require the higher levels of notational abstractness seen in the combining functors and the enclosing signs.

XII

A new device for achieving
hospitality in array

One of the most helpful advances in the notation of classification systems must be credited to Melvil Dewey: decimal numbers as against integers. The great benefit the use of decimals brings about is the possibility if infinite *hospitality in chain.* This type of *hospitality* is one of two postulated by S R Ranganathan as being necessary for successful translation from the *idea plane* of classification to the *notational plane.* The other necessary *hospitality is that in array.*

Hospitality in chain refers to that characteristic of a notation which allows unimpeded v e r t i c a l intercalation of new classes. If our classification scheme begins with two classes, 1 and 2 any new class will be subordinate to one of them, since by definition 1 + 2 exhausts the universe of knowledge. The first subordinate to 1 might thus be 1½. Further intercalations in chain (= subordinations) would be 1¼ *etc.* Dewey's contribution was in postulating the basic numbers not (as we have given them here) as integers, but as decimals. Subordination below 1 thus is first 15, intercalation in chain 105 , *etc.* (read, in order, as .1, . 105, .15).

This advantage was originally embodied in the Dewey Decimal Classification, and was adopted by the Universal Decimal Classification and the Colon Classification, but not by the Library of Congress Classification (though it has proven necessary in this last too, though in a somewhat un-overt way and for a somewhat different purpose).

However, the same notation that brings about (subordinating) hospitality in chain does not necessarily also bring about (coordinating) hospitality in array. Hospitality in array refers to that characteristic of a notation which allows unimpeded h o r i z o n t a l intercalation of new classes. If our classification begins by exhausting the universe of knowledge in classes 1 and 2 any new (*ie* previously unrecognised or unneeded) coordinate main class cannot fall anywhere but outside our numerical base; since, even in a decimal system (base: 0–9), there can be no number longer than one digit which can be on the same generic/specific level with 0, 1, ... 9.

The numerical base we have been using in illustrating the problem is admittedly unrealistically short; but even with a longer one we eventually come upon difficulties. (A short base is used just to make the problem occur at once.) No matter what our base number, even if we use the whole alphabet (as in LC, CC, and Bliss's Bibliographic Classification) there will come the moment when we need more coordinate classes than the notation supplies. Dewey tried to obviate the problem by establishing coordinate classes such as .1--.8 as specified divisions, with .9 left over for 'others' – *ie,* the unspecified divisions. But if the array .1--.8 is a systematic one (either canonically, chronologically, or even just alphabetically) it is obvious that the use of subdivisions of .9 for further coordinates to .1--.8 destroys the original order. LC tried to obviate the problem by not assigning all the available numbers when a given genus was broken up into its coordinate species; but

once these vacant numbers are exhausted, further intercalation must be accomplished by use of decimals, *etc.* [1] Ranganathan himself, using a decimal system enabling hospitality in chain, has come up with an ingenious device for the enabling of hospitality in array within the same decimal system: the *octavising* device.

With this device, the array is extendable past its base by the use of the last (or, if the last is needed for some other function, the next last) digit as the equivalent of a musical octave. The series of coordinates thus runs 1, 2, 3, 4, 5, 6, 7, 8, 91, 92, 93, 94, 95, 96, 97, 98, 991, . . . If a genus has (say) seventeen coordinate species, they can be accomodated on one coordinate level by 1–991.

But there seem to me to be heavy objections to the use of this device, either in optically or electronically scanned catalog records:

a: In the case of optically scanned records, there is the great

---

1 It is interesting to note that in a decimal system hospitality in c h a i n is achieved by (decimal) extension of numbers, whereas in an integral system (such as LC) the same device can be used to achieve hospitality in a r r a y.

difficulty which would attend its use, not only by the relatively untrained patron, but even by the relatively well trained librarian. And in the case of electronically scanned records, the desideratum of structural notation as a guide to the computer is lost, or at least would have to be regained by relatively complicated programming.

b: Even if these objections are rejected, there is still this: What is needed (if we aim at true hospitality in array) is not simply a means of e x t e n d i n g the coordinate series, but of i n t e r c a l a t i n g coordinates between extant coordinate classes. If .1 —8 is systematically arranged, and need arises to intercalate between .1 and .2, it does us no good to be able to add .91 as coordinate, because this divides the array at the wrong point. Nor can we use .15 since this is member to the array subordinate, not coordinate, to .1. So the solution must be sought in such a code as .191; and then a time will come when a new coordinate is needed between .18 and .191, yielding .1891; or between .191 and .192, yielding .19191, *etc.*

However, the use of a different punctuation (I would suggest the comma) would open the way to easy systematic intercalation of any desired generic/specific level, in a way far easier to comprehend (in an optically scanned system) and unnecessary to programme around (in an electronically scanned system).

If our original scheme were arranged thus:

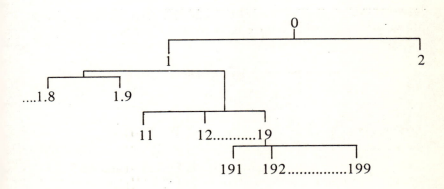

new coordinate classes at any level could be intercalated by use of commas:

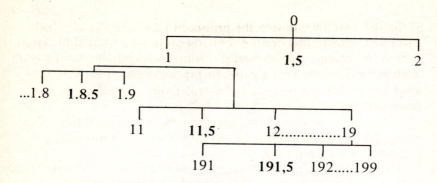

which could of course themselves be subdivided further:

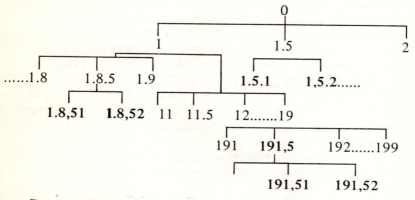

Between the original intercalations and the original order new intercalations could of course have plentiful space:

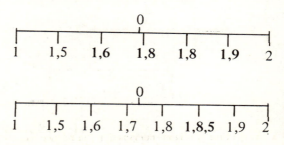

until need arose for repetition of the comma as inter-intercalators.

166

By use of such a device the proposed UDC change of main class 4 to indicate classes $5 + 6$ [2] would be rendered unnecessary: 5,5 would be superior in several obvious ways. By use of the comma device, the LC coordinating intercalator (the decimal point) could become the comma, and decimals could become s u b ordinating devices there as well[3].

3 At the time of original composition this seemed a likely goal – though after four tears there is less to fear in that direction, but little to hope for in any other.

2 For a brief discussion, see D Soergel, *Klassifikationssysteme und Thesauri; eine Anleitung zur Herstellung von Klassifikationssystemen und Thesauri im Bereich der Dokumentation* (Frankfurt am Main, Deutsche Gesellschaft für Dokumentation, 1969), 133-134.

XIII

A new notational device to replace the apostrophe in UDC

There has been a certain degree of muttering, among users of and theoreticians interested in the UDC, against the narrowness of application of the apostrophe (*n'n*). Why not, they say, achieve the same economisation outside the too-few 5- and 6-sub-classes in which (*n'n* is allowed? Instead of 141.131:141.22 *Pessimism as taught by the Neo-Platonists,* why not allow 141.131'22 ?

Thus it is recognised that *n'n* is only a shorthand colon. 546.13'33 is precisely identical in meaning with 546.13:546.33, though it is so commonly used to mean *chemical compound* that at least some of the troublesome ambiguities of the colon seem to be excluded. But of course that is not the case, since alloys, *etc ,* just as much as compounds, can be shown with the apostrophe.

In terms of a classification of the various signs used in the UDC, then, *n'n* belongs to that class which can be called Syntactical-semantic, which also includes its normal form *n:n*, as well as *n+n* and *n/n*. What I hope to justify is what follows is the expansion of a technique commonly applied to one of these to all of them. The technique to which I refer is that used for economisation of double codes joined by *n/n*.

When the two codes joined by *n/n* begin differently, the whole of each must obviously be written out, 5/6. Even when the two codes so joined begin similarly, no economisation is possible unless the two codes are more than three digits in length: 621/622 cannot be written 621/2; and 621/7 for 621/627 (or −?−for 621/67) is even worse. But 621.1/621.3 is silly when you can write 621.1/.3; 78.033.2/78.033.3 is sillier when you can write

---

1 The others are the Semantic 0/9 or the vocabulary proper, the Categoric .O*n*, −*n*, (*n*) (=*n*), "*n*", =*n* or the indicators of subordinate facets, and the purely Syntactical [*n . . .n*] . These can very easily be arranged in an order of increasing abstractness: Semantic, Categoric, Syntactical-semantic, and Syntactical − beyond which (in terms of abstractness) stand the Boolean operators as used in such techniques as are described in the AIP/UDC reports of Freeman and Atherton.

Now from these examples we can generalise a rule for the interpretation of n/n — a rule equally applicable to $n+n$ and $n:n$ —, namely

      a: What stands to the right in n/n, if it i s a numerical digit is the first digit of a code of the same category as that to which the whole code to the left in n/n belongs [examples: 5/6 "1895/1903", (7/8)] ; this code is the terminus of an aggregate class begun from the code to the left in n/n. *b*: What stands to the right in n/n, if it is n o t a numerical digit, must be a decimal point [examples: 546.1/.2, "1895.12.25/.26", (731.5/.67)] ; the partial code that follows such a decimal point has the same rank within its truncated code [example: .26" in "1895.12 .25/.26" has had truncated from it "1895.12] as that group-of-numbers-preceded-by-a-decimal which is to the left of the slash has [example: .26" is of the same rank as .25, n o t of the same rank as .12; to slash between days in d i f f e r e n t months would require "1895.11.30/.12.25"].

This may seem forced or difficult, but it is merely an explication of what everyone intuitively takes n/n to mean. (It is also explicit enough, I hope, to allow for programming of search of such codes with computer, without the need for cumbersome writing out of all the intervening codes.)

Precisely the same rules for construction and interpretation can now be applied to the $n+n$ and $n:n$. The objection that there are different meanings conveyed by each of the three signs is trivially true, but is no real deterrent.

Of course, it can be argued fairly nontrivially that the earlier classification of signs is too gross; that n/n is in a class by itself between the Syntactical-semantic $n+n$ and $n:n$ on the one hand and the purely Syntactical [$n. . .n$] on the other, or even that n/n is a purely Syntactical sign. Still, its o p e r a t i o n is so strongly similar to that governing $n+n$ and $n:n$ that I would argue from that operational similarity even were I convinced of the sign-classificatory dissimilarity.

We then get, for 19(430) + 19(438), 19(430+438); for 621.83+621.94, 621.83+.94; for 947.9+947.7, 947.0+.7; this follow follows clearly from the operational similarity that makes 19 (430/ 438) equivalent to 19(430)19(438), 621.83/.94 equivalent to 621.83/621.94, and 947.0/.7 equivalent to 947.0/947.7. Obviously, then, there is no need to export *n'n* out of 5/6 to economise 141.131:141.22; it is easy enough to write 141.131:.22, and none could misinterpret it any more than they could 141.131/.22. This of course means that *n'n* is not needed at all for the sense in which it has been used. Instead of 546.13'33 we can now write 546.13:.33, and leave *n'n* free for functions where no sign is at present available.

XIV

On the classification of multiple-attribute
events and event-like documents

In the surrogation of documents dealing with individual
members of certain classes of events it is often found either *a*:
that not all the attributes defining such an individuum can
conveniently be indicated in every case of such surrogational
mention (usually for reasons of economy), *b*: that some
documents may concern themselves only with a selected set of
attributes, while other documents concern themselves with (at
least partially) different sets of attributes, *c*: that the indexing/
classificatory language in use for surrogation normally lacks the
synthetic capability of indicating all attributes predicable of such
an individuum, or *d*: (and perhaps most important) that new
attributes may come to be noted or discovered as predicable
of such individua.

Such an analysis might at first seem most appropriate to
indexing/classification of documents in the humanities, which
themselves a r e the event-like individua. For instance, such a
document as a musical score can have predicated of it its
tonality, its *Besetzung,* its form, its period, but this certainly
does not exhaust the possibilities; conditions *a, c,* and *d* may
apply to the surrogation of such a score. Besides the obvious
economic consideration (condition *a*), and the fact that few if
any available classifications can do more than take a choice
between significant attributes [1] (condition *c*), new attributes
(or already known but apparently unimportant ones) can later
be discovered or be seen to be of value (condition *d*).

Documents a b o u t such scores (*etc*) may also embody condition *b* in that (with Strauss' *Don Quixote* as example) one such

---

1 Take as example R Strauss' *Don Quixote,* which can be classified among program
music, concerti (double) for violoncello/viola and orchestra, pieces in D major,
theme-with-variations, *etc*, or among works of its periods or among works by
German composers – but in no classification system by more than a few such
attributes.

study may concentrate on the variation-technique in terms of the period of origin of the score, another may concentrate on the modulation-style in terms of the solo-*Besetzung*[2], *etc.*

But there are event-like classes of individua in other than humanistic documentation. For instance, earthquakes are a class of events, to each of which can be attributed its epicenter; its media properties; its force on the Gutenberg scale, *etc*; its path in mantle, crust, or core; its depth of focus, *etc.* But economic considerations make it more normal to find each earthquake simply named, or the simplest available set of attributes — epicenter+time would normally be considered sufficient, along with whatever other attribute is thematic to the document being surrogated — predicated of it. This prevents the retrieval of all documents dealing with this event in searches in which an attribute is being used as i n d i c a t o r o f a l l t h e i n d i v i d u a t o w h i c h i t i s a t t r i b u t e d.

And even more important, when a new attribute is discovered to apply to an event previously not so characterised, the only way to connect it with all previous documents referring to that event would be a retrospective re-indexing of all such documents (condition *d*).

In a computerised system it is easily possible to set up a table of attributes of events and event-like documents. This would prevent the need for exhaustive attribute predications of such events at the time of each surrogation of a document referring to them (satisfying condition *a*); it would allow retrieval of documents referring to events or event-like documents even when the referring document do not mention such attributes (satisfying condition *b*); it would relieve the pressure for synthesis of classificatory notation except for thematic concerns of documents[3] (satisfying condition *c*); and it would enable attributes

2 It should be noted that events and event-like documents always possess the
t o t a l set of predicable attributes of that class of individua, whereas documents
that are merely thematically a b o u t topics may wholly ignore any but o ñ e
attribute of each such topic.
3 It should be noted that the pressure for synthetic representation of the attributes
of referred-to events and of event-like documents, in face of low capabilities in
this regard in almost all available classifications, leads to cross-classifications;
surrogation would better be severely restricted to attributes thematic to the
document (as regards secondary documents) and to nominal arrangements of one
sort or another (*cf* J M Perreault, 'The classification of philosophy', *Libri*, xiv/1
(1964) 32-39 and 'The catalog and the problems of bibliography', *Libri*, xv/4
(1965) 291-301) for those classes of documents referred to above as *event-like* —
commonly called *form-classes.*

recently discovered or recognised to be predicated of the characterised event or event-like document in the tables alone (and in the actual codification of whichever non-eventlike, secondary document for which the new attribute is thematic), thus eliminating retrospective posting (satisfying condition *d*).

It should be apparent that this technique provides a relatively inexpensive device for integration of data retrieval into an information (=citation) retrieval system, and not merely in the science (where data retrieval and indeed almost all sophisticated citation retrieval techniques are at present applied) but in the humanities and in the social sciences (as in the gradual accretion of information about an archaeological site, an election, a battle, a work of art).

The form that this technique would take would resemble that of an authority file. Attached to a conventionalised nominal entry such as 'Strauss, Richard, 1864-1949. [Don Quixote]', or to the name of an earthquake, would be a string of such attributes as were mentioned in footnote 1, or in paragraph 4; each such attribute, accessible to the computer, can call up all the embodiments of each work, or references to each event, in whose authorisation it figures, without that attribute being part of the surrogation of any particular embodiment of that work, *etc.* New attributes can be added to the authority-file for the work, or event, as they are discovered or seen to be of value, and will function just as did each member of the original set of attributes.

An attribute opined as being predicable by a secondary work will first of all be treated as an element in the thematic surrogation of that secondary work, and will then be added to the set of attributes authorised for the work or event, of which it is predicated--perhaps with an accompanying symbol indicative of its status as opinion rather than fact.

II

Two comparisons come to mind in connection with this technique. The first refers to the 'Ethnologic Atlas' planned by George P Murdock in volume 1 number 1 of the journal whose editorship he assumed upon leaving the Human Relations Area

173

Files, *Ethnology* (1962)[4]. This is not an atlas in the common sense, but a bibliographical inventory of the attributes of the tribes of interest to ethnologists, set up in a matrix in which the *yes* symbol at an intersection shows such an attribute (as defined by that column) to be predicated of such a tribe (as defined by that row). There is also a listing of the bibliographic sources of these predications, but there is no link set up between the two parts — matrix and listing.

The similarity to the earlier-suggested technique consists in the fact that the emergence of new opinions over time can gradually fill in the picture of that tribe in terms of its attributes. But notice that these secondary works express opinions which may contradict those of other secondary works; one flaw in Murdock's plan is the lack of a link between the matrix and the listing — whence we cannot determine which of the various bibliographic sources found which of the contradictory opinions. In the technique suggested earlier, the presence of such an attribute as would contradict another is traceable to its blibliographic source by virtue of the thematic posting of this attribute in the surrogate of that document.

The second comparison refers to a succession of publications: Nicholas Rescher's paper 'On the probability of nonrecurring events'[5], Phyllis Richmond's paper 'Contributions toward a new generalized theory of classification'[6], and Eric de Grolier's report *On the theoretical basis of information retrieval systems*[7]. Rescher's point that the distinction between the sciences and the humanities is founded on the higher degree of abstraction in the sciences — the humanities remaining at the level of non-recurring and hence unpredictable e v e n t s — is only incidental to his main point (which we shall not concern ourselves with),

4   Since then Murdoch has published *Ethnographic atlas* (Pittsburgh, University of Pittsburgh Press, 1967), which represents the *tribe/attribute matrix accompanies* by citations of the journal locations of the appropriate bibliographical inventory — but again only in the same undifferentiated way that was found in the journal.

5   *Current issues in the philosophy of science; symposia of scientists and philosophers* (Proceedings of Section L of the American Association for the Advancement of Science, 1959), *ed* H Feigl and G Maxwell (New York, Holt, Rinehart and Winston, 1961), 228-224.

6   *Classification research; proceedings,* International Study Conference on Classificatio Research,*ed* P A Atherton (Copenhagen, Munksgaard, 1965), 39-54.

7   Air Force Office of Scientific Research, Contract AF61(052) - 505 (Paris, 1965), 160-162; much the same point, in much the same words, occurs in the discussion following Richmond's paper (*Classification research*, 61).

but is the basis for Richmond's notion of informative classification. De Grolier takes Richmond's further point, 'that [by
the device of informative classification] levels of ideas can be
mixed with levels of "things" '8, as indicative of 'a grossly
exaggerated separation between two categories of phenomena
which are thus considered as fundamentally different and
in incommensurate'9.

He goes on to quote H J Uldall's *Outline of glossematics* 10
(in close agreement with E Benveniste's attack 11 on the Aristotelian
categories, calling them linguistic only and not ontological) to the
effect that the humanities cannot become scientific because they
cling to the distinction between things and attributes, substance
and accidents, whereas the sciences become such

> by resignation, by being willing to do one thing at a
> time, by a rigid selection of a set of functions as necessary
> and sufficient for unambiguous description, *ie* by
> abstraction.12

For deGrolier this constitutes an anticipatory refutation of
Rescher and Richmond, which is strange in view of the clear
impression one receives from reading Rescher's paper that he
sees precisely the same distance between the human sciences
and the natural sciences; again, de Grolier comes part of the way
toward the technique outlined above when he says

> that, for an historian of art, classification of 'The
> Last Supper' might, indeed, by 'illuminating', if it
> is detailed enough to show some pertinent traits
> from the point of view of the frescoe's technique, the
> Christian iconography, the style, etc. which will
> suggest explanatory comparisons.13

Nor does this really contradict Rescher, who distinguishes
between nonrecurring events, which have attributes by

8 Quoted in de Grolier, *op cit*, 160.
9 *Ibidem*, 161.
10 Pt I: *General theory* (Copenhagen: Nordisk Sprog- og Kulturforlag, 1957).
11 Emile Benveniste, 'Catégories de pensée et catégories de langue' (*Les etudes
   philosophiques*, ns,xiii/4 (1958); repr in his *Problèmes de linguistique générale*
   (Paris, Gallimard, 1966), 63-74.
12 Quoted in de Grolier, *op cit*, 161-162, referring to Uldall, *op cit*, 10-11.
13 De Grolier, *op cit*, 161.

which they can be 'grouped with others into a class', and
recurring events, whose membership, in attribute-
classes 'illuminate the classified event itself, by yielding some
additional information about it,[13] –which reveals Rescher's
concern for d i a g n o s t i c knowledge, whereas de Grolier
hopes for no more than c o m p a r a t i v e. This last is all that
the technique as outlined is intended to allow.

Finally, it should be noted that Richmond's *levels of ideas*
and *levels of things* are not intended as metaphysical (as
de Grolier seems to think), but is simply a way of articulating
her dissatisfaction with the chronologically early stages of
development of the theory of integrative levels in classification,
a stage at which all *mentefacts* were placed at the level of
human beings, while a large number of levels were given over
to *animals* and lower levels – a fact that would put a larger
proportion of classifiable documents into a single level of the
system. A means then must be found to provide levels for
i d e a s as well as for t h i n g s.

III

To return to the central point, let us attend to those headings
in LC's system of subject headings which are capable of having
individua as their immediate lower members, such as BATTLE-
SHIPS. There are three devices in which the authority-file and
the resultant public catalogue can lead the searcher to such
individua: *a*: by an unexplicit direction to also consult the
headings for such individua (without naming any of them);
b: by an explicit direction to consult the heading for such
individua (by naming each such individuum in the
sa mode); and *c*; by a compromise between *a* and *b, ie*
by giving (an) example(s) of the individua that may need to be
consulted.

Device *a* is particularly unhelpful in that the searcher must
call to mind each possible individual lower member, examining
the file to see whether it is represented by a heading; an example
of it can be seen *s v* RACE HORSES, '*also names of individual
race horses*' in LCSH$_{6-7}$. Device *b* is the most desirable, but it
must be remembered that such an example of it as can be
found *sv* INDIANS OF NORTH AMERICA is appropriate only

14 Rescher, *op cit*, 230.

to the Library of Congress itself or to a library with that diverse a collection, lest the prohibition of blind references be violated. Device *c*, as exemplified *s v* TREATIES, *also . . . names of treaties, eg* Portsmouth, Treaty of, 1905' is an appropriate solution only if it is felt that without it the searcher might well not know what is meant by the direction, and that an example is sufficient to show him how to proceed. But there can always be gained a further advantage to the searcher by going all the way to *b*.

Now note that such an individuum as ADMIRAL GRAF SPEE (BATTLESHIP) as a lower member of BATTLESHIPS might well be sought also as an individuum representing the class ARTILLERY, since it was the presence of eleven-inch artillery on it that cause it to be regarded as a treaty-violator. The authority file for this individuum might well read

ADMIRAL GRAF SPEE (BATTLESHIP)
xx
ARTILLERY.
BATTLESHIPS.

That for the sculptor-painter-architect-poet Michelangelo could read

BUONARROTI, MICHEL ANGELO, 1475-1564
xx
ARCHITECTS, ITALIAN.
ARCHITECTURE, ITALIAN.
ARCHITECTURE, RENAISSANCE.
ITALIAN POETRY–17th CENTURY.
PAINTERS, ITALIAN.
PAINTING, RENAISSANCE.
POETS, ITALIAN.
SCULTORS, ITALIAN.
SCULPTURE, ITALIAN.

The objection is not unlikely that not every document (indeed, few!) concerned with Michelangelo will thematically concern itself with his literary efforts; and thus that many of them will be irrelevant to a search for Michelangelo as poet. One solution of course is to post individual as well as specific headings, but then

the economisation that is assumed to obtain from the use of *sa*
references would disappear, since in that case virtually all
species and genera of the particular individuum would require
posting[15]. But this objection is invalidated by observation of
the fact of Michelangelo's having united these disparate attributes
in his own career-event: each document concerned with his
sculpture alone and with no mention whatsoever of his poetry
is *de facto* relevant to a search for documents relevant to his
poetry, since Michelangelo-the-sculptor i s the same 'event' as
is Michelangelo-the-poet.

In a classificatory situation (as against the subject-headings
considered above) the relative index to the schedules can be of
great utility, indicating all the contexts to which the individual ever
or event like document is subordinable; the index to the actual
classed file would of course only show such contextual subordinations as had been actualised. The structural hierarchicality
of the notation would make possible such computer retrievals as
Michelangelo when the search is for *all individua to which can
be attributed both 'madrigal-poet' and 'architect'* (which could
also retrieve, if he in fact has composed madrigal-texts, and if it
has been so recorded in our electronically searchable index/authority
file) Buckminster Fuller. Again, it is possible when we use an
ad-hoc synthesizable classification such as UDC or CC, to attach
to such index entries whole complex expressions (probably
tagged as opinion or allegation as against universally accepted
fact).

For example: Walter Hilton is alleged to be the author of the
mystical work *The cloud of unknowing,* which could be argued
to be heterodox in the direction of Montanism; this particular
heresy could be argued to have as an attribute that its origin
could be explained in terms of the over-influence of women in
theological affairs; Hilton himself was medieval (*ca* 1340-1396),
English, and Augustinian. With devices such as I suggest implanted
in such a system as UDC, and with a computer available to perform
the searches, one could retrieve the *Cloud* as the point of con-
vergence of the influences of St Augustine and of feminism in

15 It could of course be argued (as I do in the essay above, 'Reflections on the
relation between *general* and *special* in verbal search strategies') that such
generic posting is equivalent, in its effect, to u p w a r d s *sa* references from
individuum to species, from species to genera, *etc.* The use of an analytico-
synthetic classification, displayed in an appropriately structural-hierarchical
notation, automatically secures this advantage – both in terms of economisation
and (more important by far) of assistance in searching.

178

medieval southern Europe.

Examples of such computerisable association chains in the exact sciences and in the social sciences would not be difficult to formulate.

UDC AND RECLASSIFICATION

Attempts to demonstrate the superiority of UDC in a theoretical way seem to have little resonance in the chambers of bibliothecal power. Accordingly, it seemed necessary to become more openly a polemicist against the system which, at least in the USA, bids fair to become dominant. Such a dominance is particularly disharmonious with the incursion of computing devices and techniques into information retrieval work, most of all when a system which would produce far greater benefits is being ignored – and that system is of course UDC. The three essays here are presentations, for a variety of audiences, of a basic argument: f i r s t decide what system can accomplish the most for you, t h e n concern yourself with cost; and indeed, why not look for a way to beat down the cost of the best, rather than meekly accepting a cheaper but less beneficial product?

XV

Comparative classification for administrators :
a short sermon

American libraries are growing more rapidly than was
expected; perhaps even more rapidly than the libraries around
the world. Among libraries that are not growing in absolute
size, there is a more rapid rate of inclusion and exclusion, thus
requiring an even faster means of making use of the material held
there for so short a time.

Librarians managing such pressurised institutions are aware
of increasing needs for rapid and efficient access to their
monumental and/or rapidly changing collections. There can be
no sentimentality about processing departments and their
traditional (but growing) backlogs: the material must get out on
the shelves and into the catalogues so it can be used! From all
these pressures have come the movement toward automatization,
the use of simple computer-produced catalogues such as KWIC,
size-storage, and centralised catalogueing and classification.

Such devices have their uses, when their limitation are
understood. And their usefulness can be increased if ways can
be found to overstep these limitations while retaining the speed–
advantage of each basic technique. This paper (as are two longer
ones[1] upon which it is based) is primarily concerned with the
devices of automatisation and centralisation. It is the headlong
rush to reclassification with LC, as a supposedly invariable corollary of acceptance of centralised Library of Congress
cataloguing, that represents to many the great danger today,
particularly to libraries also in process of automatisation. What is
needed, as preliminaries to that decision (or to alternatives to
it), is the development of a body of insights into
comparative classification.

Such a title may suggest an austere and erudite discipline,

1 'On bibliography and automation: or, how to reinvent the catalogue' (*Libri*
  xv/4 (1965), 287-339, and 'reclassification: some warnings and a proposal'
  (Illinois University. Graduate School of Library Science. *Occasional papers*,
  no 87) (the second reprinted above).

183

and one cannot deny that, in its most developed forms, it is such. But it can perhaps be shown in a few fairly easy examples how it can be utilised, and what sort of conclusions can be drawn from it.

The two longer papers aforementioned have been concerned to develop, as the over-archingly guiding principle of all library service—whether conventional or automatised, public, or university/ research, in a single institution or in a network, in public service *per se* or in non-public service such as acquisitions searching — the principle of *search strategy*, which can best (or most economically) be phrased W h a t, t h e n, n e x t? — that is, what steps can be taken after the failure of the first attempt to provide that which will meet the patron's need.

These two key concepts, comparative classification and search strategy, are not often found among the armoury of administrators, to whom falls the decision which can be based only upon them; administrators have their own species of reasons, which need not be recited here, all presupposing a state of 'everything else being equal. . .' Comparative classification and the need for a search strategy together, though, can eliminate that only apparent state, and thus leave the administrator faced with issues other than purely administrative ones. Indeed, for administrators to have so long allowed themselves to be so little aware of the developing theory of library service as search strategy, even in such diverse thinkers as Metcalfe and Ranganathan, bespeaks a need for a new invigoration of the profession — probably possible only through the library schools.

Why do we sometimes become biased against a particular classification? If we have only one document on twentieth-century Magyar lyrical poetry, and it is all we have on Magyar literature, we may well rebel at DC_{17} which yields a code like 894.51110409003. If the document just prior is coded 894.3 ('Turkic literature'), and that just posterior is 894.6 ('Paleosiberian literature'), and may well say that the middle code is over-developed, and almost ridiculously so. Yet in our subject headings, where adjacent entries are often not conceptually related, we do not object to one entry with a couple of subdivisions coming between two unsubdivided entries, alphabetically prior and posterior[2]. Nor, in a classification where the notation is non-structural and does not attempt to represent lower classificatory orders by extensions of the code, but simply numbers each node in the tree consecutively [3], would it be resented if a document bearing a simple code for a c o m p l e x idea were preceded and succeeded by documents bearing simple codes for s i m p l e ideas.

DC is under serious attack, especially DC_{17}, and for serious reasons. Yet these reasons are not truly fundamental; nor are they leading toward solutions which are fundamentally ameliorative of a sticky situation. Since the first need in library service is for search strategy (an answer to *What, then, next?*) a structure must be provided to help patrons and reference personnel discover the next-most-relevant documents. The two major types of such structure are *syndesis* (characteristic of subject-headings) and *juxtaposition* (characteristic of notational classification).

Syndesis, and subject headings along with it, might be perfectable, but surely a great effort would be required, and the present structure would need to be replaced at one blow by its successor. It seems better then to recommend a shift to a wholly new mode of search strategy, one to be dominated by juxtaposition: in a word, the classed catalogue.

What is classification? Most American librarians can think only of shelf-arrangement as the answer, but this is far from all. And the resistance to classification as search strategy is based on dissatisfaction with currently available models, primarily DC and LC. Thus by a strange dialectic the majority of American library administrators have come to distrust all classification and to place their whole search-strategic trust in subject headings — which, however, are neither perfect for conventional libraries nor even remotely sensible for automatised searching.

Why is classification as search strategy resisted? What is one to think of a system that arranges but does not reveal its mode of

2 For instance, as chosen from *Sears$_9$*: *HUNGARY | HUNGARY–HISTORY –REVOLUTION, 1956–ADDRESSES AND ESSAYS–BIBLIOGRAPHY | HUNTING*

3 *Eg*

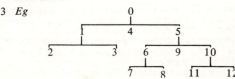

arrangement?[4] What of a system where the same concept can be predicted to be in a large number of different places, depending on relatively minor connotational differences as interpreted by cataloguers? What of a system which gives only one available search-strategic pathway, even from an initial point of attack that is complex[5], and thus m u s t require s e v e r a l such pathways?

What we do with such a system is to cease to expect such a function from it; we call is a shelf-arrangement, and thus effectively cease to need to think about it seriously.

But classification so characterised is not much of a representative of the family; where shall we find a better? In fact, several better ones are available: BC (Bliss' Bibliographic Classification), CC (Ranganathan's Colon Classification), and UDC (the Universal Decimal Classification) would all do what is needed. A few reasons are given in the aforementioned paper on 'Reclassification' for possibly opting for the last of these — primarily in terms of its strong family resemblance to DC, and hence its greater familiarity— but they will not be repeated here at any length. The one thing to be absolutely clear about however, is that the above-mentioned defects of DC and LC are not characteristic of UDC. It is nearly ideal as a search strategy[6] in that it orders concepts hierarchically (but only after having separated out the elements of complex ones), its notation is structural (so that it can be ritually manipulated) and general-categoric (following, that is, the separation of the elements of complex concepts). In other words, with it you d o know what to try next, the first point of attack having proved unsuccessful; and you know so f r o m t h e c o d e i t s e l f,

---

4 It is generally assumed that this objection cannot touch alphabetically arranged catalogues; but I will show in a subsequent work (*The idea of order: an essay in bibliographical systematics*) that this is not a really nonproblematical area at all,

5 In our earlier example, the next most relevant document is not necessarily that on twentieth-century Magyar poetry in general, since we may have no such; it may be one on twentieth-century Finno-Ugrian lyric poetry, but what do we have available in the given code to allow an economical and rapid transfer of our attention thence?

6 I cannot claim, in fairness, that any available general classification or subject-heading system is really p e r f e c t; all that is fair to do is to make a comparison in which we choose the best of the candidates in terms of the criteria recognized. It has been suggested that a thoroughly presuppositionless attempt to establish goals and criteria of performance would be advisable, and I must admit to a certain sympathy for such an undertaking; but there is a more immediate need, for which more immediate solutions are required.

not from your grasp of its semantic
contents. In the cited example. 'twentieth-century
Magyar lyrical poetry', the UDC code 894.511-14"19"
uses a sub-code for 'lyrical poetry' that is uniform in all
cases under class 8 ('literature'); thus if the best available
document is on 'twentieth-century Finno-Ugrian
lyrical poetry' the code is still recognisably relevant: 894.5-14
"19". Similarly with 'twentieth-century Magyar poetry [of all
types]', 894.511-1"19", or Magyar lyrical poetry [of all
periods]'. 894.511-14; or, varying more than one facet at a
time, 894.5-1"19"; or, adding in additional facets, 894.511-2-14
"19" (-2 means 'drama'; or, both adding in and varying) 894-2-14
"15/19". In each such code, simple programmed recognition
would indicate the degree of distance of the examined document-
surrogate from the initial search-specification. What more do we
expect from a classification, whether it be for shelf-arrangement,
as the basis for a classed catalogue, or as the basis for electronic
searching?

LC cannot do any of these things for us; it has, as mentioned,
probably been a large factor in the general disaffection with
classification in the minds of American librarians and documentalists. Why then change to it? Why indeed!

For the sake of monetary advantage, that's why! What
service outside of the Library of Congress printed cards offers
us as large a proportion[7] of classificatory work ready-done? None.
What other service offers us descriptive cataloging along with
this ready-made shelflist and shelf-arrangement information?
And do any other offer us a catalogue-arranging and search-
strategic device in addition to these other advantages? No.

But what good are these advantages in light of what we want
to accomplish? No good, if we can see significant differences
between available classifications, some better and some worse
(in terms of purpose and its achievement); a great deal, it
would seem, if we cannot see such differences, since in that
case we should look for a way to save money for purposes
which c a n be affected by excellence.

This essay argues that there are such significant differences,
and that our primary purpose is the provision of documentary
relevances; hence we must choose the means for the

7   Even though small enough to cause problems for a really large and/or
    rapidly growing library. Also see P A Richmond. 'Switch without
    deliberation' (Library journal, xci (October 15 1966), 4870).

achievement of this purpose, doing as well as we can within the financial constraints that such a choice imposes. And library administrators must do so too; they must be, in the fullest sense, librarians. This does not just mean possessors of library degrees, but rather persons oriented to the true purpose of libraries. As administrators in the narrow sense they may need to take refuge with the wise counsel of their technical personnel, but they must not rest content if these are unable to outline to them the relations between input and output, cataloging (and classification) and reference, information storage and information retrieval. If they cannot find reference librarians who know the details of classification theory nor cataloguers who know the details and needs of reference work, they must become librarians on their own and find out for themselves.

The *classed catalogue*, then, arranged by UDC, is possibly ✓ a far better solution than would be reclassification to LC, which does not really attack the central problem at all. But even if none can be persuaded to adopt the classified catalogue, a search strategy such as UDC can be extremely helpful in t h e s e a r c h o f e l e c t r o n i c a l l y s t o r e d c a t a l o g u e s which are the by-products of library automatisation. Only, however, if libraries either do their own tape-store cataloging by UDC (which those who know it would feel is not such a terrible problem), or if they can get such information externally (and centrally) ready-made. Therefore, a widespread agitation appears warranted in favour of such a centralisation of service coming about by the establishment (at the Library of Congress perhaps, or cooperatively by the Library of Congress and the British National Bibliography) of an agency to do what is now being done in terms of LC and DC codes—the assignment of UDC codes to a large proportion of the monographic literature. Indeed, this could be made an even more helpful project if such companies as Bowker and Wilson were to index by UDC, so that the card-or page-catalogue, as well as external bibliographies contributing to the same searches, were to utilise the same rather than a pointless variety of strategies. The shelves, then, could continue to be arranged by DC or by partial UDC codes, or even by LC (though the essential browsing function would be lost thereby).

The Library of Congress has always said that its classification was a private system; let's let them have it back.

XVI

Reclassification:
some warnings and a proposal

0.1   **Prelude**

Classification can be the arrangement of documents
on the shelf; it can also be the arrangement of the surrogates of those documents in the catalogue. Subject headings
can hardly be the first, though they certainly are the second. But
forgetfulness of the purpose of all these modes of arrangement
(namely, their function as a strategies for the searching out of
documentary information either known or unknown to be available) has led to non-application of over-arching guiding principles
in the arrangement of both catalogues and shelves. When these
principles are once more brought to consciousness, we can
establish criteria for the judging of all varieties of search
strategies; when they are not, criteria of wrong sorts must
instead come into play, leading to disastrous results both in
terms of quality of service and of expenditure of funds.

That the disastrousness of these results is not even noticed is
a perfect demonstration of the lack of adequate criteria and of
the principles in which they originate. The current rush to reclassify to the Library of Congress classification (LC) is one
example of such a result stemming from criteria of the wrong
sort — criteria arising in the absence of guiding principles. Such
warnings are made here in terms of the presence or absence of
such principles, criteria, and operations; but a proposal is also
made: to reclassify to the Universal Decimal Classification
(UDC). This proposal, to be as effective practically as it is
theoretically, must imply the establishment of logistical
means to compete for the market with LC, *etc*; but there
are serious hurdles to be overcome in such an establishment.

Reclassification is a problem accentuated by the present
movement to automatise general libraries; such automatisation
should call forth re-examination among librarians as well as documentalists (whatever the distinction, if any, except in terms of

willingness to re-examine) of what our fundamental purposes are and of how we can best meet them. It is often, unfortunately, only the wedge with which to insert un-reflective reclassification into the context of total change. Automatisation can lead – and perhaps must lead – to new ways of meeting old purposes as well as new; what follows should be taken as referring to the automatisation situation even more than to libraries still conventional at least in the means of service.

1.1   Occasions, of various sorts

American librarians can hardly be unaware of a galloping tendency, whenever any particular institution begins to fear that its mode of internal arrangement is inadequate, for the response to be something like: 'All right, then, we had better reclassify to LC.' This is so, whether because of unprecedented growth, because of growing demands for utilisation – with a concomitant pressure for the release of energy and money from the non-public-contact sectors of its work – or because of dissatisfaction with the mode of internal arrangement in use[1]. Why this response is so predictable is one part of what will be discussed below; why it is unfortunate in the extreme, together with what could be done as a superior alternative, is another part. It would be interesting to speculate as to whether any libraries now using LC, and in a position of saturation analogous to that of libraries now planning to change from the Dewey Decimal Classification (DC) to LC, have any clear idea of how they can escape from the analogous difficulties.

Three recent personal contacts have been additional occasions for the present essay; with Phyllis Richmond, who, in her address 'General advantages and disadvantages of using the LC system'[2], attempts to set down a foundation of more than mere expediency for the tendency to the automatic pro-LC response[3]. with Jerrold Orne, who appeals primarily to

1   See *eg* the letter by L B Archer, 'Ultimate Conversion' (*Library journal*, xci (15 Oct. 1966), 4868), which reveals the extent to which dissatisfaction with DC_{17} creates pressure for a solution – and also shows the extent to which the only solution that is even considered is change to LC.

2   P A Richmond, 'General advantages and disadvantages of using the library of congress classification' (*The Use of the Library of Congress Classification*; *proceedings,* Institute on the Use of the Library of Congress Classification, New York, 1966, *ed* R H Schimmelpfeng & C D Cook (Chicago, American Library Association, 1968), 209-220).

3   That she is also entirely aware of disadvantages – little as she concentrates on them in the cited address – is quite evident from her letter 'Switch without deliberation', (*Library journal*, xci (15 Oct 1966), 4870).

190

fiscal considerations (and to a strong scepticism about the value of classification as anything more than a 'finding device') for the decision to go from DC to LC at the University of North Carolina; and with Harry Dewey, who points out the paradoxicality of the simultaneity of this tendency and of the reawakening of interest in classification theory in America.

But unquestionably the largest reason for the automatic tendency is the enactment of the statutory means for the Library of Congress to eliminate the local classification of large numbers of foreign documents which, in the recent past, had constituted so formidable a proportion of the work of the larger and/or more specialised libraries[4]. If there had been a tendency for libraries under pressure of growth to change to LC even before the enactment of the Higher Education Act of 1965[5] the pressure to give in would become all the more tempting when one hoped that one might thereby never need catalogue again for oneself, thus releasing energy for 'public service' and money for collection building.

1.2   Some arguments in favour of LC

There are, of course, arguments in favour of LC; otherwise no one would be tempted by it. Richmond's central contention is that it is flexible because it is non-systematic, and, in the legitimate sense that the proof of the pudding is in the eating, that it simply works. Orne's is that in the absence of any overwhelming conviction of the superiority of any other classificatory system over it[6], one naturally tends to choose the system that saves money. Cronin's is that international exchange of bibliographical data is a good thing, and that if others besides the Library of Congress can profit by such cooperation, so much the better.

Richmond's central contention is based on an argument which seems to be wholly self-destructive, because it postulates a total lack of detectable or (even more important) predictable system in LC. I do not agree with so harsh a judgment against LC; but in her mind there is nothing harsh about it, since the (non-)system

4   So much so that members of the Association of Research Libraries, most with collections of more than 1,000,000 titles, often catalogue from 40 to 60 percent of their current acquisitions for themselves; cf eg R E Ellsworth, 'Another chance for centralized cataloging') (*Library journal*, lxxxix (1 Sept 1964), 3104-3107).

5   Title II, Part C, is the relevant section, as described by J W Cronin, 'The Library of Congress National Program for Acquisitions and Cataloging' (*Libri*, xvi (1966), 113-117).

6   That even if this argument be correct it leads to fallacious further conclusions will be shown in §2.2.

191

works anyway. Perhaps these contradictory points can be resolved in a clarification of what is meant by 'it works'; it is not clear what Richmond means by this when applied to a classification, but what I mean by it will be explored further in §2.1.

Richmond's most compendious statement of her thesis reads: '[O]ne does not have to look for a subject where it *ought* to be. One only has to find it where it is.. . .One may achieve a great degree of consistency in classification if one does not have to fit new material into a logical pattern but only into a precedence pattern or into loopholes in an ordinal system.'[7]

Orne evinces a thorough scepticism as to the demonstrable superiority of one classification over another, LC included; the ineluctable conclusion must then follow, other things being equal, that the classification which costs least to use is to be used. I do not agree that there is really nothing to choose among classifications, nor that (except Orne's opinion be demonstrated to be true) such considerations as he puts forward are professionally acceptable.

Cronin's point is one that cannot be so easily attacked, because its presupposition is one which none could reject, namely that work done once for all is preferable to the same job done over and over without any progressive improvement. What is really essential in the international exchange of catalogue-data that Cronin describes are the nominal and formal elements, not the conceptual[8]; it was to these first two elements that the Paris Conference directed its attention – and it is from this conference that have emanated the influence which have resulted in the Anglo-American agreement described by Cronin. But no impression derives from Cronin's article to the effect that LC classification is expected to conquer the British library world.

1.3   Experience with LC at Florida Atlantic University

The papers 'On bibliography and automatisation'[9] were directed to the problems of the interaction between the exigencies of automatisation and the principles of bibliography, particularly of conceptual bibliography; the general conclusion was that only if the latter are fully understood and adequately implemented,

7 Richmond, 'General advantages . . . ', 210.
8 For a discussion and validation of these three elements of cataloging see my set of papers 'On bibliography and automation; or, how to reinvent the catalogue' (*Libri*, xv/4 (1965), 287-339), esp 298-299.
9 Cited in footnote 8.

and only if the machine exigencies are so modified and modeled as to conform to these more fundamental goals and strategies, can what is achieved be prevented from becoming a white elephant of massive proportions and shocking cost. The mentioned papers were occasioned by both an external and an internal pressure. The external one was brought to bear mostly by Ellsworth's paper cited above[10] which, even before the enactment of HEA, seemed to suggest that the member libraries of the Association of Research Libraries were ready to accept almost any way out of their overwhelmingly expensive burden of cataloging over and over, among them as a group, what was not centrally available.

The internal pressure was that occasioned by the situation at Florida Atlantic University, where, the catalogue having been successfully automatised, need arose to consult the electronically stored information. An order had been given for an exhaustive search preparatory to the establishment of an area-study programme on the Caribbean. Two possibilities were available: consultation of the classification codes, or consultation of the subject headings. Unfortunately, neither proved to be workable as strategies for consulting the electronically stored conceptual-bibliographical information, and therefore there had to be made a manual search of the whole of the catalogue in order to guarantee exhaustiveness. The conclusion was inescapable, given at length in 'On bibliography and automation', that there should have been a far more thorough preparatory examination of the potentialities of such catalogues, including an attempt to determine whether there was a substantive difference between the various available general classifications, one which would enable more to be done with the electronically stored catalogue records than to substitute computer for typist, compositor, or filing clerk. For if these functions are all that are going to be expected, extreme problems will assuredly arise with the cost of cumulation of the resultant printed catalogue.[11]

The classification codes for the Caribbean area (and, of

10 Cited in footnote 4.
11 Consideration of the computer's printing of cards to be filed manually in an otherwise conventional card catalogue are left aside; this technique is as advocated by F Kilgour at medical and scientific library (*Proceedings,* 1964 Clinic on Library Applications on Data Processing, *ed* H Goldhor (Orbana, University of Illinois Graduate School of Library Science, 1965), 25-35).

course, any of its included parts)[12], extend from F1601 to
F2175. It would be a very simple matter to have the computer
print out whatever nominal and formal elements were desired
for all documents which had had any such codes assigned them.
Unfortunately, though, such a search would still be a very long
way from exhaustive, since the mentioned span of codes
relates only to documents in which the Caribbean area is
treated geographically or historically; documents on education,
art, government, biography (or any other primary headings under
which 'relative' such as the Caribbean area might be 'distributed'),
would be found only by searching though the appropriate span
of codes, and then by accepting only those codes to which had
been of fixed the alphabetical or tablular code representing the
Caribbean area or its parts. Thus:

LC1071 (examinations in professional schools) is divided
alphabetically b y c o u n t r y, so that for Cuba it becomes
LC1071.C8;

LE15-17 is individual educational institutions in the West
Indies, semi-enumerated alphabetically b y c i t y, p r o v i n c e,
i s l a n d, *etc* in the main scheduies;

N910 (art galleries in the Western hemisphere outside the
USA) is divided alphabetically b y c i t y, so that for Havana
it becomes N910.H3;

NE501-794 (history of engraving) is divided systematically
by a r e a and then alphabetically b y c o u n t r y in Table III-A
of the N-schedules, giving NE568-586 for the West Indies.

JA84 (history of political science b y c o u n t r y) is
divided alphabetically, so that for Cuba it becomes JA84.C8;

JL590-1169 includes all the West Indies as related to
constitutional history and administration, but also many
irrelevant places, so that a precise search would have to accept
only JL590-669, JL740-779, JL790-799, JL820-840, and
JL1000-1169

JS1851-2059 is local government in the Caribbean area,

12 It should also be noted that those codes which represent concepts of which the
Caribbean area form. in extension. a part of the first order. should also be
predictability relevant. A convention which would enforce such a predictability
is described in my papers 'Documentary relevance and structural hierarchy'
(Information storage and retrieval, iii/1 (1966), 13-18, reprinted above) and
'Coterminous or specific; a rejoinder to *Headings and canons'* (*Journal of
Documentation*, xxxii/4 (1966), 319-328), but it is not rigidly enough conformed
to in the practice of cataloging at the Library of Congress to have been considered
as a potentially fruitful angle of attack

enumerated in the main tables (paradoxically, it does not include the irrelevant Guianas, as found in JL590-1169)

CT330-548 includes all the West Indies as related to biography, but includes the same irrelevant places as we saw in JL590-1169, so that a precise search would have to accept only CT330-398, CT430-448, CT470-498, and CT510-548. It may not be expected, for one who is familiar only for primarily with LC, that there be any such predictable similarity among these various correlated codes which would make them recognisable by a computer without extensive and expensive re-programming for each subject for which there could be a correlation with the desired idea. But such a lack would not be acceptable to those who see the possibility of a positive solution of the problem.

The other possible lines of approach was through the subject headings. Here we might expect that we could start from the term 'Caribbean area' or 'West Indies' and proceed thence, via the *see also* references to the locating of all included terms. But first it is necessary to remember that the *see also* references in LC subject headings (and in Sears as well, of course, based as it is upon LC) are not thoroughly organised to provide chains from broadest to narrowest, especially when the terms are proper names. Nor are LC *see also* references unambiguous; they indiscriminately refer to subordinates, coordinates, correlates, and even occasionally to superordinates. In addition, there is the phenomenon described in an unpublished paper by Ritvars Bregzis, 'Automation and bibliographic control', of 'loops' in the *see also* reference structure, which would, unless prevented by programme-error-detection, cause trouble in computer searching. The first of these problems is the really serious one in the case at hand, as can be seen from such a heading as ' MAILU', a tribe in New Guinea which is not connected by *see also* references to any including or included headings, either ethnic or geographic. We cannot then expect to make an exhaustive search for New Guinea (and the same is true of any other geographic area) unless a preliminary search be made for all the potentially productive headings n o t connected by *see also* references. Thus the computer search of LC subject headings was abandoned, since it would be successful only if a manual search were made first.

1.4   The demands of professionalism

The reasoning that leads to the decision to reclassify to
LC is acceptable (even though not, in my opinion, correct) and
only if it is based on the conviction that LC is a system
intrinsically superior to DC (or whatever other systems are being
abandoned—Cutters Expansive Classification is still around in a
few places waiting to be phased out, and there may even be a
few American libraries using Brown's Subject Classification or
Bliss's Bibliographic Classification (BC). And, though Richmond's
cited address is so oriented, such reasoning is probably not a
large determinant in the minds of administrators, who tend to
put administrative reasons before all else. By 'administrative
reasons' is meant cost differentials and associated factors such
as proportion of staff time spent on non-public-contact
operations, or the ever smaller proportion of the budget spent
directly on the collection.

Thus, even the administrative reason in its purest form is not
at all something we could judge to be in bad faith; that it is,
nevertheless, incorrect, is the principal point of this essay.

But, whatever be our judgment on the good faith of
administrative reasons, there are other professional reasons
that must enter in. And it is in the very nature of any
opposition between these two that the one which must win out
is the professional, if we who are involved in the choice wish to
retain claim to professionality—even those of us who are administrators.

Professionality is not necessarily a good quality. Another
paper[13] describes both sides of this coin at more length, and
the general point is that the idea of professionality derives from
the verbal sense of professing, and that what the p r o fessor
professes is something which he, in common with the commun-
ity at large, c o n fesses to be a value. The something, characterised by a value worth the dedication implied in the risk of
professing[14], is the logical intersection of inscriptions and
communication: d o c u m e n t a r y i n f o r m a t i o n. This
is our pro-fession, that documentary information is something of
value, and that we are dedicated to this value: we are its instruments.
If we do not accomplish this communication[15] we have either

13 J M Perreault, 'What it is to be 'Professional', (unpublished).
14 To p r o fess is to take risk, to be willing to be sacrificed, whereas the c o n fessor
    is (liturgically) one who is n o t a martyr.
15 As Ranganathán so well summarises it: Every book its reader; Every reader his
    book.

ignored or betrayed our profession. There are of course higher
values, for which we should be willing (at the risk of demon-
strating to the sceptic that professionalism is a bad quality
rather than a good one) to set aside our professional values; we
could well be charged, otherwise, with a sort of fanaticism.
But money as such is surely n o t such a higher value; and
purely administrative reasons, unless they appeal to a truly
higher value, are precisely such an anti-professional betrayal.

There is no such anti-professional betrayal involved in reclassification, to LC or whatever, when the administrator
does not see classification as an integral and essential part of
the value he professes. As Orne puts it, he has very little faith
in classification except as a finding device; when a patron wants
information but does not know whether there is a document
which can communicate it to him, he can discover its
presence (or absence) directly through the catalogue, without
using the classification as a guide. Such an attitude clearly
embodies an unawareness of the extent to which 'the catalogue',
namely the subject headings in it, do not find needed document
automatically, but o n l y i n s o f a r a s t h e y (the subject
headings) a r e a n a d e q u a t e c l a s s i f i c a t i o n,
presented fragmentarily [16]. There is no reason why
American librarians should, in such overwhelming
proportions, remain unaware that classification is a

total phenomenon, not one restricted to shelf-arrangement—
unless we can brand library education with a lack of commitment to its purpose of instilling principles along with particulars.

What classification (in the sense of a total phenomenon) can
and must accomplish if we are to uphold our commitment to
the communication of documentary information, will be the
burden of §2, concentrating in §2.2 on refutation of the idea
of subject headings as non-classificatory. What must be held in
mind during the following description and analysis is that the
conflict between the reasons characterised here as 'administrative' and 'professional' must be resolved in favour of the latter,
if there is less than absolute proof that any classification can do
as well as any other. The burden of proof is thus upon the
administrators, but the negative part of the case will be presented
anyway, in the hope of showing that the positive side could not

16 See *eg* P A Richmond, 'Cats : an example of concealed classification in subject
   headings' (*Library resources & technical services,* iii (1959), 102-112).

be argued successfully.

2.1   The qualities of a classification worth changing to

If one wishes, for professional reasons (generated, that is, by commitment to furtherance of the professed value of documentary information), to reclassify the collection of documents committed to one's care, one must look to the characteristics of each classification that may bring about improvement – and of course do so in comparison with whichever classification is now in use. What, then, are the characteristics of any one classification such that it should be preferred?

At least on the idea plane, the comparison of extant classifications is largely a matter of difference in collocation; but for all the argument over various collations, and the general agreement that BC and Ranganathan's Colon Classification (CC) are more elegant and logical in collocation than the other system, this agreement is not accompanied by any similar agreement about efficaciousness as a correlate to this elegance. There is of course the further difference – one very similar to that of collocation, but finer in detail – of what concepts are subordinated to what main classes. There is thus, on the idea plane, primarily the problem of order among concepts, a variation which can of course (as pointed out in 'Documentary relevance and structural hierarchy'[17]) cause failure or success in retrieval. And finally, more than any other aspect of conceptual order (or of any aspect of classification on any plane), the structure of the relationships which constitute the hierarchical subordination determines the ability of a classification system to respond well to the ineluctably central question of all reference service: i f   w e   h a v e   n o t   f o u n d   w h a t   w e   n e e d ,   w h a t d o   w e   d o   n e x t ?

On the notational plane there is of course the general problem of hospitality, in array and in chain[18]; and in general the whole

17 Cited in footnote 12; see also the later essay 'Citation order – presuppositions, structure, and function, (*Marine sciences literature and data processing techniques; proceedings* of the International Marine Information Symposium, Washington, 1968 (Washington Marine Technology Society, 1968), 15-24) reprinted above.
18 The latter of these is adequately solved by the radix-fraction principle discovered by M Dewey, but the former is not really solved in any available classification; but see my essays 'A new device for achieving hospitality in array' (*American documentation*, xvi/3 (1965), 245-246), reprinted above.

problem associated therewith, of the primacy of idea-order considerations over notational ones. Then there is the not wholly resolved dispute over the desirability of a structurally hierarchical ('expressive') notation[19]. There are theorists who see no possibility of a notation capable of satisfactory structurality. They may be right, and they may have problem-examples in mind such as to defy all attempted solutions; but I doubt it, if we combine Ranganathan's sector (formerly 'octave') notation[20] with my comma-device. It seems to me no less than self-evident that, if feasible, structurality is desirable, because only in this way do we achieve a ritual substitute for the intuitive decision as to w h a t s h a l l w e d o n e x t ?

The verbal plane, insofar as it is represented in systematic conceptual organisations (=classifications) by their indices, is not a central factor in the excellence of retrieval results; it is more an aid for the cataloguer. Insofar as it is represented by the final products of alphabetical conceptual organisations (=subject headings, thesauri) it is more debatable within the present frame of reference, since it is more clearly an influencing factor in retrieval but — this will be dealt with at greater length in §2.2 because of its peculiar hold on the imagination of the American library administrator.

What is the purpose of conceptual organisation (whether systematic or alphabetical) in libraries? It is to provide a search strategy for documents relevant to needs, even when it is not known whether such documents exist within the corpus to be searched. But since, as enunciated above, the most fundamental question when names of documents are unknown is one that calls for something besides one-for-one matching, there must be the means for moving from the most specific concept(s) relevant to the need, to those most nearly relevant—to the next-most specific or general, in a word. Ranganathan's notion of APUPA (Alien, Penumbral, Umbral, Penumbral, Alien) represents this desideratum diagrammatically; when we see that we must give up the hope for the desired specificity, we hope for the next most

19 See, in convenient near-juxtaposition, E J Coates, 'Notation in classification' and
   J E L Farradane, 'Classification and mechanical selection' (*Proceedings,*
   International Study Conference on Classification for Information Retrieval,
   Dorking, 1957 (London), ASLIB, 1957), 51-64, 100-102; 65-69, 106-108).
20 For the most compendious statement by its originator, see S R Ranganathan,
   The Colon Classification (New Brunswick, Rutgers University Graduate School
   of Library Service, 1965) (=Rutgers Series on Systems for the Intellectual
   Organisation of Information, vol IV), 117-130.

relevant generality or specificity to be as close to our first point of attack as possible, and for there to be a gradual progression to the non-relevant, the 'alien'.

Two more factors enter in here, though; the first is that the APUPA principle cannot prevent the presence of relevances else-where ('distributed relatives'); the second is that specificity is not enough. Thought is correlation[21] and specificity is one kind of correlation, but surely far from all of correlation.[22] What is needed, then, is not mere specificity but t h e a b i l i t y t o p r o d u c e c o d e s e q u i v a l e n t t o a n y c o r r e l a t i o n i m p l i e d b y a n y d o c u m e n t. This ability is here dubbed the *concreteness* of the classification, and I look upon it as the quality whose presence or absence is the most important of all in the evaluation of classification, largely because it represents the nexus of most of the crucial characteristics mentioned above. The opposite characteristic is *cross-classification*, which occurs whenever only part of the document's conceptual correlation can be presented by the codes of the classification[23], or when the correlates must be broken into several groups rather than concatenated into a single, *concrete* correlation. Every document which forces the classification-or subject-heading system to apply to it more than one classification code or one subject heading (or one or more of each) reveals the deficiencies of the classification in use.

We must be careful to understand the terms in the foregoing pronouncement. The 'single code' does not of course mean a single digit, since by definition thought is correlation, and correlation implies mutiplicity of correlates; besides, 'every document' must be interpreted variably in terms of the principle of cotermineity, sometimes mapping macro-, sometimes micro-documents onto the conceptual organisation, but in each

21 As so often stated and clarified by S Ceccato; *cf eg* 'Concepts for a new systematics' (*Proceedings*, International Symposium on Relational Factors in Classification (Oxford, Pergamon, 1967) (=*Information storage and retrieval, iii/4*).

22 The variety of subsumptions deduced in my essay 'Categories and relators: a new schema' (*Revenue internationale de la documentation*, xxxii/4 (1965), 136-144, reprinted above) shows this clearly enough; genus/species is only one of a whole family of such relations.

23 It is almost ironic to see the welcoming smiles accorded to total non-correlation by those who so gladly accept unitermic indexing and the like; classification and what makes it valuable have not even come over their horizons, probably because they have had such poor examplars in view so long as to have been almost blinded by them.

case doing so at the level of the document being catalogued, and on the level of that document a s a w h o l e.

In light of the examination of the flaws of LC as a strategy for the Caribbean search we would hope for a classification that would make any occurrence of an idea easily recognisable by computer (or, for that matter, by patron), and likewise make each idea part of an expandable or contractable chain of subsumptions. Traditional enumerative classification tries to do these things, but does them in too simplified a manner, without preliminary analysis of complexes into elementary concepts. It is only with the advent of classifications that make use (both on the idea and the notational plane) of general categories that over-simplification can, even only hopefully, be eliminated. The seminal ideas for this development came from Mclvil Dewey, but they did not reach fruition until the development of UDC, CC, and BC. And in light of the over-arching need for concreteness we could ask how LC (or, for that matter, DC) would handle correlations that go beyond mere 'topic + place'. To 'art galleries — Havana' could well be added 'administration' or 'Italian renaissance painting and sculptures–restoration'. LC's way out of this is to decide whether to classify under Italian renaissance art in general [24], or Italian paintings [25], or Italian renaissance sculptures [26], or restoration of works of art [27], or Havana art galleries [28]; whichever terms have not been chosen for the (shelf-)classification can (perhaps) be rendered as subject headings. But this device, which is defended by some as the 'multi-pronged' approach, is only an escape from the read need, namely for an economical, intelligible, memorable, and (most of all, and in the sense explicated above) strategic and concrete code. LC cannot do it, as we have just seen; UDC can. The complex heading 'sculpture + painting of the renaissance in Italy–its restoration in the art galleries of Havana' reads as [73+75].034(45).025:727·7(729·11).

24 N650-7413 is modern (= non-ancient) art by country; Italy, in the appropriate Table IV, is 411-423, divided the same as is Greece, 391-403, where renaissance (14th-16th cent.) =395; by analogy, then, Italian renaissance =415, which, when added to the base number, gives N6915.

25 ND201-1113 is modern painting by country; we go through the same computation (with the same Table) to get ND615.

26 NB201-113 is modern sculpture by country; for once there is a resemblance between analogous complexes: NB615.

27 N8560.

28 N910.H3, as explained in §1.3.

201

Such a number, it must be admitted, is long–longer than most DC or LC codes. But it is short in comparison to the words necessary (as in subject headings) to represent the same concepts. It is longer, in fact, than would be the total number of digits necessary to represent all its aspects in LC codes: 35 in UDC, 27 in LC ([NB615+ND615]+N8560+N910.H3), but this loss in economy must be balanced against the gain in structurality of notation and memorability for search. Such a UDC code, it must also be remembered, is not merely a number for shelf-arrangement, but is also the basis for a classed arrangement of the catalogue; indeed, it can be used for this purpose along, with the shelves arranged on some entirely different principle (say, by size for economy of space-utilisation, or by broad subject-classes and then directly by author code).

Finally, the UDC code, if used as the arranging system for the catalogue, provides clerically recognisable permutation points. The cited number could also create entries at [75+73] .034 . . . (painting and sculpture. . .), .034 (45) .025.4: 727.7 (729.11)* [7+75] [29] (renaissance in Italy . . .), (45).025.4: 727.7(729.11)* [73+75] .034 (Italy. . .), .025.4: . . . (restoration. . .), 727.7 . . . (art galleries. . .), and finally (729.11) * [73+75] . . . (Havana . . .) This last (as well as the entry for Italy), both being place-indications and likely to be unsought, could have been omitted in the printed or card catalogue; but if the record had been stored electronically, all the entries containing (729) and all extensions of it would have been easily retrieved, along with those at 972.9 and its extensions and correlations (in which last are found historical and geographical treatments of the Caribbean area).

Although considerable emphasis is placed throughout this essay on the classified catalogue as an alternative to the alphabetical subject catalogue, the presence of the computer and of the possibilities it opens up call for even greater emphasis on search strategy for the consultation of non-conventional catalogue Librarians must not allow themselves to be branded as reactionary in moving from their previous attitudes about construction and utilisation of search strategies; nor can we afford to continue to take refuge in such excuses as are used to shield our subject headings and classifications from criticism, such

29 The asterisks are inserted to indicate the normal heading-element of the whole code, so that misinterpretation arising from re-ordering will be avoided (see the essay above 'Citation order–presuppositions, structures and function'),

as is being given here. It has been urged (in conversation with Henry Dubester of the National Science Foundation's Office of Science Information Service) that what is being attacked here is something LC subject headings admittedly cannot do[30] and that the attack is therefore not justified. Are they above criticism just because they are modest in the face of new and greater demands?

The computer offers a great deal; but before we can take fullest advantage of it we must put our own house in order. We librarians must become more fully aware of what our purposes are and of the theoretic bases of how we have been trying to accomplish them. When (and if) this is achieved, it ceases to matter what someone has said he does not expect his system to accomplish—except in the light of what we see it o u g h t to accomplish or at least attempt to accomplish.

2.2   Various fallacies about classification in the broad sense

It is often said that 'classification' is not really possible, and that since this is so we should rely on the catalogue as the search mechanism. By this is meant the subject headings in the catalogue. But it has been shown that search strategy is based primarily on the question: W h a t s h a l l we t r y n o w, o u r f i r s t t r y h a v i n g f a i l e d?

Thus what makes a subjevt-heading catalogue (alphabetical conceptual organisation as against systematic) strategic is the structure implicit in it, by which we are led from Umbra to Penumbra. It was to show the possibility of an analysis of subject headings into the form of an enumerative classification (and perhaps in some cases into that of a general-categoric one[31]) that the subject headings for epistemology, ontology, and cosmology were diagrammed, as found on pp 305-308 of 'On bibliography and automation '. Such a diagram makes explicit and intelligible the step-wise organisation of LC subject headings. It maps out the whole of a strategy, rather than giving it to the searcher one step at a time.

30 *Cf eg* D J Haykin, *Subject headings: a practical guide* (Washington, USGPO, 1951), 1-11.

31 This conclusion is at least implicit in my discussion of the groups of subdivisions under the heading ART; see J M Perreault, 'Approaches to library filing by computer' (*Proceedings*, 1966 Clinic of Library Applications of Data Processing (Urbana, University of Illinois Graduate School of Library Science, 1966), 47-90, reprinted in *The indexer*, (1967), 169-187).

To operate with a classification, even an enumerative one without general categories, is (compared to operating with an LC subject-heading catalogue) like finding one's way across town with the aid of a map, as against asking directions at each street corner. In this sense we can exclude subject headings from the domain of classification; but we should not forget that classification in the strict sense of s y s t e m a t i c conceptual organisation, and subject headings in that of a l p h a b e t i c a l conceptual organisation, are search strategies both - and are thus subject to the same criteria.

One argument against strenuous efforts to improve subject headings, as well as against the substitution for them of a classed catalogue, is that they are only appropriate to searches by the inexpert. That this argument is entirely fallacious can be seen from the degree of concern shown by a good many profess-ional associations and governmental technical information agencies for the development of thesauri – which are merely more sophist-icated versions of the subject-heading approach. Such thesauri are developed for the searching of groups of documents, in which searches it is postulated that the searchers, even though experts, do not know whether or not relevant documents will be produced as the result of the search. Thus the very development of thesauri belies the assertion that alphabetical conceptual organisation is only worth the trouble in an environment of term-papers and how-to-do-it books. And the fact that it is experts who demand such developments also belies the associated fallacy that experts need no subject-catalogue guidance—they know what they want, we are told, from citations and the like, and hence need only nominal-bibliographical catalogues.

Another fallacy is that of change from one classification to another, when neither is demonstrably inferior or superior, for the sake of monetary economy. That this is a fallacy can best be seen by the next step in the argument – or rather by the next step that is n o t in the argument: If one classification is as good or as bad as any other, this may be because they are both examples of 'artificial' languages, and should both be avoided in favour of a 'direct, natural' approach to bibliographical conceptualities, if such is available.

This is of course not obvious; otherwise, if there were advantages to be gained from HEA Title II-C, it would not accrue from the LC classification any more than from the DC—if neither is superior. But since there is supposed to be simultaneously available a direct and natural mode of strategic access, and if both other modes of access are inferior because of their artificiality, it would seem that there is as much reason f o r welcoming the subject headings as there is a g a i n s t change from one inadequate classification to another.

This argument is particularly potent when it is remembered that classification means, to most American librarians, only the shelf-arrangement, and hence that reclassification implies the changing of document labels, circulation cards, circulation card pockets, *etc*; whereas change from one search strategy (as catalogue-arrangement) to another, while it surely requires some physical alterations, can at least be accomplished without changing the shelf-arrangement. However, we cannot really be sure that leaving the shelves untouched in the course of search strategy change would be wise, at least in public libraries, since it has been found that a far higher proportion of their patrons expect the shelf-arrangement to assist them than do those of other types of libraries who seek assistance through the catalogue. (The research data on which this conclusion is based is from a project conducted by M L Bundy for the state of Maryland, in 1966. The number of persons surveyed was 21,138; 43.1 per cent used the shelf-arrangement for searching and 19 per cent the catalogue. The remaining 53 per cent used the periodical indices, had discussions with librarians, used record players, *etc*; it is significant that the 43.1 per cent was the highest single type of use, with 22.1 per cent for use of reference books next highest[32].)

Working back through these arguments, then, it seems that subject headings provide an inferior search strategy--were this not so it would be the most efficient provision of them which would represent the main advantage provided by HEA. But the fact that subject headings are inferior is demonstrated by the current development of essentially similar strategies, in the form of technical thesauri; and this development simultaneously demonstrates the need for improvement of search strategy for the sake of expert and inexpert alike. But that the 'natural' search strategy is in fact superior to the 'artificial' is only another fallacy of the same sort, because it is subject to exactly the same criteria as

32 M L Bundy, *Metropolitan library users: a report of a survey of adult library use in the Maryland Baltimore – Washington area* (Maryland State Department of Education, 1968), 44-46.

those by which we can judge classifications (in both the strict and the popular sense). And such criteria cast a light which shows that since the fundamental problem of retrieval is W h a t , t h e n , n e x t ? and since this problem requires a wide-range strategy, alphabetical conceptual organisation is inferior to systematic just insofar as it does not offer a good a solution to the fundamental problem.

2.3.   'A place for everything is good enough'

An opinion at least apparently shared by Richmond and Orne, and surely by a great many others as well, is that systematic perfection is a less important characteristic of a search strategy than i the *ad hoc* provision of a place for everything. In a sense that is true — in the sense that we store away our own collection, of documents or whatever else, in an order and in locations which in no way reflect their meaningful contents or usefulness. But this situation obtains only up to the capacity of the memory of the individual; when that limit is exceeded, surrogates must be created to assist the memory. And when the 'memory' that is being thus supplemented is shared by all those who are cataloguing documents by thousands each year, it is necessary that there be more than merely *ad hoc* ways of getting back to these documents upon demand. Thus are developed both codes of author/title cataloguing and systems of conceptual search strategy. Both such sets of rules are designed, not for analytical bibliography with its concern for the b o o k —and even for the individual c o p y — but the systematic bibliography with its concern for the w o r k and for the relations between works within the corpus. Author/title codes and classification system provide the systematic foresight that prevents the one-by-one incorporation of documents from forming not an organic corpus but a disorganised mass.

An example of conflict in citation order and predictability can be helpful here; the point of departure will be DC (since, while I am horrified at the idea or reclassification to LC, I am not too happy about the permanent retention of DC either). Our test document is an Australian union catalogue of scientific periodicals, arranged by subject. We recognise Bibliography at once as the main class, and the most obvious order of analysis of terms runs: Bibliography–Catalogues–Union–Science–Periodicals–Australia. When we look for a beginning point in the index we find 017, and since it is a catalogue of libraries as such, we extend this to 017.1, 'union catalogues of public subject arranged libraries.' And we see that the topic 'scientific periodicals' cannot be attached to 017.1: however, we can at least add on 'Australia', giving 017.10994, but the central point, the topics covered in the collections indicated, cannot be shown. So instead of starting from 'union catalogues' we can start from 'subject bibliographies', 016, to which can be added 'scientific' 016.5, but n o t 'periodicals' and 'Australia', which would give 016.5050994, since 016.505 would be read back as 'a periodical on the bibliographies of science'. Since two of the first duties of an information language are explication of homonyms and consolidation of synonyms—namely, in a word, the elimination of ambiguity—no such misreading of the original analysis can be allowed. (Such a misreading might be defended by those who propose that classification is no more than pigeon holes—places for everything but nothing more than places—in terms like: 'Well, when or if someone finds this document, he'll understand what the code r e a l l y means, and until then, it gives us a unique place to keep it.'

So we can go only to 017.10994 or to 016.5, neither of which represents the full concreteness of intersecting categories which the document defines. But there is a way, if our citation order analysis is altered to Science—Periodicals—Bibliographies—Australia. Then a code can be constructed to accommodate all present categories: 505.0160994. But, assuming that we have a policy that dictates placement of all bibliographical items together, such a solution results in radical unpredictability, and thus cannot be tolerated.

What can be done with this problem in LC? First of all, of course, we do not even have the official option of moving it out of Z into Q; and in Z we can code it as Z7403 (Bibliography —Science—Periodicals) only, certainly not as Z695.83 (Library science—Union catalogues); for a classification whose 'specificity' is so much vaunted, this is highly un-concrete. We might choose Z975 (Library science—Catalogues—Australia) but that too is too un-concrete. With LC subject headings we can have *Catalogues Union,* but it cannot be extended for greater concreteness. A better solution (not led to from *Catalogues, Union* by sa, though) would probably be *Periodicals—Bibliography—Union lists,*

which can be divided by place, unlike the first heading,
giving *Periodicals–Bibliography–Union lists–Australia.* But
there is still no mention of 'Science'. To get this essential point
in we must have another heading: Science–Periodicals–
Bibliography. (It is interesting to note the distance that
these headings lie from the *beau ideal* of alphabetico-direct theory

Now, before we go on to coding this in UDC, we must
examine why there is restriction in DC on going all the way
when we begin with 017.1 or 016. The third duty of an information language (after the first two given above) is to establish
rules of formation: a systematic conceptual organisation is an
artificial l a n g u a g e, and must therefore have both a vocabulary and a s y n t a x. But there are no rules of formation
(syntax) in DC, except the implicit one that can be stated algebraically thus: (A), $((A)B)$, $(((A)B)C)$, $((((A)B)C)D)$, etc, which ca
be interpreted that each last term is a modification of the complex
that precedes it. This situation obtains in DC largely because of
the original (and still obeyed) desired to have a *pure* notation,
which desire prevents the use of any overtly relational or
syntactical codes.

In UDC, the various aspects are similar to those of DC except
in the use of punctuational symbols in place of DC's purely
numerical facet indicators. Catalogues–Subject arranged–Public
collections–Union, is coded as 017.11; Australia is (94);
Science is 5; Periodicals is (05) or :05. (This last distinction is
an advance over DC, allowing as it does a choice between
'periodical' as a form and 'periodicals' as a form-topic. If such
a distinction (along with the colon) had been available in DC, it
would seem that we could have gone beyond 016.5, not to
016.505, which would necessarily involve us in an ambiguity,
but to 016.5:05. But even this would be subject to ambiguous
misinterpretation as '[the topic of] Periodicals dealing with the
bibliography of science'. The only escape from this trap is the
use of square brackets, as emplified below and fully discussed
elsewhere [33].

---

33 J M Perreault, 'Towards explication of the rules of formation in UDC', in
On the Perreault schema of relators and on the rules of formation in UDC
(Copenhagen, Danish Centre for Documentation, 1966) (=FID/CR Report no 4),
reprinted above.

If we utilise the inverse of the filing order of the UDC symbols[34], we would find the basic subject, put place (n) after it, then outer form (On); but we have here not one but two basic subjects, 017.11 and 5. (Note that 'union catalogues' or 'subject bibliography' cannot be used as terminal sub-divisions, as in DC.) These two basic subjects (as is the case with any multiplicity of basic subjects drawn from various parts of the schedules, and treated intersectedly in the document at hand) can be joined by the symbol $n{:}n$, which is interpreted as 'logical intersection', giving 017.11:5 for 'union catalogues . . . in science'. We have seen from our attempt to do all this in DC that 'Australia' must modify 'union catalogues', not 'scientific periodicals'; so we can modify as needed, 017.11(94), and then intersect this with the other basic subject, giving 017:11(94): 5. Now we wish to add the further concreteness, namely that the content of this Australian union catalogue is not merely 'science', but 'scientific periodicals', so we try to add :05 to 5, giving 017.11 (94): 5:05. But this formulation is also subject to a misinterpretation, namely as 'periodicals (as a topic) o n Australian union catalogues in science'. But there is a solution. Instead of stopping us, like DC, with $((A)B)$, the $n{:}n$ has allowed us to go on to $(((A)B)C)$[35]; but we still cannot simply add D at the end, if we wish to avoid the given misinterpretation. Instead, we can explicitly use

34 As given in *Universal Decimal Classification* 3d abr Eng ed (London, British Standards Institution, 1961) (=BS 1000A =FID no 289), 10; the substantive codes given here are drawn from the same edition.
35 Note that there has been a change in the semantic filling of each algebraic symbol, as against the (ambiguous) DC order 505.0160994.

algebraic sub-groupers (square brackets)[36] thus: 017.11(94): [5:05], which is interpreted so that only 5 is modified by :05 and the whole complex reads back 'union catalogues, Australian, on science periodicals'; algebraically, then, $(((A)B) [(C)D])$.

We can far more nearly exactly predict the main classified entry for such a document in UDC than in either DC, LC, or (though this is added only hypothetically) LC subject headings. In DC and LC, one of several only partially concrete codes can be chosen, and it is therefore impossible to predict which will be used; this is a sort of cross-classification, which is thus seen as not merely an abstract horror in the minds of classificationists but as a horror in use as well.

2.4   Some problems relative to UDC filing order

One aspect of the use of UDC that comes under fire most often (though erroneously) is connected with the problem of predict-

36 "It will be seen that this is Fill's use of the square brackets, rather than its more common use as an intercalator; cf K Fill, *Einführung in das Wesen der Dezimalklassifikation* (Berlin, Beuth, 1960), 20-21, as well as J M Perreault, 'Towards explication of the rules of formation in UDC', cited in footnote 33. That the intercalator-usage of the square brackets as proposed in UDC 3 abr (cited in footnote 34), is unofficial, is argued by Öhman in a private communication to G A Lloyd (dated 15.1.1968):
... In 'Categories and Relators', Perreault calls the square bracket a 'sub-grouper', and gives several examples of its use. Wesseling writes ('The Universal Decimal Classification and the Perreault System' FID/CR Report No. 4)' . . . the square brackets appear to be an invention of Perreault's'. This is clearly a mistake, the authority is undoubtedly the 2nd French edition. Of this fact Perreault seems to be ignorant, but he does cite an authority [whose examples are in part] taken from the 2nd French edition p.1537. . . .
In 1952 Lorphèvre pointed out to me the possibility of using the square bracket as a sub-grouper, and I have used it ever since. . . .
The 2nd French edition gives examples of the use of the square bracket as an intercalating device, but as far as I can see there is no mention of its use as a subordinating connective. . . .
In the first English abridged edition (1948) the square brackets are treated as an official sign on p. 108, significance 'Relation (subordinate)' . . . I assume that this is [borrowed] from the [6th?] Dutch edition . . . [T] he uses as a sub-grouper, so clearly exemplified in the 2nd French edition, has entirely disappeared in the Dutch and English abridged editions of 1950 and 1948. It would be very interesting to know the reasons for this rather major change.
. . .Probably the use of the square bracket as a sign for a subordinate relation has grown out from its use as a sign for intercalation. It may have been(wrongly?) assumed, that only a subordinate concept should be intercalated.
It should be clear that I consider the use of the square bracket as a sub-grouper the only important one. I see no reason why it should not be made entirely official and appear in published notations where it makes the notation clearer"

ability – namely, the filing order between UDC codes. As against a DC code with its absolutely pure notation (which only appears to be mixed because of the presence of the wholly content-empty decimal point), a UDC code utilises a mixed notation which makes possible the easy indication and interpretation of the various facets represented within it. This factor should indeed make the filing and locating of documents and/or surrogates far easier. And there is certainly no virtue in the filing order of LC codes, even though it i s programmable – since they only locate, as if we were back before the days of relative classification, *ie* back when a shelf-code was just that, an assignment of a particular document to a particular place on a particular shelf in a particular cabinet in a particular room. What is gained by the mixed notation in UDC is the ability to file by 'empty', 'partially empty', and 'full' facets.

The DC code 894.51110409003 ('20th-century Magyar lyrical poetry'; see §3.21) places its document in order after that coded 894.51110409002 (894.51110409004 does not occur, since there has as yet been no such period of time); its facets can be shown by spacing out, thus: 894.511 104 09003. But a code for '20th-century Magyar poetry', which, being obviously more general, must come before in the file, cannot do so except by facet by facet comparison (*ie*, partially empty compared with full):

894.511   104 09003.   894.511   1   09003

– but the fact is that such a preliminary operation is not normally performed nor even recognised as necessary, so that the more general document comes later:

894.51110409003   894.511109003,

– because of the accidental and misleading comparison between the ninth digits of each code. With UDC codes for the same concepts, on the othe hand, the presence of the facets is entirely clear; 894.511-1"19" cannot come anywhere but before 894.511-14"19", because -1 (partially empty) comes necessarily before -14 (full). This phenomenon can be referred to analogously: DC filing is 'letter-by-letter', UDC 'word-by-word'.

The occurrence of wholly 'empty' facets too can be a problem in a classification using either a pure notation or a mixed notation without facet indicators. An analogous case here is the filing of main entries for Biblical documents: **Bible.** *New Testament.*

211

Greek . . . comes after **Bible.** *English.* . . n o t a t a l l because
N comes after *E,* but rather because whole comes before part;
this can be realised quite easily if we just imagine where **Bible.**
Swahili . . .' comes in relation to the two mentioned entries,
namely between them. Since classification too is a species of
systematic bibliography, it must also seek such groupings, and is
assumed to be able to do so more easily because it uses a
notation and an index, whereas author/title cataloging must rely
on the natural language and on supposedly self-interpretable
terminology. But what happens in DC is that ritual interpretation is impossible because of the need for several levels of
generality, which forces the use of multiple introductory zeroes;
thus at 942, the first enumerated sub-heading is for the most
ancient historical period, 942.01, forcing the standard subdivisions to adopt an extra zero: 942.001—942.009. And it is not
impossible to find that even double-zero is pre-empted for more
concrete tasks, so that the standard subdivisions require three
zeroes.

Other charges against the filing order of UDC complex
codes, especially when formed with the colon device, are brought
by Metcalfe[37] but his examples of chaos seem to me as lucid as
could be hoped for (though not his use of the .00, auxiliaries
as intermediaries). What makes his example at least
apparently chaotic in its file order is the very paucity of
coloned-on numbers which Metcalfe comes up with; certainly
if he had used a base number like 016, to which very nearly every
other number may be added, he would have had no objections
to make. What it comes down to in the end is that he rejects
non-alphabetical collocation, and does so all the more
vehemently when it is represented by only a partial selection of
such coloned-on secondary numbers. It is even implied that if,
instead of retaining these borrowed secondary numbers, sub-
classes were directly enumerated, all would be well, but this
is one of the defects of other systems that UDC is particularly
fortunate in being able to avoid, and justifies calling it at least a
partially faceted classification.

The easy interpretation of the explicit complexity of UDC
codes compares very favourably indeed, in my opinion, to the
tricky interpretation of the only implicit complexity of DC
codes; this makes one wonder what constitute filing problems to

37 J W Metcalfe, *Subject classifying and indexing of libraries and literature*
(New York, Scarecrow Press, 1959), 152-155.

those who find fault with UDC order. There follows a comparison
of order between UDC codes and DC codes for the same
conceptual complexes (it will be noted that DC is often either
un-concrete or unspecific).

UDC	DC
894.5 [Finno-Ugrian literature] -	894.5
894.5"19" [20th century]	894.509003
894.5.085 [its oral presentation]	[oral presentation is not
894.5.085"19"	specifiable]
894.5-1 [poetry]	[forms of the family of
894.5-1"19"	literatures are not specifiable,
894.5-1.085	since they would take the
894.5-1.085"19"	form 894.51, which is already
894.5-14 [lyrical]	enumerated for Ugrian lit-
894.5-14"19"	eratures]
894.5-14.085	
894.5-14.085"19"	
894.511 [Magyar]	894.511
894.511"19"	894.51109003
894.511.085	
894.511.085"19"	
894.511-1	894.5111
894.511-1"19"	894.511104
894.511-1.085	894.51110409003
894.511-1.085"19"	894.511109003
894.511-14	
894.511-14"19"	
894.511-14.085	
894.511-14.085"19"	
894.511-2	894.5112
894.511-2"19"	894.511209003
894.511-2.085	
894.511-2.085"19"	
894.511-2-14	
894.511-2-14"19"	
894.511-2-14.085	
894.511-2-14.085"19"	
894.541 [Finnish Suomi]	894.541

3.11 A counter proposal: centralised classification by UDC

LC has a great many more enumerated classes than does any other available general classification, in particular DC. DC has fewer than UDC or BC as well. CC probably has fewer than DC, though. So, conclude the naive, LC must be the·most specific, and UDC next so. This would be like believing that a language with $2x$ words in its total vocabulary, but with no formations possible but those of the pattern $x_i + x_j$, has twice the expression possibilities of another language with only x words but with formations of the patterns $x_i + x_j$, $x_i X x_j$, x_i/x_j, $x_i - x_j$, $x_i + x_k$, $x_i X x_k$ x_i/x_k, and $x_i - x_k$ possible. Thus it is the capacity for concreteness, defined above as the ability to produce codes equivalent to any correlation implied by any document, which is the most powerful factor in the expansion of the total number of expressions possible in any language, natural or artificial[38];with its powers of expression in levels and rounds, CC might well have a larger gamut of developed expressions than any other information language; despite the smallness of its list of elementary terms. In any case, there is no reason, when we add syntax to vocabularv in our computations, to accept LC as more specific than UDC even though it may well be far more so than DC.

But there is need for more than additional specificity; there is need for more than just a stop-gap solution, more than just monetary economy (especially if the main advantage rests in a different sort of change than that contemplated). This problem is not one that needs to be solved just for the sake of incipiently large collections; it needs solution for that of a l r e a d y large collections, in order for them to be used to their fullest. It is often proposed that the smaller the collection, the more thoroughly it must be strategised for sufficiently numerous relevances to be produced when the need arises. This is nothing if not trivial; the larger the collection, the m o r e the need for a thoroughly developed search strategy.

What is proposed, then, is that UDC be the classification to which libraries change when their seams beging to burst, whether

---

38 Or, as the Netherlands Study Committee 'Grondslagen UDC' (affiliated with the FID) says in its report D66-196 (10.May 1966):
(1) The Committee has diagnosed an increasing need of a more exhaustive consideration of unlocking potentialities through the UDC (depth classification or facet classification).
(2) The Committee is of the opinion that the most effective way is to extend relations, rather than reconsidering or extending hierarchy.'

they are now using DC or even LC. For those using DC now, the change can be relatively painless (see §3.21); there would be at least the possibility of intercalation of new and old, instead of the usual technique of creation of two side-by-side collections, differently arranged. With collections now arranged by LC, of course, intercalation would not be possible – but service-improvements would be.

This is only an abstract proposal, at least up to this point; but the problem is not abstract, it is very real. What makes the new situation so new (with HEA Title II-C) is that classification effort is reduced by its centralised provision. So, what can make UDC reclassification similarly attractive may well need to be the same sort of provision; what is needed may be a return to a function proposed for itself by the Institut Internationale de Bibliographie, the ancestor of the present Fédération Internationale de Documentation: the function of centralised classification of the research-journal articles of the world. (Attendant difficulties will be outlined in §3.4.)

This is a tall order, even when one's hope is only for centralised classification of books, not for journal articles. But as a stage just below that of centralised UDC classification, I propose change to UDC classification done by each instruction for its own purposes. The fact that this, despite the lack of the economies of centralisation, can produce the desired results, is largely due to the theoretical superiorities of the UDC over both DC and LC; problems of implementation will be summarily discussed in §3.3.

3.12   Why not a proposal in favour of CC or BC?

Since what is needed for the improvement of search strategi-sation is a change from enumerative (LC) and semi-enumerative (DC) to general-categoric classification, it may well be asked why CC is not being advocated, since it is the most thoroughgoing exemplar of the general-categoric approach. However, both it and UDC (but not BC) are rigorously criticised in regard to their general-categoric structures in de Grolier's excellent *Study of general categories*[39]. The fact, though, that neither CC nor UDC is without flaw (as de Grolier surely shows), and that their flaws' are differential, is not what leads to a preference for UDC. The

39 E de Grolier, *A study of general categories applicable to classification and coding in documentation* (Paris UNESCO, 1962).

215

major reason for not advocating CC or BC is their notations; not that they do not do what is expected of them (namely, primarily, that they 'mechanise' the order – in array and in chain – of concepts), but that they are so alien to what we expect a library notation to look like, that it would be very surprising if they could be widely acceptable in American libraries. An additional advantage of UDC is its close resemblance to DC; a policy of 'osmosis'[40] could be adopted in reclassification from DC to UDC which, while it would be less than perfect in having on the same shelf documents collocated somewhat differently, could at least allow intercalation–as against the necessity of parallel and separate collections when reclassification from DC is to LC or CC.

It might be argued that there is a fairly strong resemblance between LC and BC, and that the same advantages would accrue to a change along that axis as would be the case for DC/UDC change. The resemblance is there, surely, but it is almost entirely a formal one, depending on the fact that both use a mixed notation beginning with capital Roman, then Arabic numerals, *etc.* But the collocation of main classes is far less similar than with DC/UDC: only class Z is anywhere close to similarity in content.

3.21   A brief comparison of UDC and DC

UDC is a classification governed by the FID: it is modeled on the DC, but considerably modified both in collocation and synthetic structure; its notation is mixed (consisting of the same sort of numericals found in DC, plus punctuationals; generally without alphabeticals; decimal; highly flexible). Many of these points can be seen from examples given above and below.

But UDC varies from DC in other things. It is without as pronounced a Western slant, since the intention was to be universal. The United States likewise is given less predominance than in DC. The one class that is most fully developed (in terms of enumerated specifics) is 6, 'Applied Sciences. Medicine. Technology'. In the abridged English edition, class 0 occupies three pages, 1 three, 2 three, 3 twenty two, 4 (currently being vacated and transferred to 8) two, 5 twenty, 6 *fifty-two,*

40 See e g S R Ranganathan (with A Neelameghan), *Classified catalogue code, with additional rules for dictionary catalogue code* 5 (London, Asia Publishing House, 1964), 71-73.

7 eight, 8 one, 9 two, and the general auxiliaries thirteen. There is great need, obviously, for further development in the humanistic and (to a lesser extent) the social-scientific classes, but even the sparse enumeration here listed is very greatly expandable by the synthetic formation possibilities. The 78 schedule ('Music') occupies only one page, yet it is capable, by internal combination, of representing such a concrete topic as 'performance practice of baroque liturgical organ music', giving 783.1:786.6 .091.034.7; DC can only come close, with 786.60932 (Organ—History—Baroque) or 783.073 (Sacred music—Performance); LC is no better, giving ML554 (Organ=History=Baroque), ML604 (Organ=Performance=Baroque), or BX9187 (only applicable if the document deals with instrumental music — including the organ — in the Presbyterian church; there is no general class nor any special classes for other church bodies); LC subject headings give *Organ—History; Music, Baroque; Music—Performance;* and *Church music—History and criticism;* some of which would be likely to be excluded for the sake of economy.

The largest present body of utilisers of UDC[41] consists of European special libraries, primarily in the scientific and technical areas; the examples used here should show, though, that there is no reason to fear that it is incapable, because of less enumerative specificity, of handling humanistic subjects well too.

The revision of UDC is constant, and is vested in committees of-subject-and classification-experts (some of very broad responsibility like that dealing with 1/2, others narrow like that for 621.3). There is no likelihood that either retention of DC or change to LC will gain the concerned library anything at all in greater currency of inclusions or of terminology.

The codes that are created by UDC are often longer than those created by DC—for the same document, of course. However. the DC code is not shorter because it represents the same concreteness more compactly; it is shorter o n l y because of its lack of concreteness.

DC is also quite clumsy to interpret because of its reliance upon pure-numerical notation and fractioning by threes; for a code like 505.0160994 this gives a book-spine code that looks like

41 An informative table of user-institutions is to be found in J Mills, *Guide to the Universal Decimal Classification (UDC)* (London, British Standards Institution, 1963) (=BS 1000C =FID no 345), 115-128.

505, or even·505 - whereas it ought to be   505
.016   .01   .016
 988   609   0994
4   94   5
or (as permuted in UDC)   :05
                                      :017
                                      .11
                                   (94)

The UDC code has been re-arranged to beging with·the same element that the DC codes m u s t begin with if it is to succeed in being concrete. Note that the UDC advantáge is that it can be precise within the limitations of the policy of main (classified) entry under 0, while DC cannot. Part of the difficulty in interpreting a code like 505.0160994[42] is in knowing w h e r e each new facet begins, and in knowing w h a t it means. In the given case a single 0 begins each facet, but if there were a different semantic filling demanding a change in order to Science–Periodicals--Australia--Bibliography, the 016 could not be retained in that form, since it would have to be interpreted as a time qualifier of 994 (='early period'); it would need to become 0016, giving 505.09940016. A UDC code, on the contrary, is unalterable in semantic filling.

Another example of the difficulty of interpretation (by a reference librarian or a patron) of a DC code which succeeds in representing the whole correlation with concreteness is '20th-century Magyar lyrics', 894.51110409003 (§2.4). The multiplicity of 0's and the clump of 1's would make this far harder to interpret than the same correlation expressed in UDC– 894.511-14"19". The conclusion (suggested in conversation by A J Wells, editor of the British National Bibliography) may well be that UDC, with its clear facets and easy permutability, is so much better for catalogue arrangement as to make consideration of DC for that function pointless, whereas DC (at least in its pre-17th-edition form) might well be better for shelf-arrangement, where thorough going concreteness (in my sense) is not as necessary. My personal response to this suggestion would be partly favourable, except in regard to the variation between the

42 We must guard against comparing UDC 5:05:017.11 (94) with 505 since that
                                                      .016
                                                      0994
is not the way DC is used; we must compare current recommended practices in each system. (Accents graves are now being used to separate facets at the LC DC Office; this gives 505.'016 '0994 or the like.)

two collocations; it would seem more logical to arrange the catalogue by the full UDC code, permuted, the shelf by the first (or first two) facet(s).

The primary (and original) function of UDC was for the ordering of surrogates, not of documents; indeed this was once the case with DC. The presence of clear facet indicators, though, makes UDC (and CC too, of course) ideal as a catalogue-classifier. An example of how this could work is given at the end of §2.1; such a device eliminates subject headings with their total unpredictability and ignoring of the APUPA desideratum. And, since it makes the catalogue itself far more effectively browsable, it frees the shelves from the necessity of being a search strategy on their own, and brings the surrogate- and the document-arrangement under the same rubric; the catalogue then simply provides all the multiple (main + added) access vistas that the shelf arrangement obviously cannot, and all is done in terms of one and the same set of principles [43].

3.22   A brief comparison of UDC and LC

We have already discussed the virtual impossibility of computerised search of an LC file (§1.3). Here we will take up some of the logistical difficulties involved in preference of UDC over LC. There is, more than anything else, the difficulty of obtaining a complete full English UDC [44]. There is reason to hope, though, that the current research project on UDC and mech-anised searching—especially in its preliminary phase of collation of a current full English edition on magnetic tape—will provide the copyright-holder, the British Standards Institution, with the basis for a complete full edition in main class volumes,

---

43 It is one of the strangest developments in American librarianship that we have made so little attempt to unify the strategy of shelf and of catalogue. DC and Sears, LC and LC subject headings, DC and LC subject headings — none of these pairings has anything to recommend it except simultaneous availability; LC and Sears would make every bit as much sense.

44 There are full schedules for some classes and sub-classes, but not for all 0/9; hence what can be obtained is full but not complete. On the other hand, there is not too much difficulty in obtaining complete abridged schedules — these might do for small to medium-sized libraries, but few of them are under pressure to reclassify — at least prior to HEA. (See also the essay below, 'The Universal Decimal Classification as candidate for reclassification either on the shelf or in the catalogue' (*Reclassification — rationale and problems* (College Park, School of Library and Information Services [of the] University of Maryland, 1968). 79-95), reprinted below.

perhaps within the coming year[45]. When this occurs there will not need to be as much concern over the apparent 'absolute' size-superiority of LC over UDC–though §3.11 has shown how little such a comparison means.

That LC is unprogrammable is not, and cannot be, proven–and I shall make no such attempt. What is clear enough, given the description of search strategy provided above, is the relative ease of doing so for CC and for UDC. An experimental programme on the seismological section of UDC has been reported on by Caless[46]; it is no surprise at all that he concludes that electronic searching is feasible in actuality as well as in theory.

It is thus definitely shown that coordinate or post-coordinate (a better term would be 'unarticulated', or 'discrete') indexing, with its denial of all correlational value, is not by any means the only search strategy adapted to sophisticated mechanised use. Classification – hierarchical, artificial, intellectual, and the rest – henceforth to be excluded from the progress towards information retrieval o n l y insofar as it is inflexible, unstrategic, and inhospitable – such, in other words, as has been described above and in 'On bibliography and automation'. And the capital instance of all these defects, as clearly as anyone might ever hope or fear, is LC.

3.3 What if centralised UDC classification cannot come about-

There are various solutions to the problem of classification and re classification, and they can, in many cases, be stated in sets of bifurcations or dichotomies. We have the dichotomy Classified Shelves/Unclassified Shelves; the bifurcations Alphabetical Catalog Systematic Catalogue, Institutional Surrogation/Centralised Surrogation, Card Catalogue/Book Catalogue, Dictionary Catalogu. Divided Catalogue, *etc.* While there is a tendence for some of the limbs of pairs of these choice situations to become rigidly associated, there are more such popularly associated pairs than is logically necessary. For instance, a library with classified

---

45 See the summarisation, along with compendious bibliographical reference, of the work of R R Freeman and P A Atherton on modernising the management of UDC in *Final report of the research project for the evaluation of the UDC as the index language for a mechanised reference retrieval system* (American Institute of Physics, 1969) (=its AIP/UDC-9).

46 T W Caless & D B Kirk, ' An application of UDC to machine searching (*Journal of documentation*, xxiii/3 (1967), 208-215).

shelves is expected to have an alphabetical catalogue; one with
a book(-form) catalogue is expected to have a divided catalogue.
The situation at hand, though, is to decide what goes along
(logically, though not necessarily popularly) with the choice of
Institutional as against Centralised Surrogation.

My observation of classification students at the School of
Library and Information Services, University of Maryland, as well as
my own remembrances from working with DC (at Milwaukee
Public Library) and with LC (at Florida Atlantic University)
would lead to the conclusion that, in the absence of any outside
(centralised or cooperative) assistance in conceptual bibliography,
the use of UDC is both more economical of time and energy,
and more consistent in results over time and/or among multiple
personnel.

It is m o r e   e c o n o m i c a l   o f   t i m e a: in that its
index, while not perfect, is far superior to that of DC[17];
and the more compact layout of the schedules enables a more
rapid survey of the general/specific situation. The same is also
true b: because of the faceting and the unambiguous notation,
which conspire to prevent the need for going from place to place
seeking solutions by analogy.

To obtain the DC code 894.51110409003 (§§2.4, 3,21) it is
necessary to go from p 1848 to p 1728 to p 472 to p 1140
(without any explicit lead to this last); we are now at the f i r s t
class code 894.511; then to p 1120, which tentatively lets
us add the next facet 104, giving 894.511104, though to verify
it we go on to p 1114 (note under 811.02-08), to p 1104,
none of which changes our original tentative decision except to
make us wonder why 'lyric' is 82*1.04* on p.1120 and 81*1.04* on
p 1114, but 808.8*14* on p 1104; then back to p 1148 to add
the last facet '20th century', giving the whole code 894.5111040-
9003. By contrast, in UDC$_3$ abr. we go from p 203 to p 192
to p 143 (main class) to p 142 (literary form) to p 22 (period),
accumulating 894.511,−14 and "19", which together give the
whole code (better anyway, as well as easier) 894.511–14"19".

It is m o r e   e c o n o m i c a l   o f   e n e r g y in that its
flexibility prevents the frequent occurrence of cross-classification
by arbitrary choice of a facet to be excluded. It thus prevents
frustration, the greatest energy-drain on the classifier using
either LC or DC (see examples in §§2.1, 2.3, and 3.21).

It is m o r e   c o n s i s t e n t   o v e r   t i m e   a n d / o r

221

among multiple personnel because its use can be taught (as with CC as well) in terms of guiding principles, rather than by gradual accretion of particular problem-cases and of their *ad hoc* solutions—this last being a technique better fitted to in-service training anyway. In particular, the availability of a notation that allows an undiluted citation order (the example of the union catalogue in §§2.3 and 3.21 is sufficient here) leads to such consistency.

It must be admitted that high flexibility can lead to bizarre results—but only if the classifier has no grasp of the fundamental principles of search strategy. If he does not, he may produce such a code as 017.1(94):5:05, *ie* without the necessary sub-grouping square brackets at the end; or he might assume that the same square brackets are needed even when the citation-order policy calls for 5:05..., which is not the case (though it is not positively harmful); or he might come up with an order than seriously distorts the correlation of the intended semantic filling, such as 994:05:5:017.1.

3.4   How can centralised UDC classification come about?

The set of advantages given in §3.3 is better, by quite a distance, than nothing, but it cannot compare with the advantages of work once done and in need of no meliorative repetition. How is this desideratum to be encompassed?

One possibility, suggested in §3.11, would be for the FID to undertake to return to its original function of a central document-classification-provision agency. But it is highly doubtful that FID will be able to do more than provide moral support, plus (perhaps) consultative services. In any case, it is the coupling of classification with author/title and descriptive-cataloguing centralisation that makes LC and LCSH such an administratively attractive solution. Who, then, will be the 'sub-contractor' in this enterprise?

There seem to be two ways most likely to lead to a profitable conclusion. The first is quite unrevolutionary; it would be for a cooperative network of libraries to undertake, between them, to create a consolidated set of surrogates classified by UDC. If this set of surrogates were stored on magnetic tape, the diversity between the various collections would create a totality which might well be marketable and easily distributable. An electronic network arrangement could also eliminate the simultaneous classification of the same document by the several cooperating libraries. Perhaps the first step toward such a network would be the demonstration, in a manageably middle-sized g e n e r a l collection, preferably automatised, of the high utility of such an effort. (It would be most advisable, of course, for there to be outside funding for such a public-spirited experimental effort). Once this is accomplished, the chances for the establishment of the network might well be stronger.

The second way is more revolutionary; let the Library of Congress establish an office for centralised UDC classification in cooperation with FID (or possibly with the British National Bibliography), thereby causing Title II-C of HEA to provide four sorts of search-strategic information instead of three. For the Library itself, then, or for libraries immovably attached to LC and the dictionary catalogue, the LC classification codes and subject headings will continue their traditional, if disputable, service. For those using DC now but aware of the imperfections of it (and of Sears or LC subject headings used in tandem with it) as a search strategy, there would be opened up the wholly new prospect of a differently arranged catalogue, which either on magnetic tape or on cards would provide throughgoing correlation, clerical permutability (multiple access), and the APUPA principle (for browsing)– and they may continue to use DC (as suggested by Wells; see §3.21) for shelf-arrangement.

Or, to go one more logical step, the UDC Office might well (even if not at once) entirely supplant the DC office, since the differences in collocation between the two, and the resultant disparities between the classified-catalogue code and the shelf-arranging code, might prove more disturbing to the patron than a more thorough divergence.

Such a wider (and more easily acceptable) divergence would emerge if UDC were used to organise a classified catalogue of documents arranged on the shelf by LC. This solution would not be acceptable, however, because the Bundy findings (reported in §2.2) cannot but prevent us from acting as if shelf order w i t h o u t a n y s y m b o l i s a t i o n o f s e m a n t i c f i l l i n g (as in LC, where the semantic filling of the codes is entirely opaque without the appropriate schedule to refer to for each and every code) is good enough for our patrons, who (it might be cynically said) 'don't know what they want anyway, so it really doesn't matter.

An example of the divergence in collocation between DC and UDC would be the codes for 'history of philosophy', which in DC (and thus on the shelves) occupy 180 through 199, in UDC only 19 through 199, thus clearing 18 for 'philosophy of beauty' (although it is not too effectively used for that).

4.0   Epilogue

Is it too late? Many libraries have already changed from DC to LC and are unlikely to be willing to spend the additional funds necessary to rectify the mistake (hopefully, it has been shown here to be such).

But the availability of centralised cataloguing, if accompanied by UDC classification, might rectify even this desperate situation, since it would eventually produce the basis for a change in the catalogue — which after all, n o t the shelves, is the crucial nexus for search strategy, since shelf-arrangement cannot help but be dominated by the problem of distributed relatives and that of the physical unavailability; it is the multiple access vistas of the catalogue, together with adequate correlation (concreteness), APUPA, and notational structurality, which solve the problem of classification — or more broadly, of search strategy — namely: W h a t , t h e n , n e x t ? [47].

47 The question of how we can know, if we are unsuccessful in our first attempt to find precisely what we seek, whether our further efforts are getting us any closer to it, will be explored more thoroughly in my forthcoming book *The idea of order; an essay in bibliographical systematics.*

XVII

The universal decimal classification as candidate for reclassification on the shelves and in the catalog

Introduction

The Universal Decimal Classification (UDC) is a system derived from Dewey's Decimal Classification (DC) largely by *a*: increase in specificity to enable the treatment of smaller and more particularised documents, by *b*: internationalisation, away from the American bias of DC, but still retaining a fairly strong Western bias, and by *c*: addition of devices aimed at separation of the elements of a complex classificatory expression, together with notational changes to allow recognition of the elements of such complexes[1].

UDC can thus be called a faceted classification, though its origin in DC prevents the thoroughgoing analytico-syntheticity of Ranganathan's Colon Classification (CC).

UDC is aimed more at the organisation of the catalogue than of the shelf. It should be remembered that the primary purpose of the catalogue is the enabling of searches in depth, as against that of the shelf-order, the enabling of browsing. Classification is what makes either approach (or we might better say: either terminus of the spectrum of queries) possible, even when the catalogue is organised by subject headings — since these last are only a concealed classification[2].

It is essential to remember that classification is not merely a shelf-organiser. *Classification* is another way of saying *search strategy,* or *information language,* and a language is a means of revealing meaning. I would venture a definition of *meaning* as *correlation within structure.* A classification is excellent, within these specifications, by virtue of the fineness of the discriminations it can allow, and of the complexities allowed in the

---

1   See W Boyd Tayward, 'The UDC and FID — a historical perspective', *Library quarterly,* xxxvii (1967), 259-278.

2   See for instance J M Perreault, 'The conceptual level in bibliography' (part III of 'On bibliography and automation; or, how to reinvent the catalogue), *Libri,* xv/4 (1965), 287-339.

expressions that can be constructed with it. When these two aspects are considered under their briefer titles of *specificity* and *concreteness*, we see that the various information languages can be characterised in terms of their provision for these needs; DC is tolerably specific and rather less so in synthetic concreteness, Library of Congress Subject Headings (LCSH) somewhat more specific but about the same in synthesis, LC considerably more specific than either but far less satisfactory in terms of synthetic devices. UDC has several levels of fullness at which it can be compared to these other three: the abridged edition is in about the same range of specificity as are DC and LCSH, the full edition falls between these and LC in terms of specificity, and both abridged and full editions are far more capable of synthetic concreteness than any of the others.

(It can be pointed out in passing that only CC exceeds UDC in this capacity for synthesis, and that its specificity is in the same range as abridged UDC, DC, or LCSH. Thus the total repertory of expressions available by the use of these various information languages can be seen to fall into three strata, each containing two systems that are roughly equivalent; DC and LCSH (lowest level); CC and UDC-abridged (middle level); LC and UDC-full (highest level).)

Facets in UDC

The most significant conceptual advantage of UDC over DC, LCSH, and LC, is in the clearer provision of facets. Now it cannot be denied that facets are present in the other three systems. An example in LCSH can be seen among the subdivisions of the term ART — as I have discussed it in 'Approaches to library filing by computer' [3] —, one can be seen in DC at 738, and one in LC at ML1400-3275. But more is needed than a mere abstract and vague recognition that the restrictions on a broader subject fall more or less naturally into groups. The editors of LCSH saw it in setting up the several alphabets under ART: form, place found, type (style), place of origin, period of time. The editors of DC saw it in setting up the Processes facet for ceramics at 738.1, the Specific Types from 738.2 to 738.8. The editors of LC saw it, or they would not have recurrently

3 J M Perreault, 'Approaches to library filing by computer', *Proceedings*, Urbana Clinic on Library Applications of Data Processing, 1966 (Champaign, Illini Union Bookstore, 1966), 47-90; repr in *The indexer*. v/4 (1968), 169-187.

grouped periods, before places, before Kinds and Forms, in *history and criticism of vocal and choral music* (ML1400-3275). But more than this is necessary, and the founders of UDC were most to be thanked for having taken Melvil Dewey's insight (that geographical area and period of time are subordinate concepts in relation to almost any other concept) and for broadening the application of this insight so that the schedule can be economised without lessening the discriminations allowed — discriminations that arise not only from enumeration (specificity) but also from the combination of elements from various facets of one class or even of elements from the various classes themselves (concreteness).

As an example, let us take such a conceptual complex as *electrically powered rudders for barges,* which is coded into UDC as 692.122.3.014.6-83. 629.122.3 is *barges,* .014.6 (when attached to any 629.12-code) is *rudders,* −83 (when attached to any 629.1-code) is *electric motive power.* The schedule lay-out for this class, 629.1 *transport engineering,* is in facets: first are listed general aspects (including *motive power*), then *parts* [and] *equipment of vehicles or craft,* then *types of vehicles or craft* — each facet with its characteristic notation. In DC[17], on the other hand, *towed barges* is 623.829 (a code which also expresses *canoes, rowboats,* and the like); *rudders* is 623.862 (a code which also expresses *masts, anchors,* and the like; and *electrical special systems in naval engineering* is 623.8503. None of these are combinable, as were the UDC code elements. In LC *barge construction* is VM311.B3 (too concrete, but in the wrong direction); *rudders* is taken care of as *steering gear,* VM841-845; and *electrical equipment* must similarly be over-generalised to *miscellaneous uses of electricity on ships,* VM479, or joined up to the class containing *barges,* namely as *electric and electronic equipment on small craft,* VM325. These codes, too, are not combinable.

The two possible forms of the classed catalogue

UDC is not an information language of one sole utility. LCSH is only of use for organising the catalogue; DC is of use primarily to organise the shelves, though with a good chain-index it could be used as the basis for organising the classed catalogue; LC is for the shelves alone, for all practical purposes (though any system, after all, can have chain-indexing attached to it). UDC, on the other hand, can be used on the shelves, o r as the basis for the classed catalogue with chain-index and single systematic entry, o r as the basis for the classed catalogue with an elementary index and entries permuted.

This last distinction is the least familiar, so I shall expand on it a bit. The classed catalogue with chain-index has only a single entry for each document, in the systematic part; multiple access is provided through the chain-index entries. The classed catalogue with permuted entry has a larger systematic part and an index that can be called elementary, in a sense demonstrated in Figure 2. If a good many conceptual complexes recur, the more economical format, over-all, is single entry with chain-indexing, since the set of chain-index entries constructed for the first occurrence of that complex will suffice for all later occurrences of the same complex. With permuted entry the same conceptual complex would have to be broken up into its elements and entered in the appropriate places over and over; but the index would be vastly economised in that once each element in it had been recognised, it would not need to be entered again at all. Thus it seems that the best over-all economy with the chain-index would be gained in a collection wherein the same conceptual complexes could be counted on to recur with considerable frequency; whereas the best situation for economy with permuted entry would be a collection of a more diffuse character, wherein the same complexes do not so often recur, but wherein the elements of these complexes d o recur in different complexes.

It can be seen why UDC is the only system under consideration which encourages permuted-entry classed cataloging: DC and LC do not possess faceted conceptual order matched by a notation showing the presence of facet-elements in the whole classificatory expression. The chain-index is the necessary complement to the systematic part of a DC- or LC- organised classed catalogue, since no one could permute an LC-code, and a DC-code could often cause considerable difficulty in this regard. With UDC (or CC, of course) chain-indexing is not necessary except where a specific term needs mention of its generic term to suppress ambiguity.

If you want to use DC, or LC, or LCSH, or even CC, it is an easy enough task to obtain the necessary documentation, including instructions (though they are scanty for LC) and schedules. But it is not quite so easy with UDC, at least not at every level of fullness. As mentioned before, UDC in the abridged edition has roughly the same discriminatory power (specificity + concreteness) of CC, in the full edition roughly the same as LC. Now, the abridged edition is easy enough to obtain[4], but the improvement therewith effected may well not be dramatic enough to convince the potential customer of value for his trouble and cost. And the full edition in English has never been completely published, though hope is renewed by the work done by the American Institute of Physics UDC project under Pauline Atherton and Bob Freeman. There is also a compromise on the way soon, a medium English edition[5]. The UDC schedules (full edition) are published by class, somewhat like LC; the usual pattern (in the German full edition, at least) is for each volume to have its own index, and for a cumulated index also to be published. The German medium edition recently published[6] has 440 pages in one volume of schedules; the index is due to appear soon in a separate volume[6a]. The abridged English edition is in one volume of 254 pages: 119 of schedules + 107 of index: the English medium edition will probably represent an increase of size over the abridged of around four-to-one.

Up-to-dateness in UDC is maintained by the appointment, to each more-or-less equivalent class, of a committee of experts, some of them subject specialists, some classificationists. 'Integrity' is approximately on a par with LC: the task of the committee is only infrequently to wholly recast a class or to recommend its relocation or that of any large proportion of

---

4 *Universal Decimal Classification:* abridged English edition, 3d ed, rev (London, British Standards Institution, 1961) (=BSI 1000A:1961) (=FID 289), 60s.

5 See R R Freeman, *Modern approaches to the management of a classification* (New York, American Institute of Physics, 1966) (=Report no AIP/UDC-3); repr in *Journal of documentation*, xxiii (1967), 304-320.

6 Volume I only; the schedules: *Dezimalklassifikation, D K– Handausgabe:* 'Systematische Tafeln'(Berlin, Deutscher Normenausschuss, 1967) (=FID 396), DM 101.50.

6a It has since appeared: 'Alphabetisches Sachverzeichnis' (Berlin, Deutscher Normenansschuss, 1968), DM 67.50; the errors caused by careless programming for its computer-production may well give it the same bad reputation as has plagued the index to D C_{17}.

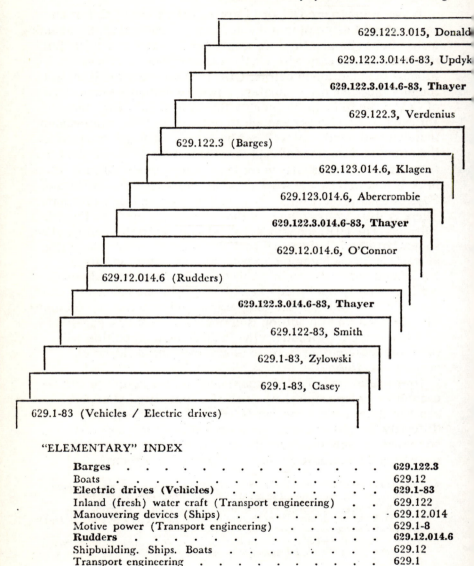

Figure 1

Permuted—entry systematic classed catalogue

629.122.3.015, Donald

629.122.3.014.6-83, Updyk

629.122.3.014.6-83, Thayer

629.122.3, Verdenius

629.122.3 (Barges)

629.123.014.6, Klagen

629.123.014.6, Abercrombie

629.122.3.014.6-83, Thayer

629.12.014.6, O'Connor

629.12.014.6 (Rudders)

629.122.3.014.6-83, Thayer

629.122-83, Smith

629.1-83, Zylowski

629.1-83, Casey

629.1-83 (Vehicles / Electric drives)

"ELEMENTARY" INDEX

Barges	**629.122.3**
Boats	629.12
Electric drives (Vehicles)	**629.1-83**
Inland (fresh) water craft (Transport engineering) . .	629.122
Manouvering devices (Ships)	629.12.014
Motive power (Transport engineering)	629.1-8
Rudders	**629.12.014.6**
Shipbuilding. Ships. Boats	629.12
Transport engineering	629.1

(Note that the emphasized index entries may well have all already have been in use upon arrival of the document by Thayer, and would in that case only need to be checked to determine establishment.)

230

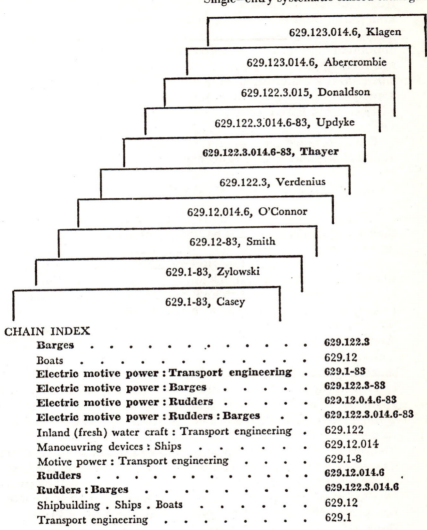

Figure 2
Single—entry systematic classed catalogue

629.123.014.6, Klagen

629.123.014.6, Abercrombie

629.122.3.015, Donaldson

629.122.3.014.6-83, Updyke

629.122.3.014.6-83, Thayer

629.122.3, Verdenius

629.12.014.6, O'Connor

629.12-83, Smith

629.1-83, Zylowski

629.1-83, Casey

CHAIN INDEX

Barges	**629.122.3**
Boats	629.12
Electric motive power : Transport engineering .	**629.1-83**
Electric motive power : Barges	**629.122.3-83**
Electric motive power : Rudders	**629.12.0.4.6-83**
Electric motive power : Rudders : Barges . .	**629.122.3.014.6-83**
Inland (fresh) water craft : Transport engineering .	629.122
Manoeuvring devices : Ships	629.12.014
Motive power : Transport engineering	629.1-8
Rudders	**629.12.014.6**
Rudders : Barges	**629.122.3.014.6**
Shipbuilding . Ships . Boats	629.12
Transport engineering	629.1

(Note that all the emphasized index entries could have arisen from the arrival of the document by Updyke; when that by Thayer arrived, no new entries would be needed; and of course the other index entries could have been generated by earlier and more general documents. Aside from the index entries common to both systems, the "elementary" index needs only three entries as against seven for the chain index, but thirteen permuted systematic entries are needed as against ten non-permuted.)

231

its sub classes. Suggestions for improvement also originate
from individual members and member-organisations of the
Fédération Internationale de Documentation (FID), the parent
body; these suggestions (as well as the recommendations of
appointed committees) are circulated for the approval of the
membership before official adoption. *Extensions and
corrections* are published semi-annually and cumulated in
three-year periods; and all extensions and corrections from
1949 to 1964 have recently been cumulated into a six-volume
set[7].

The picture we get is of caution: a good thing except where
a radical or rapid change is needed.

Need for centralisation

If I may slightly mis-use a pregnant expression of Ranganathan's, a classification must be 'self-perpetuating' to succeed.[8]
As an example of how the lack of this characteristic can cause
death, think of Cutter's fine (but virtually extinct) Expansive
Classification. All the systems under present consideration
are self-perpetuating; but there is another feature which helps
to keep a classification system thriving: it needs to be s e l f-
p r o v i d i n g. If there is only one brand of flour for sale in
Aunt Minnie's town, and if a packet of yeast is attached to each
sack of that flour, and if other brands of yeast must be bought
separately, how many loaves of bread is Aunt Minnie likely to
bake with the self-providing brand of yeast, and how many with
any other brand? LC, LCSH, and DC are all brands of yeast
coming along with the only available American flour (printed
card service) that appeals to academic and larger public
libraries. FID has not managed to find a brand of flour to attach
its own yeast to. (It must be realised, too, that it is on the basis
of the quality of the product primary in the mind of the buyer
that the secondary product is bought. Good flour with second-
rate yeast will out-sell (if the price is the same) second-rate
flour with good yeast.)

7 See p 34 of the 1969 *FID Publications catalogue* (=FID 427).
8· S R Ranganathan, 'Self-perpetuating scheme of classification', *Journal of
   documentation,* iv (1949), 223-244; repr in R K Olding *(ed), Readings in library
   cataloguing* (Hamden, Archon, 1966), 193-221.

Knowing this complex of reasons, it seems to me most unfortunate that UDC be in such a poor selling position, with nothing attached to it to help appeal to the customer; I have therefore suggested [9] that a centralised UDC classification service be set up, preferably to be issued along with descriptive cataloging (as at the Library of Congress or the British National Bibliography).

Assimilation during reclassification

Since the overwhelming majority of libraries reclassifying or planning to reclassify are abandoning DC, and are (in terms of today's earlier discussions) likely to be adopting LC (unless they are keeping DC for the shelves and are putting greater effort into the subject catalogue — where it is most needed —, there is a comparison between LC and UDC in terms not so much of conceptual characteristic as of assimilation to DC. UDC uses (except for the recently emptied class 4) the same order of main classes as does DC. Below that level, while there is considerable agreement, there is also plenty of disagreement. However, this much c a n be said, despite the imperfect agreement: the reclassified material in UDC can intelligibly be shelved right with the unreclassified material still in DC. This cannot be done with LC and DC: a complicated system of physical relocations is necessary as the change progresses. But an even more important factor than administrative non-flap is that the patrons need not be disturbed in their search by having material on e v e r y class in two places for at least s o m e period of time.

Conclusion

This whole point must not, though, conceal from us that UDC is under consideration here primarily in its role of catalogue-organiser, parallel to LCSH. And it must not be forgotten that a great many are convinced that UDC has too complicated a notational system for use on the shelf. By this may be meant that a UDC code, worked out to its fullest possible conformity to a conceptual complex, may be quite long; and that a DC code similarly fully applied to the same conceptual complex, is less

9   J M Perreault, *Reclassification: some warnings and a proposal* (Urbana, Graduate School of Library Service, 1967 (=Illinois University. Graduate School of Library Science. *Occasional papers,* no 87), reprinted above.

long; and an LC one shorter yet. I will not deny that the most part this is true; but what is true too, but all too often not noted, is that the shortening of the code in DC and LC is not accomplished by a more economical translation of the s a m e conceptual complex, but by the unavoidable elimination of some needed or at least desirable elements in the translation. (Think, for instance, of the earlier example about *electrically powered rudders for barges:* no one can deny that 623.829 is shorter than 629.122.3.3.014.6-83, and so is VM315. But you cannot miss the fact that these shorter codes convey less meaning than does the longer; and, within their respective systems, the smaller ones cannot be expanded to convey that additional meaning.) When DC is capable of giving the same full translation as UDC, its code is generally found to be longer, not shorter[10]. This is not the case with an ordinal notation system like LC, but the lack of the capacity for *ad hoc* syntheses in LC means that such adequacy of translation from conceptual complex to classificatory expression depends on the precise case having occurred in the past.

And it should also be held in mind that what is needed, for all but the smallest libraries, is a classification capable of discriminating between documents dealing with unusual and narrow topics whenever they occur; such a classification will almost certainly also be capable of dealing with documents on ordinary and/or broad topics. The recognition of this fact is a major source of the impetus to reclassify to a more specific, more discriminating, and more current system. What needs to be kept in mind, if UDC is to be thought of as in the running as a candidate for adoption through reclassification, is that the system that is best able to handle the unforeseen is that most appropriate as our reclassificatory choice, and in this UDC is ahead of DC, LC, or LCSH.

10 See for example *ibidem*, 18.

ANALYSIS OF L C AND D C CODES ASSIGNED,
WITH COMPARABLE U D C CODES

(1) H. Hager: A bibliography of works published by Estonian ethnologists in exile, 1945-1965. (1. Ethnology—Estonia—Bibl.)

[ANALYSIS: bibliography / ethnologists, Estonian, exiled / 1945-1965]

DC: (no code assigned)

LC:
```
 ┌ printing + library science + bibliography
 │    │  bibliography by subject: anthropology and ethnology of Europe
 │    └    ┴
 └ Z   5117
```

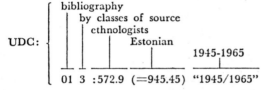

UDC:
```
 ┌ bibliography
 │   │ by classes of source
 │   │   │ ethnologists
 │   │   │   │ Estonian
 │   │   │   │        │ 1945-1965
 │   │   │   │        │      │
 │   ┴   ┴   ┴────────┴──────┴──────
 └ 01  3  :572.9 (=945.45) "1945/1965"
```

(2) B. Häring: Bernard Häring replies; answers to 50 moral and religious questions. (1. Questions and answers—Theology. 2. Catholic Church—Doctrinal and controversial works—Catholic authors.)

[ANALYSIS: religion / Christianity / theology, doctrinal ∟ moral / Catholic / questions and answers]

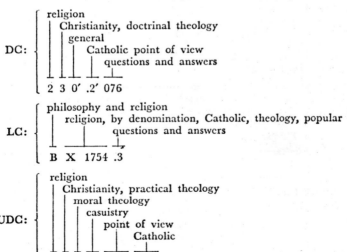

DC:
```
 ┌ religion
 │  │ Christianity, doctrinal theology
 │  │  │ general
 │  │  │  │ Catholic point of view
 │  │  │  │   │ questions and answers
 │  ┴  ┴  ┴   ┴   ┴
 └ 2  3  0'  .2'  076
```

LC:
```
 ┌ philosophy and religion
 │   │ religion, by denomination, Catholic, theology, popular
 │   │         │ questions and answers
 │   ┴────────┴
 └ B  X  1754 .3
```

UDC:
```
 ┌ religion
 │  │ Christianity, practical theology
 │  │  │ moral theology
 │  │  │  │ casuistry
 │  │  │  │  │ point of view
 │  │  │  │  │   │ Catholic
 │  ┴  ┴  ┴  ┴   ┴
 └ 2  4  1  .01 .00: 282
```

235

(3) C. Moeller: Der Mensch vor dem Heil; eine Untersuchung moderner Literatur. (1. Salvation—Addresses, essays, lectures. 2. Retreats for members of religious orders.)

[ANALYSIS: religion / Christianity / theology, doctrinal / salvation / belles lettres / 20th century / lectures]

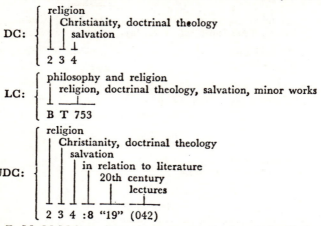

DC:
religion
Christianity, doctrinal theology
salvation
2 3 4

LC:
philosophy and religion
religion, doctrinal theology, salvation, minor works
B T 753

UDC:
religion
Christianity, doctrinal theology
salvation
in relation to literature
20th century
lectures
2 3 4 :8 "19" (042)

(4) E. M. McMahon: Becoming a person in the whole Christ. (1. Spiritual life—Catholic authors. 2. Monasticism and religious life—Psychology.)

[ANALYSIS: religion / Christianity / monastic life / theology, moral / personal / Catholic]

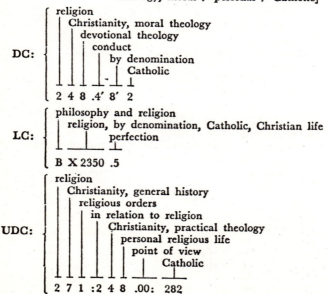

DC:
religion
Christianity, moral theology
devotional theology
conduct
by denomination
Catholic
2 4 8 .4' 8' 2

LC:
philosophy and religion
religion, by denomination, Catholic, Christian life
perfection
B X 2350 .5

UDC:
religion
Christianity, general history
religious orders
in relation to religion
Christianity, practical theology
personal religious life
point of view
Catholic
2 7 1 :2 4 8 .00: 282

(5) I. Birnie: Encounter. (1. Adolescence.   2. Gt. Brit.—Social conditions—
1945-   3. Interpersonal relations. 4. Teaching.)

[ANALYSIS: sociology / youth / relations, interpersonal / improvement / education / Gt. Brit. / 1945-   ]

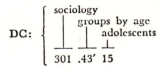

DC:
sociology
    groups by age
        adolescents
301 .43′ 15

LC:
sociology, family, youth, both sexes
HQ 796

UDC:
sociology
    social relations
        youth
            in relation to education
                Gt. Brit.
                    1945-
301 .16 -053.7 :37 (42) "1945/"

(6) M. Bisgyer: Challenge and encounter; behind the scenes in the struggle
for Jewish survival. (1. Jews in the U.S. 2. Jews—Political
and social conditions.)

[ANALYSIS: sociology / Jews / assimilation / U.S.]

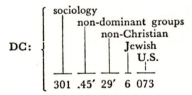

DC:
sociology
    non-dominant groups
        non-Christian
            Jewish
                U.S.
301 .45′ 29′ 6 073

LC:
history and description, New World, U.S., elements in the population
    Jewish
E 184 .J5

UDC:
sociology
    groups
        hereditary
            Jewish
                U.S.
301 .18 5 (=924) (73)

(7) R. Egger: Das praetorium als Ansitz und Quartier römischer Spitzen-
funktionäre. (1. Praetors. 2. Rome—Provinces—Administration.
3. Rome—Antiq.)

[ANALYSIS: administration / colonial / military / officers,
higher / Rome / ancient]

DC: (no code assigned)

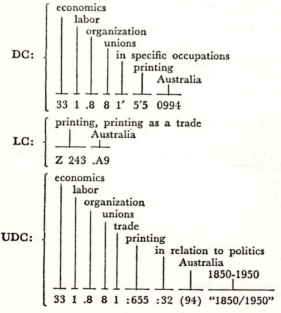

LC:
```
┌ political theory
│   │ Rome, special topics
│   │   │ provincial administration
│ └───┴───┴──
└ J C 85 .P9
```

UDC:
```
┌ political science
│   │ colonial policy
│   │   │ administration
│   │   │   │ in relation to administration
│   │   │   │   │ army
│   │   │   │   │   │ general staff
│   │   │   │   │   │   Rome, ancient
│ └──┴───┴──┴───┴──┴────
└ 32 5.3 5 :35 6.2 (37)
```

(8) J. S. Hagan: Printers and politics; a history of the Australian printing
unions, 1850-1950. (1. Printing industry—Australia.
2. Trade unions—Australia—Political activity.)

[ANALYSIS: unions, trade / printing / politics / Australia / 1850-1950]

DC:
```
┌ economics
│   │ labor
│   │   │ organization
│   │   │   │ unions
│   │   │   │   │ in specific occupations
│   │   │   │   │   │ printing
│   │   │   │   │   │   Australia
│ └──┴───┴──┴──┴───┴──
└ 33 1 .8 8 1' 5'5 0994
```

LC:
```
┌ printing, printing as a trade
│   │ Australia
│ └───┴──
└ Z 243 .A9
```

UDC:
```
┌ economics
│   │ labor
│   │   │ organization
│   │   │   │ unions
│   │   │   │   │ trade
│   │   │   │   │   │ printing
│   │   │   │   │   │   │ in relation to politics
│   │   │   │   │   │   │   Australia
│   │   │   │   │   │   │   │ 1850-1950
│ └──┴───┴──┴──┴───┴──┴───┴──────
└ 33 1 .8 8 1 :655 :32 (94) "1850/1950"
```

(9) E. Hultman: Studies on muscle metabolism of glycogen and active phosphate in man with special reference to exercise and diet. (1. Glycogen. 2. Muscle. 3. Exercise—Physiological effect. 4. Phosphorus in the body.)

[ANALYSIS: physiology / man / muscle / metabolism / glycogen + active phosphate / exercise + diet]

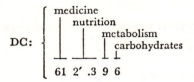

DC:
medicine
nutrition
metabolism
carbohydrates
61 2′ .3 9 6

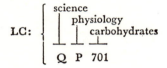

LC:
science
physiology
carbohydrates
Q P 701

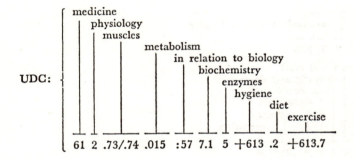

UDC:
medicine
physiology
muscles
metabolism
in relation to biology
biochemistry
enzymes
hygiene
diet
exercise
61 2 .73/.74 .015 :57 7.1 5 +613 .2 +613.7

(10) G. R. Cooper: Methods of signal and system analysis. (1. System analysis. 2. Signal theory (Telecommunications).)

[ANALYSIS: engineering / analysis + Engineering / telecommunications / signals]

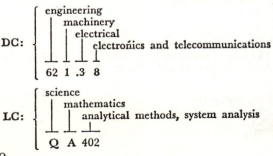

DC:
engineering
machinery
electrical
electronics and telecommunications
62 1 .3 8

LC:
science
mathematics
analytical methods, system analysis
Q A 402

239

(10) Continued

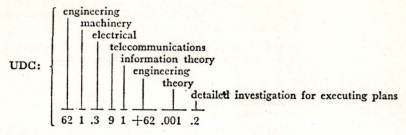

UDC:

```
       engineering
         machinery
           electrical
             telecommunications
               information theory
                 engineering
                   theory
                       detailed investigation for executing plans

       62 1 .3  9 1 +62 .001 .2
```

(11) E. John: Filling stitches. (1. Embroidery.)

[ANALYSIS: handicrafts / textile / embroidery / technique]

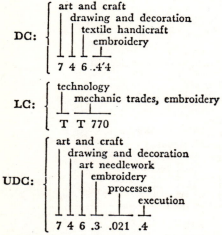

DC:

```
       art and craft
         drawing and decoration
           textile handicraft
             embroidery

       7 4 6 .4′4
```

LC:

```
       technology
         mechanic trades, embroidery

       T  T 770
```

UDC:

```
       art and craft
         drawing and decoration
           art needlework
             embroidery
               processes
                 execution

       7 4 6 .3 .021 .4
```

(12) H. Krellmann: Studien zu den Bearbeitungen F. Busonis. (1. Busoni...)

[ANALYSIS: music / arrangements / Busoni]

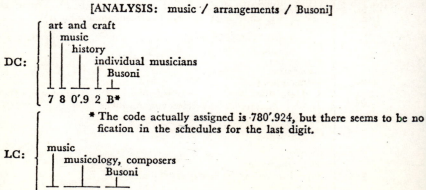

DC:

```
       art and craft
         music
           history
             individual musicians
               Busoni

       7 8 0′.9 2 B*
```

LC:

* The code actually assigned is 780′.924, but there seems to be no ~~justi~~fication in the schedules for the last digit.

```
       music
         musicology, composers
               Busoni

       M  L 410  .B98
```

240

(12) Continued

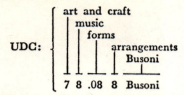

UDC:
```
      art and craft
      | music
      |  | forms
      |  |  | arrangements
      |  |  |  Busoni
      |  |  |  |
      7  8  .08  8  Busoni
```

(13) F.v.d. Meer: Shorter atlas of Western civilization. (1. Geography, Historical—Maps. 2. Civilization, Occidental.)

[ANALYSIS: generalia / civilization, Western / atlases]

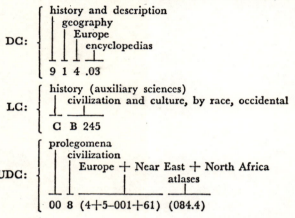

DC:
```
      history and description
      | geography
      |  | Europe
      |  |  | encyclopedias
      |  |  |  |
      9  1  4  .03
```

LC:
```
      history (auxiliary sciences)
      |  civilization and culture, by race, occidental
      |  |
      C  B 245
```

UDC:
```
      prolegomena
      | civilization
      |  | Europe + Near East + North Africa
      |  |              atlases
      |  |                 |
      00 8  (4+5–001+61)  (084.4)
```

(14) The Nineties; glimpses of a lost but lively world. (1. U.S.—Social life and customs—1865-1918.)

[ANALYSIS: description / U.S. / 1890-1900]

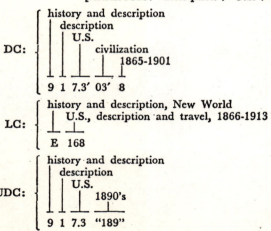

DC:
```
      history and description
      | description
      |  | U.S.
      |  |  | civilization
      |  |  |  | 1865-1901
      |  |  |  |  |
      9  1  7.3'  03'  8
```

LC:
```
      history and description, New World
      |  U.S., description and travel, 1866-1913
      |  |
      E  168
```

UDC:
```
      history and description
      | description
      |  | U.S.
      |  |  | 1890's
      |  |  |
      9  1  7.3  "189"
```